T0303629

We Conquered All of Europe

We Conquered All of Europe

Red Odyssey II

JEFF GOULDING

pitch

First published by Pitch Publishing, 2019

Pitch Publishing
A2 Yeoman Gate
Yeoman Way
Worthing
Sussex
BN13 3QZ
www.pitchpublishing.co.uk
info@pitchpublishing.co.uk

© 2019, Jeff Goulding

Every effort has been made to trace the copyright.
Any oversight will be rectified in future editions at the
earliest opportunity by the publisher.

All rights reserved. No part of this book may be reproduced,
sold or utilised in any form or transmitted in any form or by
any means, electronic or mechanical, including photocopying,
recording or by any information storage and retrieval system,
without prior permission in writing from the Publisher.

A CIP catalogue record is available for this book
from the British Library.

ISBN 978-1-78531-599-2

Typesetting and origination by Pitch Publishing

Printed and bound in India by Replika Press Pvt. Ltd.

Contents

Dedicated to the Reds we lost along the way; Gerry Byrne, Tommy Lawrence, Ronnie Moran, Peter Thompson, Tommy Smith, Lee Walker, Peter Nolan and Jimmy Fitzmaurice

Rest in Peace, Red Men.

Acknowledgements

I have always set out to chronicle the history of the club through the lens of the people who built it, served it and supported it. In attempting to tell the stories that shaped this era, I have drawn on many people's experiences and perspectives as well as my own.

So, to former players Jamie Carragher, Jimmy Case, John Barnes and Johnny Wheeler; and supporters Ray Carrick, Phil Roberts, Ian Byrne, Tony Zeverona, Steven Scragg, Matt Ladson, Terry Murphy, Joe Goulding, Sean Macgregor, Graeme James Strain, Sue Taylor, Dave Usher, Lee Walker, Peter Kenny Jones and Katie Price, I thank you all for your time and for sharing your thoughts and experiences of playing for and following our beloved club.

Foreword

I published *Red Odyssey: Liverpool FC 1892–2017* in order to celebrate the 125th anniversary of what I believe is a magnificent footballing institution. As I drew down the curtain on that tremendous epoch, laden with drama, intrigue, great victories and crushing defeats, tragedy, comedy and of course trophies galore, I suggested we were merely pausing for breath.

Of course, we all suspected that even more thrilling stories lay in wait for us, and we were right. I just didn't expect there to be so many, in such a short space of time.

The last four years have seen new heroes emerge. Old foes have faded from view, only to be replaced by new villains. And, with Jürgen Klopp at the helm, we have experienced a thrill ride of heavy metal football, breath-taking highs and lows and eventually the euphoria of another great victory.

In my first book, I pointed to Klopp's remarkable leadership powers, particularly in the aftermath of defeat to Seville in the UEFA Europa League Final in 2016. I pointed to the enormous talent in the squad and marvelled at how Anfield itself had been transformed.

Players like Trent Alexander-Arnold, Mo Salah and Sadio Mané would pick up the mantle and take the club to new heights, I suggested. And of course, I knew that the supporters would continue to create their own stories and drive the club on to ever greater success. They would do so regardless of any setbacks that came their way. At Liverpool we never walk alone and always carry hope in our hearts.

That I felt this way at the end of the book was a surprise to me. In it I described my own journey from youthful optimism and devotion to the club, to cynical middle age. Somewhere on the way to my fifth decade on earth, I had almost fallen out of love with Liverpool FC. However, writing the book and discovering how wonderfully rich its history is, had helped me to rediscover what it was that made me fall in love with it all those years ago.

People and stories, memories and passion are the lifeblood of this great club; not money or buildings or branding. Anyone with an affection or affinity with Liverpool Football Club knows that our supply of these is inexhaustible. No defeat on the pitch or calamity off it can blow us off course, because we are Liverpool and we will always have dreams, songs to sing and stories to tell.

Our rivals mock us because they will never understand this fundamental truth. When others lose a game or a final, they are crushed. Yet we can revel in the occasion. The journey is as glorious as the destination for us. It always will be, because in the adventure we find new heroes and create new stories to pass on to the next generation.

The last four years have only served to strengthen my belief in this fact. How else can we explain how Kopites were able to rejoice in their experiences at Wembley, Basel and Kiev, despite witnessing disappointing defeats. How did we all find the strength to keep singing our songs when others sneered at us. It's because we love the ride, no matter where it ends up. We know that if we support and believe, we will get our rewards eventually.

In this sense, the people who follow the club today find themselves in perfect harmony with its manager and players. Klopp has spoken continuously of creating new memories and moments for the supporters to enjoy. In recent years we have certainly been blessed in this department.

Seville may have inflicted heartache on us in Switzerland, but the memories of Lovren's late winner against Dortmund and the humiliation of United in that epic two-legged Europa League battle will keep us amused forever. On the road to Kiev we witnessed incredible scenes, home and away and have joyous memories that will always eclipse the pain of losing the final.

We have rediscovered the old ways. When I grew up on the Kop, in the 1970s and '80s, it was the most natural thing in the world for us to serenade the players, one by one. We invented new songs with relentless regularity. Somehow, we lost that art through the barren years of the '90s and the rampant commercialism of the noughties. As I reflect on the Klopp years, I am struck by the explosion of new songs. From the wonderfully haunting 'Allez, Allez, Allez' to 'We're going to Madrid', the songsmiths on the Kop have reached new heights.

When Jürgen Klopp noticed that Bobby Firmino didn't have a song of his own, he simply ordered one and the supporters dutifully obliged. Bobby's song is one of the best created. It joins similarly brilliant, and quintessentially Liverpool, ditties crafted in honour of Mo Salah, Virgil van Dijk and Divock Origi.

We have found a way to enjoy football again, no matter what happens. We are not just supporters now. We have become believers again. And, at the end of the 2018/19 season we received our reward. We have now conquered all of Europe.

The first book took in 125 years of Liverpool history. This one encompasses just four. However, so rich are the stories, they fill almost as many pages. You will read of our European adventures, the great games as well as the despair of defeat. You'll see how the bond with our manager and the players he leads has been tested and forged in the fire of conquest and loss.

However, *Red Odyssey II: We Conquered All of Europe* will give you the whole story. In its pages you will witness a transformation of spirit, attitude and the reclaiming of belief. The sweet taste of victory sometimes masks the bitter despair we sampled on the road to glory. So, this book will take you from moments of doubt to the dawning of belief, and eventually to the promised land of Madrid and that epic homecoming, remembering every step of the journey.

Along the way we'll relive the dark moments and rejoice in the glorious ones, we'll share the moments off the pitch that are as important as the games on it. Throughout it all, we'll hear the voice of the people who lived it and the insights of former players.

Enjoy this next chapter in our glorious history.

Introduction

On 8 October 2015, Liverpool FC announced the appointment of Jürgen Norbert Klopp as manager. It would end the Anfield reign of Brendan Rodgers who, despite receiving a vote of confidence in the summer, was enduring a miserable time.

The king is dead, long live the king! Well that's not quite how the news of Rodgers's sacking was greeted by Liverpool supporters. Sadly, for the Irishman, his departure was greeted with relief and rather than being viewed as a fallen king, his legacy had become so tarnished that many saw him as a clown prince.

For me, that is a shame. Rodgers led Liverpool to one of their most exciting seasons in decades. Yes, he had the mercurial and tempestuous talents of Luis Suárez to count on, but you still have to manage players like that and get the most out of them. It's worth noting that prior to that first explosive season under Brendan, Luis was thought to be a wasteful striker who needed too many chances to score. Pundits even suggested he wasn't a natural goalscorer.

Amazing with hindsight, but nonetheless true. If you add in Suárez's troublesome behaviour, then you have to concede that he will have been a challenge as well as a blessing to his manager. The trouble for Rodgers was that he was always punching above his weight. Maybe the Liverpool job came too soon for him. The almost impossible job of following up that title near-miss in 2014 was always going to weigh heavy, and with the owners casting covetous eyes towards Dortmund's eccentric genius, Jürgen Klopp, Brendan was living on borrowed time.

The writing had been on the wall for Brendan for some time – he'd won just three of the first ten games of the season, drawing five and losing two. Liverpool had lost Suárez the year before and had inevitably struggled to replace him. However, Rodgers had signed a few players whose careers would blossom under his successor – Roberto Firmino, Joe Gomez and James Milner.

When the Merseyside derby came around, on 4 October 2015, the game had become even more of a must-win encounter than usual. Many Reds felt the Blues were odds-on to end their miserable run against Liverpool. It was all such a far cry from the heady days of the 2013/14 season.

The gloom surrounding the club was all too briefly lifted in the 41st minute when Danny Ings struck to put Liverpool in front. Coming just before half-time, it was the perfect boost, or so it seemed. In what had become a hallmark of the Rodgers era, his charges would squander an advantage in frustrating circumstances. With the dressing room beckoning and an opportunity to rally the troops in the offing, Rodgers watched on helplessly as Romelu Lukaku levelled in the 45th minute.

The game was there for the taking, for both sides, but a derby classic failed to materialise and instead it became merely a footnote. *The Times* summed it up perfectly, 'Liverpool started well, flirted with success and then faded, the Northern Irishman powerless to stop it, before petering out in the mire of mediocrity. In the distorting focus of hindsight, it is hard to avoid a suspicion there is a metaphor in there, somewhere.'

It was therefore a forlorn Brendan Rodgers who greeted the press in the mixed zone at full time. His comments suggested he knew that his fate had been sealed that afternoon, telling *The Guardian*, 'If we are to replicate what we did two years ago, we will have to build something. Unfortunately, that will take time. That is frustrating for supporters but there are new players to come in. That will take time, whether that is me or someone else in the job.'

Within the hour the call had come, and Brendan's dream was over. He had wanted Liverpool to be a destination, instead, for him, it would be a stepping stone to other places. Who knows, greater success may lie ahead for the Irishman, but it would not be at Anfield. He would go on to set new benchmarks in Scottish football, and while some may decry the quality of the game north of the border – with some justification – it's still true to say that Rodgers has achieved things in the Scottish game that nobody before him has managed to do.

Speculation filled TV studios and radio airwaves and fan forums exploded with excitement. Who would Liverpool appoint next? For me, there are always mixed feelings at the departure of a manager. There is the initial sadness that it didn't work out, followed by anticipation and hope of better things to come. Only with the sacking of Roy Hodgson did I experience only relief and happiness.

Almost immediately thoughts turned to Jürgen Klopp. It was known that he was taking a break from football and therefore available after a successful spell as manager of Borussia Dortmund. But could a club like Liverpool, locked in a malaise of its own making, attract a manager of his undoubted quality.

So far had expectations fallen, many of us – me included – felt Jürgen would have bigger and better options. Speculation surrounded the jobs of several managers at clubs with bigger pockets, including Chelsea. If the Reds were to get their man, they would have to move quickly. Liverpool though, had developed a reputation for being ponderous and always a day late and a dollar short when it came to the big decisions.

We were all doubters back then.

It seems we were wrong to be. Liverpool supporters now know that the club's hierarchy moved with hitherto unseen speed to contact their target and he needed even less time to say yes. His holiday was over, and the king of Dortmund would set up court at Anfield.

Like many great managers before him, Klopp was an unremarkable footballer. A one-club man at Mainz, he went on to manage them and lead them to their first top-flight promotion in the club's history and becoming their longest-serving manager into the bargain. On the eve of Liverpool's Champions League victory in Madrid, he would describe that as the greatest moment of his life.

His achievements would soon draw the attention of bigger fish and in the summer of 2008, Borussia Dortmund came calling. It proved a historic appointment. He steadied the team's league position, moving them from 13th to sixth place in two seasons and securing a trophy, winning the DFL Supercup in his first season.

In 2011 Klopp would make himself one of the most sought-after managers in German and European football by winning Dortmund's first league title in almost a decade, with a couple of games to spare. He repeated the feat in the following season, shattering points records as he rampaged across the Bundesliga. His second title came after an astonishing 28-game unbeaten run.

He would then take Dortmund to the pinnacle of European football, setting up a heroic defeat to arch rivals Bayern Munich. His response to this defeat was perhaps a glorious illustration of Klopp's greatest asset, his ability to communicate in a way that cuts through to ordinary people.

There is nothing cliché about Jürgen Klopp. Bill Shankly once said, 'There are those who like to use big words, so that they make themselves sound important and special. We speak the language of the people. Whereas someone might say a man was avaricious, we'd say he was bloody greedy.' Shanks was displaying both his intellect and his ability to speak directly to his people, no flowery language, just absolute clarity. This is who we are, and this is what we stand for.

Klopp it seems is cut from similar cloth. In summing up that defeat to Bayern, he would say, 'The only thing I can say is that it was great. London is the town of the Olympic Games. The weather was good, everything is okay. Only the result is shit.'

Klopp is the anti-cliché. If anything, he seems irritated by attempts to manufacture stories or headlines. He's often bemused by fake controversy and – just like Shankly before him – prefers to live in the real world. Football is a simple game after all.

His first press conference showed how he was plugged into the psyche at Anfield. We were a giant, dining out on past glories and no longer believing the future had anything to offer. The past was like a great millstone around our necks, dragging us down and preventing forward momentum.

His diagnosis was as incisive as his prescription, 'You must change from doubters to believers – now!'

None of us knew if it would work, but we strapped ourselves in for the ride, nonetheless. And, oh what a rollercoaster it proved to be. It would involve spectacular adventures, wild rides and impossible victories, and of course, we could conquer all of Europe.

So, sit back, grab a beer or a coffee and brace yourself for the journey of your life. Our Red Odyssey continues.

LIVERPOOL FC 2015/2016

Klopp, the Kop and the army of doubters

Stamford Bridge is falling down; a tantalising glimpse of things to come

By 31 October 2015, Jürgen Klopp had been in charge for four matches and next up was difficult game against Chelsea. While the performances had been encouraging, the results had done little to set the pulses racing. There had been scant evidence of the much vaunted 'heavy metal football' yet. The media had latched on to the catchphrase and run with it. However, three draws and a nervy 1-0 home League Cup win over Bournemouth had threatened to turn it into something of a millstone around the German's neck.

All this meant that few supporters were expecting an emphatic victory at Stamford Bridge. Even though Jose Mourinho, who had led Chelsea to a league title in the previous season, was in the process of blowing up and losing yet another expensively assembled dressing room, he would not have expected what would become his sixth defeat of the season.

The clock was already ticking and soon Roman Abramovich's patience would run out and Guus Hiddink would replace the Portuguese in the dugout. Maybe Klopp sensed blood, because this would prove to be a much more compelling vision of his brand of football than anything on offer since he took over from Brendan Rodgers.

In what would become a season of ups and downs, this particular high point gave the travelling Kop a glimpse into the future under Jürgen Klopp. It was one in which hard work would play a part, along with belief in each other and resilience in the face of set-backs.

One player who epitomised this most was Phillipe Coutinho. He had been struggling in previous outings and things just weren't working for him. Yet Klopp kept faith in his own ability to get the best out of his charges and in the quality of the player. It was an approach that would pay dividends.

The Brazilian's contribution to the game proved pivotal, and Jürgen, addressing the post-match media scrum at full time, was effusive in his praise.

'Sometimes you have to work really hard to make football look easy,' he said. 'That is what he did. It was not a perfect start for Phil. But he came back and was cool enough to shoot at the right moment. He knows the last three games were not perfect, but he needs the games. I love this player. Who can't love Phil Coutinho? I don't expect all-day perfection. I expect you to work and try to get better every day. That is what Phil is doing and the team are doing.'

Of course, things would later sour between the German and the Brazilian, but during Klopp's first tentative steps in the Premier League, Coutinho was beginning to thrive. It's a fact he would later forget, to his apparent cost and Liverpool's profit.

Jürgen had raised a few eyebrows with his team selection, choosing to start with another Brazilian, Roberto (the man who would become Bobby to the Kop) Firmino spearheading the Reds attacking line, with Christian Benteke settling for a place on the bench and Coutinho playing a supportive role from the left.

The idea of the Liverpool number nine at the tip of a front three may have seemed strange to journalists back then, but it would soon prove to be a masterstroke. Phillipe would score two and, of course, Benteke would emerge as a substitute to grab the decisive third goal.

However, from the point of view of the 3,000 Reds in the away end, the game got off to a terrible start. Just four minutes in they were behind to a Ramires goal. James Milner had been far too easily beaten on the wing by César Azpilicueta and, on the touchline, Klopp fumed and raged as he sent the ball goalward.

Brazilian Ramires headed the ball home with relish. The Chelsea players celebrated wildly, but Klopp's grimace spoke volumes. Here we were treated to all sides of the German's personality, his moods as changeable as the English weather. He spent the whole game dancing in the technical area, beseeching his players to think, to work harder and roaring them on to greater things. For the referee and the fourth official, it was a different story entirely.

Who knows if he got under their skin, but the amount of injury time awarded at the end of the first half drew fierce protests from the Chelsea bench. Liverpool took full advantage.

Roared on as much by the manager as the away end, Liverpool had refused to buckle to Chelsea's opener. Adam Lallana and Lucas Leiva had both tested Begovic, and then

Coutinho delivered a moment of magic that rattled Stamford Bridge. Twenty yards from goal and with no right to score, he skipped past his marker and unleashed a curling left-footed drive that sailed past the despairing keeper and into the net.

It was an absolute beauty and with it belief began to surge. As both sets of players left the field at the interval, they were facing two very different team talks. For Liverpool they would doubtless have heard how Chelsea were there for the taking. Mourinho, on the other hand, would face a mission impossible as he tried to lift a dressing room staring its sixth defeat in a row in the face.

The second half would continue as the first left off, with the match as fiery off the field as it was on it. Klopp would continue to berate the officials and even got into a row with one of Jose's staff, before telling him to 'take a time out'. On the pitch Lucas was flirting with danger, twice lunging into dangerous tackles, only to escape with just a yellow card.

Jose complained that referee Mark Clattenburg was giving his counterpart preferential treatment, after he was told to sit back down. His protests were falling on deaf ears and he'd dug deep down into his box of tricks but could only find his petulant child routine.

The Mourinho sob-story was in stark contrast to Klopp's performance. While Jose's bore all the hallmarks of a two-year-old in the grip of a temper tantrum, Jürgen was all about fire and brimstone.

Perhaps inflamed by their manager's passion, Liverpool's players dug their claws into the vulnerable Chelsea rearguard and it wouldn't be long before they capitulated again. James Milner had made way for Benteke, and Firmino was swapped out for Jordon Ibe. The Belgian headed down a crossed ball and it was swept up by Coutinho. The resultant shot cannoned off John Terry and into the net. The travelling Kop exploded and Mourinho slumped into his seat.

There were 16 minutes left. Perhaps a previous Reds team would have thought about clinging on. Not this one. It wouldn't be until the 90th minute, with Liverpool 3-1 up, that the boss chose to make a defensive substitution. But before Dejan Lovren could make his cameo, Ibe had seen Benteke's assist and delivered one of his own for the Belgian to dispatch with calm ease.

It was a truly satisfying victory, but the league table spoke of even greater challenges ahead for Klopp and much hard work for his players. Liverpool were in seventh place and they had beaten a team in 15th. Still, that didn't stop some journalists asking whether this win signalled a charge for the top four, even the title?

Klopp expressed disbelief that English football could be so impatient. He also dismissed suggestions of a plunge into the January transfer market. In his own inimitable style, he batted away the curve balls from the press pack.

'I have been here three weeks. Everyone tells me 'you want to buy this player, this player, this player'. But development is to work with the players you have. It's like if you have a problem with your wife, you don't want to change every day, you just work and work and get better.'

That faith in his squad and belief in his method would prove to be the cornerstone of Liverpool's rise from the ashes of the Brendan Rodgers era. It would see Liverpool not only survive the loss of Coutinho, who played such a pivotal role in this victory, but go on to reach new heights.

Klopp walks alone at home to Palace and sends a message to supporters who leave early

The annoying thing about stereotypes and cliché is that there's occasionally a morsel of truth in them. On Sunday, 8 November 2015 anyone in or around Anfield would have found it hard to argue that it wasn't 'grim up north.' It was a miserable day on the Mersey and not just because of the footy.

Alan Pardew was bringing his Crystal Palace team to Liverpool, with only a point separating the two teams. When they left for the capital at 4.45pm, they had washed away any lingering euphoria from the Reds' Stamford Bridge raid and left Jürgen Klopp walking alone.

Earlier that day, I'd opted to walk to the game despite the dark skies and drizzle, partly because the washing machine had started shrinking my pants and because the kids had begun to shrink my bank balance. It's a decent walk; roughly 8,000 steps according to the pedometer on my mobile phone.

By the time I reached the ground I was in a decent mood. I'd been lifted by recent results. It seemed that Klopp's philosophy was slowly sinking in. Our 1-0 long-haul victory over Rubin Kazan in the Europa League group stage was a decent one and the 3-1 demolition of Chelsea, from a goal down no less, both had me convinced Klopp's men could overcome their jet lag.

To hell with the fact that Palace had proven a bogey team in recent seasons, I thought. The pain of the 3-3 which effectively ended our title challenge in 2013/14 may still take a while to ease, but my optimism knew no bounds. Besides, Jürgen was standing on the brink of an incredible record; avoid defeat and his Reds would remain unbeaten for the first eight games of his tenure. This would equal a standard set by the great Bob Paisley, and I had no doubt he would do it. I was a believer, just 8,000 steps from heaven.

Pardew had organised his charges well. They were also big and strong, and he had clearly set them up to claim more than a point that day. From the moment the game kicked off it was obvious this wasn't going to be a stroll.

Coutinho and Cabaye both put efforts high and wide as the sides traded punches early on. Still, I recall feeling reasonably comfortable. I even commented to the guy next to me that Klopp seemed to have sorted the defence out. In the pre-van Dijk era such hubris was unforgivable and often punished.

Right on cue Liverpool were beset by yet more uncertainty in the box. Liverpool could and should have dealt with the threat from Palace far more decisively. Instead, from where I sat, Yannick Bolasie seemed to be given way too much space and time.

In an instant it was 1-0 and Red hearts sank. Still, the trouncing of Chelsea had given us all hope that the Reds had rediscovered their once-famed resilience. In fact, the setback did seem to spark a fightback, but it never reached the heights scaled against the men from Chelsea.

The game was descending into a scrappy affair, when it looked like we were about to lose a key man. Mamadou Sakho had picked up a knock. He seemed to be struggling badly but opted to fight on through the pain. This was long before a drug test controversy robbed him of a place in the run-in and in the Europa League Final. At this stage he was a cult figure and an integral cog in Klopp's team.

Tension rose as he went off the field of play to receive treatment, replaced by a palpable sense of relief as he chose to battle on. Loud applause accompanied his charge back on to the pitch along with chants of 'Sakho, Sakho, Sakho.'

Behind me, someone joked, 'He was going off there, until he saw Lovren pulling his shirt on and then he thought "fuck that".'

Dejan Lovren was as divisive a figure then as he is now. The comment provoked nervous laughter. Such was the importance of Sakho to the Reds' backline and paucity of cover on the bench, nobody wanted to contemplate losing the Frenchman while we were a goal down to a team full of giants with a penchant for set-piece goals.

Unfortunately, our worst fears were realised and Mamadou would be forced to make way for Lovren. Klopp had asked us to become believers, but belief was in short supply and very fragile during the genesis of his reign.

The change of personnel somehow sparked a momentary revival though, and within two minutes any feelings of trepidation were blown away. Phillipe Coutinho gleefully accepted an Adam Lallana assist and buried his shot into the centre of the goal.

The Reds had again responded positively to going a goal down and hope sprang eternal as they besieged the Palace goalmouth, winning a succession of corners. Had they converted one of them as the half petered out, the result may have been very different. Sadly, this was the season of promise and what ifs. Anfield seemed to be a place where corners go to die, and the mutterings around me spoke of a frustration borne out of too many false dawns.

Klopp's task of turning an at times rancorous and discordant Kop into believers probably never felt as enormous as it did that day.

Liverpool weren't bad in the second half. They created enough goal-scoring opportunities to take the three points, but they were far too blunt in attack. A goal seemed as distant a prospect as a 19th league title at times, and from Palace's point of view it would have felt like a comfortable afternoon.

The disjointed and nervous football on the pitch, coupled with the angst off it served to suck the life out of the game. As the final ten minutes approached, I started to think that a draw wouldn't have been the worst result ever. Disappointing? Yes, but given the long journey in midweek, coupled with a short recovery period; it would have at least been understandable. Klopp may yet equal Paisley's astonishing record.

Palace hadn't come for a draw though, and they hadn't read the pre-match script. Pardew had gambled on Liverpool tiring towards the end of the game and his side rallied in the final stages. They won a corner and anxiety levels began to rise once more. Liverpool were like American action heroes in reverse when it came to corners; none of our bullets could hit the target, but the bad guys scored a direct hit almost every time.

From where I sat it was hard to see exactly what went on in the box, but it's far way that you couldn't see that this was another self-inflicted wound. Klopp cut a miserable figure on the touchline, as all around him seats began to empty fast.

He will have come to Liverpool believing the Anfield faithful to be soul brothers of their Dortmund counterparts. Maybe once, but not this day. Liverpool's home support felt broken. The weight of 25 years of disappointment had sapped the will of even the most ardent supporters.

Klopp would later bemoan the exodus, which began with fully eight minutes left on the clock. This was more than enough time to turn things around, surely? Maybe this was true of previous Liverpool incarnations. Time would prove that the future would see the restoration of that fighting spirit, but nobody leaving early that day could see it. Neither, in truth, could those who stayed.

Klopp was right to identify this as an issue in his first interview. However, even he seemed taken aback by the scale of the problem. Earlier in the game I had been lambasting the Palace supporters for their moronic and predictable chants. It's like they work off a script and you could run a sweep on what minute they'll start the 'Where's your famous atmosphere?' chant.

Trouble is, when it comes to stereotypes and clichés, there's often a grain of truth in them. Anfield had reached a low point in this game. It shocked the manager, and as we look back on the evolution of Klopp's Liverpool, I believe we may well see this game as a turning point.

In the pub, after the game, I was told that 'it's up to the players to give the fans something to shout about'. Well that's partly true, I suppose. 'So, are we mere spectators or supporters?' I asked. 'Fans or customers?' Surely, it's a two-way street. My words were lost in the despondency of the result.

When I heard of Klopp's comments, criticising his own supporters for leaving him in his hour of need, I felt strangely uplifted. At last, I thought, Liverpool have a manager of genuine quality who gets what it means to support Liverpool and what our history has taught us. He was perhaps the only man with the credibility and bottle to put Liverpool fans in our place. How fortunate that our fates had collided with the arrival of Jürgen Klopp, precisely the type of manager we needed.

You might say he was made for Liverpool, and Liverpool was made for him. Too soon for a Shankly reference? Maybe, but it felt right in that moment.

Something in Klopp's chastening words seemed to resonate with me and other Liverpool supporters. We knew we had to stop believing our own hype, stop living on past glories and start creating some new ones. The Palace debacle became a watershed, a new dawn. It had to be. Had it not, we would have remained forever 8,000 steps from heaven.

Jürgen takes a bow as late goal seals draw with the Baggies

In the winter of 2015, Jürgen Klopp provoked much debate by leading his charges in a triumphant bow in front of the Kop at the end of a game against West Bromwich Albion. This was no response to a title-deciding victory, but to a home draw that decided nothing. Liverpool were in ninth place when the final whistle sounded.

All revolutions have their pivotal moments. They need them. When the initial euphoria and hope settles into drudgery, you need something that shakes things up. It doesn't have to be much, but it must convince the troops that their dreams can become reality, if only they keep fighting for them. Once that happens, whole new vistas can be imagined.

Admittedly, a freezing cold Sunday in December and a meaningless home game against the Baggies seems an unlikely candidate for such a turning point. A last-gasp equaliser on home soil against a supposedly inferior enemy doesn't seem like a cosmic signpost for that greater glory. It may have been even less a justification for leading your team in a triumphant bow in front of the Kop. However, that's exactly what Klopp did at full time. The reaction to his moment of abandon shocked even him.

The BBC called it a 'madcap celebration' but Jürgen was emphatic in his response: 'The atmosphere was the best since I've been here. We need moments like this, we need moments like this at home ... I have no problem in football; if you lose a game you have to accept it but this was not a game to lose.'

Klopp of course is right. How can we explain such exuberance in the face of apparent mediocrity? A better question would be why do we need to? It was just how everyone felt, and it seemed to make perfect sense at the time.

Liverpool had struggled for much of the game. Tony Pulis's gameplan relied entirely on set pieces and long balls. Liverpool had taken the lead after 20 minutes thanks to Jordan Henderson, but West Brom struck back within ten minutes. They could even have been ahead on half-time, but for a disallowed goal.

In the 73rd minute they went in front thanks to Jonas Olsson. It could have deflated the crowd, but instead the noise levels simply rose. On the touchline Klopp urged the supporters to climb to new heights and they responded magnificently.

However, as chances came and went and the seconds slid inexorably into the bottom half of the hour glass, anxiety grew. Doubters were once more everywhere, and there was nary a believer to be found.

What happened next would define Klopp and his relationship with the supporters, it would crystallise the bond he had with them and his team.

For those who have reason to fear or loathe his Liverpool, it would become an object of scorn. Jürgen didn't care, because he knew that football is about joyous moments as well as heroic victories.

It was a moment when all of us realised that Jürgen was one of us. The only difference was he has control over the squad, we just think we do.

Deep into the fifth minute of injury time, Origi picked up the ball about 30 yards out. He stumbled and then found his footing, took the ball on a few yards before unleashing a looping diagonal shot into the bottom right corner of the goal. The Kop exploded and, on the touchline, Klopp was imagining a victory, let alone a point.

He turned to the supporters in the main stand and beckoned them to roar the team to an improbable winner. We used to believe such things were possible once, he was reminding us of that.

Just imagine a Kopite in the dugout. Imagine his every tick, twitch and grimace mirroring every sliding tackle and each kick of the ball. Imagine his internal maelstrom bubbling away throughout 90 minutes of football, his emotions crashing then soaring, before finally, upon the referee's whistle they erupt in a magnificent celebratory explosion of euphoric irrationality. If you can, then you might as well be imagining Jürgen Klopp.

It's the only way I can explain him and the team linking arms and celebrating in front of us in that way. Cold, hard logic had disappeared, tactical analysis was redundant. All that was left was the joyous abandon of the fanatic.

Even with the distance of time I can still see the beauty of Origi's leveller. Even after absorbing the text messages from Bluenoses, and facing down the taunts on social media, I can't lose the warm glow. According to rival supporters, such emotions should be reserved for only the biggest of sporting victories. Of course, they would know all about those. After all, they'd seen them on the telly.

To be fair they're probably right. Let's face it, a draw at home to West Brom doesn't compare to Everton's last-minute 'winner' at Bournemouth that season, which provoked the travelling Blues to storm the pitch only to see their heroes succumb to an immediate sucker punch, losing the game in the process. Compared to that, surely, we can celebrate snatching a point, where defeat had seemed certain.

I've never suggested that such results are a benchmark. Rather, I see them as staging posts on a longer journey. In the months and years that followed this game, there would be many more moments like this. It has always amused me how much our response to them infuriates our rivals. They expect us to be despondent, to wallow in self-doubt. When they see us in revelry regardless of the outcome it seems to short-circuit their brains.

The game against West Brom had been a difficult one, as all games against a Tony Pulis side are. Pressure had been building throughout the second half. Chance after chance missed the target, ramping up the frustration levels with each passing minute. Often these tensions leave the confines of the ground. They play out in bars and homes all over the globe and find voice on social media. The entire fanbase becomes one hive-mind in meltdown.

It's tough watching your team from afar but believe me, because I've done both, nothing matches being in the stadium when it comes to the shredding of nerves. I can't imagine what it's like in the dugout.

The see-saw of emotions really must be experienced to be believed. I am sure there are other walks of life that match it; I just haven't experience them yet.

I am a survivor of many an encounter in which the clock seems to eat up the seconds, while I desperately cling to hope and pray that I won't be going home to lick my wounds for the coming week. It's an experience that does strange things to a supporter.

All of us go to the game wanting, expecting or even demanding nothing less than three points. The thought of accepting a draw against a team like West Bromwich Albion is an anathema; never mind celebrating one. After all we are Liverpool. We should be comfortably dispatching teams like this routinely, right?

Except we don't.

Football doesn't work like that does it? Ask Chelsea, Manchester United or City. Football can be wonderfully unpredictable sometimes.

During a match you modify your aspirations. You start off flushed with optimism. Three points is the minimum expectation. You've already noted the scores affecting rival teams. You've plotted where a win will take the men in red and mapped out a strategy for the remainder of the season.

Unfortunately, no strategy ever survives contact with the enemy.

So, when you go a goal down you just pray for an equaliser. It doesn't matter how you get it. It could go in off the referee's backside for all you care, so long as it ends up in the net. If you find yourself behind as full time approaches that feeling only intensifies.

I often find myself bargaining with imaginary deities, promising the earth in return for a precious point. Let's face it, draws at home aren't ideal, but they're better than nothing. After all, there's a club's honour at stake. Well not really, but that's how it feels to all of us.

Football is an irrational game. If you don't agree with that, consider this next time you're at the game. You're watching 22 men you don't know kicking a ball around a pitch, while paying a princely sum for the privilege. Would you do that if you weren't convinced you were part of something bigger than yourself? Something magical and life affirming?

So, is it really that surprising that in the mad world of the football supporter, a draw can feel like both a defeat and a victory, even though objective reality tells us it really is just a draw? It just depends on the context.

Sadly, for many, such romance has no place in football. Instead it's a case of hiding your love away for fear of invoking the scorn of your rivals. How boring.

Give me passion over the sanitised sport we are served up today any time. I say let the blue-noses invade the pitch in a meaningless game on the south coast if they want. It is just a symbol of the bond between them and their club. So too is the sight of Jürgen's men taking a bow in front of an exultant Kop, after a meaningless point against a team of also-rans.

Against West Brom it looked like Klopp and the players felt a little of the old magic that older Kopites once took for granted. Origi said he had never experienced support like it. 'They pushed us on,' he said.

The boss echoed those sentiments and talked about an explosion of emotion at the end of the game. All he could think of was running to the supporters and celebrating with them. What's not to love about that?

On Sunday, 13 December 2015 Klopp reminded the Kop that it was okay to find joy in supporting your team – win, lose or draw. They would never forget that lesson in the years that lay ahead. For that, I say take a bow Jürgen Klopp.

Firmino opens his account against Manchester City, as Liverpool run riot at the Etihad

It's 21 November 2015. Liverpool, who sit tenth in the Premier League, face a visit to the champions Manchester City. Amid winter, Britain had enjoyed the warmest day on record at the start of the month, but within a matter of days, the country had been battered by Storm Abigail.

Liverpool's form was eerily like the British climate – they were blowing hot and cold. The 3-1 victory over Chelsea at Stamford Bridge at the end of October had promised so much, but a subsequent narrow win away to Rubin Kazan in the Europa League, and a frustrating 2-1 defeat at home to Crystal Palace, meant that Liverpool supporters would travel with trepidation as they made their way to the Etihad.

The transfer of Raheem Sterling to Manchester City in the summer for a fee of £50m had swelled Liverpool's coffers, but the circumstances surrounding the deal and the behaviour of his agent had angered many supporters. There was a sense that the player thought he was bigger than the club and was holding his employers to ransom. Whatever the merits of that argument, it all added to the pre-match hype. This was potentially Raheem's first outing against the Reds since leaving the club.

Looking back, we needn't have worried. Sterling did little to trouble Liverpool, and in any case the Reds had a penchant for punishing the top four sides, while struggling against teams they should beat comfortably. It was an annoying habit and it took Jürgen a couple of seasons to put that right. Back in 2015, the travelling Kop had more to fear on a trip to Newcastle than they ever did at the Etihad.

This was a fact borne out by Liverpool's blistering start to the game. They were 3-0 up after 30 minutes in a half in which they could have recorded double that. The first came courtesy of an Eliaquim Mangala own goal after just seven minutes, which had the away end in raptures and Klopp ecstatic on the touchline.

Jürgen can celebrate a tackle in the middle of the park with the same ferocity and passion as he does a glorious goal. The sight of Philippe Coutinho harrying and hassling Bacary Sagna off the ball in the centre circle and then breaking forward with pace had the German in raptures. His joy, though, would reach fever pitch, as the 'little magician' fed his Brazilian compatriot, Roberto Firmino, who slung a dangerous cross into the box, which the despairing defender could only turn into his own net.

Despite his assist, Firmino would encounter his manager's wrath soon after. Klopp would later reveal that he had given the man who would become Bobby, to countless adoring Reds, strict instructions that he wanted him to play 'as a striker who is sometimes a midfielder, not a midfielder who is sometimes a striker'. However, with around 20 minutes gone the boss had become frustrated that his player was dropping too deep.

Those sitting in the dugout and watching from the press box would see him remonstrating angrily with Firmino and giving him the bollocking of a lifetime. It was a very one-sided discussion and the Brazilian clearly took it to heart.

He immediately raced up the field and delivered a delightful assist for Coutinho to make it 2-0. The greatest coaches in the modern game all share an uncanny knack for profoundly altering the course of a match, during the game.

Whether it's a timely or insightful substitution or, as Klopp demonstrated, the ability to get into a player's head and influence his play, their contributions can be the difference between success and failure.

The goal and his manager's celebrations on the touchline drove Bobby on to even greater heights. Less than ten minutes later, he was on the scoresheet himself. It was his first goal for the club, and with the scoreline at 3-0, he had made a telling contribution to all three of the Reds' goals.

He was then denied twice by the brilliance of Joe Hart and sent another shot sailing inches wide of the post. When a moment of incredible brilliance by Sergio Agüero who in the 44th minute shook off a six-week injury layoff to convert a chance he had no right to score, 3-1 looked very flattering for City indeed.

The players could scarcely believe their dominance over the champions and their expressions as they entered the dressing room gave them away. Klopp smiled and gently remonstrated with them for being doubters in their own ability. 'Believe, don't be surprised,' he told them.

Psychology is so critical in sport. Mental toughness is key in football. Klopp showed he had this in spades and crucially knew how to transmit it to his players. In times gone by, after conceding late in the first half like that, Liverpool sides would have succumbed to a late onslaught, perhaps drawing or worse still losing the game. It was an affliction that would plague them again before Klopp's work was complete, but on this day they would be resolute.

In the second half, Liverpool showed tremendous quality and belief. Whereas City showed little. Manuel Pellegrini would struggle to explain his side's performance, simply agreeing it was the worst he had seen. Liverpool might have had something to do with it of course. In the 81st minute Martin Skrtel wrapped up the points and gave the scoreline the convincing look his team's performance merited.

The assorted press eulogised over Liverpool's pressing style and ability to turn defence into attack so effectively. Many wondered whether the Reds could maintain their ferocity week in, week out. Klopp's answers to these questions were both entertaining and incredibly informative.

'If you are stuck in the forest and it's dark and you are afraid, and someone tells you not to be then it doesn't work. It's about your own mind. Only you can affect that. We need the confidence in ourselves, but we cannot switch the lamp on and off, on and off. This was very good, but we have to keep working at it,' he said.

There was that theme again. It's not about what anybody else says or does, it's about what you believe in your own mind. You have to become a believer in yourself. The power of mentality; it would become a cornerstone of the Klopp era, and it is so in tune with the philosophy that drove Liverpool to unparalleled success in decades gone by. The glory of Anfield has forever been built on a strong sense of inner confidence, hard work and togetherness. Klopp's philosophy would be instantly recognisable to any Liverpool manager or player of yesteryear.

The transformation under the German coach had not been lost on the media, with *The Telegraph* commenting, 'Where there was turgidity there is vibrancy; where there was cowardice there is courage; where there was dourness there is now ebullience. Most reassuring for Jürgen Klopp, where there was doubt there is now belief – soaring, uncontainable belief.'

American broadcaster NBC described the performance as, 'One of the finest performances we've seen in recent years.'

However, speaking to *The Times,* Klopp was more measured. He could see that to become a great Liverpool side his players would need to do this against all comers, and not simply raise their game against seemingly superior opposition. He argued that if the Reds were to take the next step, they'd have to play with such bravery and passion against lowlier opposition.

He explained, 'I would love to win a game like this at Anfield. That's the next challenge. We have Swansea coming but I don't know that much about them yet. We lost to Palace so we have to find a solution and we will.'

Jürgen would deliver a less than emphatic triumph against Swansea in the next game, claiming a 1-0 win. It wouldn't be enough to make him happy, but it was a start. The thrashing of the champions, though, gave us all a taste of the bounty to come.

No vintage red, but Klopp's Liverpool rebirth takes shape with win against Bordeaux

We arrive at 26 November 2015. Jürgen Klopp's reign is only just beginning, but already we've had momentous moments and we've seen enough to warrant a new surge of optimism around Anfield. Our visitors for this moment in Reds history are French outfit Bordeaux, and the competition is the Europa League.

Of course, as we know only too well, football is not played in a vacuum. Our French visitors are traumatised by the horrific events in Paris, which saw 130 innocent civilians killed in a terrorist attack, many of them at a concert in the Bataclan Theatre.

Naturally, security concerns dominated the game, with reports of a major security operation around the ground and delays at turnstiles, as supporters were searched going into the game. In the end this didn't materialise, and policing appeared relatively low-key, given the circumstances. Fans mingled freely, posed for photos and joked with friends, just like they always do.

The atmosphere outside the Kop was buoyant and the Park and Albert pubs looked packed. Kopites, it seemed, were undaunted by events overseas. Not so my 11-year-old daughter, who grabbed hold of me as I left for the match that night. She hugged me tightly and said, 'If anything happens, run for your life.'

However, instead of fear and terror, Anfield saw an outpouring of solidarity with the French people. It was gratefully accepted by the French supporters. A Bordeaux delegation paraded a banner, thanking the British people for their support after the massacre, to huge applause from all four corners of the ground.

Then came the traditional rendition of 'You'll Never Walk Alone'. It felt like it was sung directly at the French contingent, and it was repeated *a capella* as Bordeaux entered the pitch. Their fans held their scarves aloft and joined in, applauding enthusiastically when it finished. This was ordinary people united in a common passion and a belief in liberty, equality and fraternity. In the end there is not much that divides us all.

This was a game Liverpool just needed to win, by any means necessary. Still, after the sumptuous display dished out at the Etihad, expectation had once again been raised. That said, while it would have been great to dish out another thrashing to confirm our revival, I confess, as I walked through the turnstile that night, I didn't really care how we progressed, just as long as we did.

In the last couple of years Liverpool have never looked like they belonged in continental contests. Even forgiving the capitulation against Real Madrid, we couldn't ignore the fact that Liverpool had succumbed to lesser opposition too many times.

I found this particularly painful as I have always seen Europe as the pinnacle. The Reds built their reputation on the European stage, and in my lifetime we have been the most feared team on the continent. In 2015 though, even the heady nights of Istanbul and Athens seemed like ancient history. Liverpool were once again facing the prospect of rebuilding an empire from crumbling ruins. As Klopp said on his arrival, 'It's time to restart.'

So be it. This game could be the foundation stone in the mother of all reconstructions, I thought, and got ready to sing my heart out for the Reds.

From the kick-off Liverpool went on the attack. They ran at the Bordeaux defence with pace, they chased and harried for every ball. Liverpool, once criticised under Rodgers for not being nasty enough, were a model of controlled aggression.

The referee didn't quite see it that way though. I'd have called him fussy, as he awarded several decisions Bordeaux's way. The lad behind me was more emphatic and declared him 'shocking'. Still, Anfield loves nothing more than a siege mentality, even one conjured in the minds of biased supporters. It only ferments the atmosphere and with each perceived injustice the cauldron bubbles and spits into life.

The point was graphically illustrated on the half-hour mark when Mignolet inexplicably decided to slow the game down by holding the ball for a full 22 seconds. To us it felt like 22 minutes. It must have felt longer for the referee as he booked the keeper for time-wasting. Goalkeepers are rarely punished for this, and the Kop was outraged. Trouble was, half of them were venting their fury on Mignolet, the other half on the match official.

Whatever the object of their scorn, it had the effect of raising the decibel count. Sadly though, that wasn't the last piece of indecisiveness from our stopper as the French team squandered a gilt-edged chance to capitalise on his dithering.

Liverpool began to look nervous defensively, and another mistake by Mignolet was punished ruthlessly. The Belgian conceded a free kick in a dangerous position, and as he lined up his wall, there was little doubt among supporters around me that this would go straight into the net. Of course, it did.

The visitors went 1-0 up and for a second it felt like the atmosphere would crack, and the supporters would collapse into bitter recriminations and wallow in anger and self-loathing. It happens so many times in league fixtures, but not that night. Maybe it's the floodlights, maybe it's the continental accents in the away end, and maybe it's because it's a European fixture, who knows. But on nights like this the Kop possesses an ability to give itself a slap and roar the team back into life.

If only we could do it on a rainy Saturday against Bournemouth. That would come, in time.

Fortunately, we didn't wait too long for the leveller. Just five minutes later, Benteke was hauled down in the box. After reviewing the replays later from the comfort of my armchair, I have to say the decision was generous. Who cared, Liverpool had won a penalty. Up stepped the captain, James Milner. The crowd held its breath, as the away supporters did everything in their power to put him off. But Milner has ice in his veins and he coolly slotted the ball into the bottom right-hand corner.

Liverpool were beginning to display something Brendan Rodgers turned into a buzzword but never managed to develop in his charges – character. You could knock them down, but they got straight back up again.

As the half drew to a close, we'd have all been content to go in at 1-1, but thankfully Benteke had other ideas. The referee had awarded just one minute of injury time at the end of the first period. Given the time wasted by Mignolet and the resultant free kick, that seemed strange. However, Liverpool only needed 30 seconds of it to go in front.

It was a superb finish by the Belgian following a great assist from Nathaniel Clyne. Suddenly, we looked to the second half with growing optimism. We would be attacking the Kop and a comfortable win seemed on the cards. Instead it was 45 minutes of frustration and angst, as the Reds seemed to back off, apparently settling for a 2-1 win.

In the end they got what they wanted and as the game petered out, the Kop launched into a rendition of its famous anthem. It was sung more out of relief than triumphalism.

As the players left the field of battle and Bordeaux saluted their fans, we were left to reflect on what had seemed at one stage to be an unlikely qualification from our Europa League group, and with a game to spare.

This was no vintage red, but it was enough to allow some of us to dream of the final in Basel, and the possibility of a fourth triumph in the competition previously known as the UEFA Cup. That wouldn't have been a bad start to Klopp's reign. More about that later though.

Liverpool's hardest player, Gerry Byrne, bows out, but his story will live on forever

Gerry Byrne passed away on 28 November 2015. A tough defender and a Shankly original, he played in a total of 333 games for Liverpool, scoring four times.

Byrne also won major honours with the club, including two First Division titles and was involved in two promotion campaigns from the Second Division. However, his most prized medal was earned in the 1965 FA Cup Final, during which the Reds finally clinched a trophy that had eluded them since the club's foundation in 1892.

Born in Liverpool in 1938, he joined Liverpool at the age of 15 in 1953. He would sign professional papers for manager Don Welsh two years later in 1955.

Byrne's debut came in 1957, a 5-1 thrashing by Charlton Athletic. It would be his only game that season. His first goal wouldn't come until 1962, in a 3-1 victory over Brighton and Hove Albion.

In 1959 Bill Shankly arrived and Byrne would survive a cull of 24 players by the Scotsman, and it would be under the great man that he would get his real opportunity at the club. Shanks would recognise the player's grit and determination to play for Liverpool.

Growing up in the city, Gerry will have been acutely aware of how much it hurt Reds supporters that they had never tasted success in England's premier cup competition. He must have dreamed of one day playing at Wembley and bringing the cup home.

He would get the chance to do just that in 1965, but his dream was almost snatched from him in the cruellest of circumstances. He would, however, overcome the odds in remarkable circumstances.

The Reds' hopes of ending their FA Cup hoodoo soared after they defeated Chelsea 2-0 in the semi-final at Villa Park.

They'd been on an incredible journey and almost 68,000 supporters would cram into the old ground to witness Byrne and his team-mates keep a clean sheet. That solidity proved to be the perfect platform for Peter Thompson and Willie Stevenson to grab the goals that took Shankly and his men to Wembley.

Liverpool's second and decisive goal was a penalty. Ordinarily Gordon Milne would have taken it, but as he stared at the goal, it seemed to shrink before his eyes. Deciding that he didn't fancy taking it, he handed over the duty to Willie Stevenson. Much to everybody's shock and surprise, Willie accepted the challenge and slotted the ball home to guarantee the win.

However, it was anything but a confident pen. He would later tell a legends night at the Liverpool Devonshire Hotel, 'I thought I was having quite a good game, so I told Gordon, "No problem, I'll take it." I meant to put it in the bottom right-hand corner, but my foot slipped, and the ball went about six feet up in the air and straight back into the net. It didn't matter though when a goal takes you to a final, it's a great goal no matter how it goes in.'

Gerry Byrne and Liverpool were in the final and the city was gripped by Wembley fever. Of course, the Reds went on to win the game, but it's worth reflecting once more on what happened early in that match, and in particular the injury to Gerry Byrne.

After a crunching tackle, Byrne collapsed to the turf, clearly in distress. Bob Paisley, the then club trainer, was sent on to tend to him. What happened next will be spoken of for as long as the club exists.

Back then substitutes weren't allowed, so had he left the field injured Liverpool would have had to contest the match with ten men. This would surely have been an impossible task against a great Leeds side.

Recalling the events in his book, *My 50 Golden Reds*, Paisley wrote, 'I knew as soon as Gerry Byrne went down on that lush Wembley turf that something was seriously wrong. All my training over the years had taught me to recognise the difference between a player who was simply going down for a rest and one who had been hurt. Gerry was as hard as nails but as I ran across from the Wembley benches to where he lay on the pitch, I didn't need telling that we could be in a fix.'

Watching archive footage of the game, it's possible to get a sense of Byrne's pain. Paisley would have to deliver the seemingly heartbreaking news that the player may have to miss the rest of the game. In a typically understated manner, Bob said, 'Gerry it's broke,' but Byrne simply got up and replied, 'I'll get by Bob.'

In an act of sheer heroism and remarkable strength, he would go on to finish the game, including extra time and even had a hand in Liverpool's winner. His contribution to that game and Liverpool FC was immense.

In recalling Gerry's qualities and that incredible day at Wembley in 1965, Ian Callaghan had this to say to lfchistory.net 'I was listening to a tape recently about the 1965 Cup final and on it Bill Shankly said Gerry Byrne should have got all 11 medals for what he did in that cup final. Bill was saying Gerry was one of the best players he had. And he was. He was a tremendous player, one of the best two-footed players around at that time without a doubt. He could play left-back and right-back without any problem.'

We can take heart in the fact that our history contains men of such conspicuous valour and skill as Gerry Byrne. If the Reds are to reclaim but a fraction of the glory his eyes saw, they will need to show the same courage he displayed throughout his playing days.

Origi treble sees Reds into the semi-final of the League Cup in emphatic style

A terrible November had come to an end with the world weeping for the victims of a horrendous terrorist attack in Paris. December began with the UK's politicians seemingly hungry for war, and on a night when Liverpool's strike force would lay waste to the Southampton backline, Parliament was voting to drop yet more bombs on Syria.

Against such a backdrop football risks being irrelevant. At best it is an escape from the horrors of the real world. At worst it can feel like a distraction. In the context of such madness on the global stage, all footballers can do, all supporters can do, is their jobs. The players must simply compete. They must use the platform they are given to entertain. Their fans can only support and believe.

On 2 December, at St Mary's Stadium on the south coast, Liverpool's players delivered. The travelling Kop would make the trek home having witnessed an utter demolition job and with hope in their hearts that they had discovered another strike sensation in Divock Origi.

At stake was a place in the semi-final of the League Cup. The glimmer of silverware could be seen on the horizon. It was in that spirit that thousands of Liverpool supporters made the mammoth trip south on a wintery Wednesday. That guaranteed a bumper crowd for the Saints, which at 31,592 would be just shy of a record for the season.

Liverpool would be facing two players who would go on to play pivotal roles in Klopp's quest for glory. One would perhaps leave the field happier than the other with his display. Mané's powerful header past a despairing Bogdan was a tantalising advertisement of the talents that would light up Anfield in future years, while Virgil van Dijk will have committed the six-goal mauling suffered by his defence to a locked box somewhere in the depths of his subconscious.

By the end of the game, the Southampton manager Ronald Koeman cut a dejected figure as he shook hands with his opposite number. He had served up the Saints' worst defeat in 56 years. Not until he took over at Goodison and opted to decorate his Christmas tree in red and white would his decision making be so ruthlessly criticised. In truth, his team had simply been taken apart by a Liverpool side slowly coming to terms with their manager's philosophy.

However, within a minute of the start it would all look and feel so different. It was Klopp who had most cause for concern as he watched a future Reds star, Sadio Mané, wheel away in celebration, after powering the home side in front.

With their first attack of the game, Southampton tested the left side of Liverpool's defensive line. Dušan Tadić slid the ball to Ryan Bertrand who shaped to cross. A trio of Reds players failed to prevent the inevitable, with Emre Can, Alberto Moreno and Connor Randall all watching on in despair as the ball sailed towards the head of Mané.

Bogdan in goal had little chance as the bullet header rippled the net and the Saints fans erupted in joy. It was the worst possible start and suddenly that 237-mile trip home for the travelling Kop was looking ominous. Such is the life of the away supporter.

The only good thing you can say about conceding a goal in the first 60 seconds of a game is that you have 89 minutes to put it right. Liverpool would do that with aplomb.

They went on to dish out an emphatic six-goal riposte with their first six shots on goal. There would be joy on those coach trips home after all, and sore heads in the morning of course.

All the talk in the run-up to this fixture had been about Jürgen Klopp's not so veiled criticism of Daniel Sturridge's injury record. The manager had seemingly implied that the striker had something of a low pain threshold.

Sturridge would answer in the only way a footballer can, with his performance on the pitch. His reply would prompt Klopp to reflect, 'Now I know what everybody is talking about.' His words had wound up his forward, and he knew it. The rebuke it seemed had served its purpose.

Liverpool's equaliser and Sturridge's first would originate down the same flank some 24 minutes later. Joe Allen, a leftover from the Brendan Rodgers era, sent a delightful cross for Sturridge to latch on to. At first, he seemed to take the ball too wide and the chance seemed to have gone. However, he turned and bore down on goal, the defender not knowing how to handle him. With the tightest of angles, he smashed the ball past the outstretched arm of Maarten Stekelenburg in the Saints' goal.

Daniel was mobbed and in the stands a banner, draped over an exit, among the Red throng, read 'MY ENDLESS LOVE'. The crowd danced and sang as the Southampton supporters held their heads in their hands. 'Oh Liverpool, we love you.'

This was merely the beginning though, and a rout was on its way. Just three minutes later the horde from the Mersey were in sheer delirium. Not merely because their side were now in front, but the sheer quality of the goal that had put them there.

Allen's sumptuous pass had led to Liverpool's first. This time Can became the provider, first with a delightful flick to create the space, then a glorious lobbed through-ball to the waiting Sturridge. Again the striker had much to do, and again he delivered in emphatic style. It was a goal of utter brilliance.

If the first half belonged to Sturridge, the number 15 would be magnificently upstaged by Divock Origi. The Belgian striker had arrived more than a year earlier. There were high hopes for him. Jürgen Klopp had even talked of how he had watched the player while at Dortmund. However, he had yet to score a single goal for the Reds. He was about to put that right in emphatic fashion.

Deep into first-half injury time, Origi got his toe to Moreno's thunderbolt and flicked the ball past the Southampton keeper to make it 3-1. Adam Lallana had whipped in a corner from the left, which was only half cleared by van Dijk. The ball fell to Moreno who was some 20 yards from goal. He unleashed a shot that skimmed through a packed defence and went in with the faintest of touches from Origi.

In truth countless replays are needed to convince me that the ball didn't go straight in from Moreno's shot, but the press would credit the Belgian with the goal. He was stood in front of the goalkeeper as the ball came in, which led to appeals for offside from Saints' players. They were still incensed at not being awarded a penalty after a clumsy challenge in the Reds' box by Connor Randall.

In truth the game was now over at the interval, but there was still time for the Belgian to grab a couple more. The second half would turn a convincing victory into a mauling.

In the 68th minute he found himself with acres of space in the Southampton penalty area, after a glorious through-ball from Jordon Ibe. The resultant shot almost burst the net and Liverpool had planted their flag in the semi-final.

Ibe would smash in a fifth for the Reds before Divock wrapped it up with Liverpool's sixth and his third just four minutes later. The away supporters behind the goal exploded and chose to serenade Adam Lallana who, as an ex Saints player, had been given a torrid time by the home support.

'He's winning 5-1, he's winning 5-1, Adam Lallana, he's winning 5-1!'

On the touchline, Jordan Henderson, who was waiting to come on as a substitute, punched the air with delight and Klopp roared into the floodlit sky. This was his Liverpool now. There would be setbacks to come but there could be no doubt he had stamped his style on this team.

Liverpool weren't finished though, and Origi would power home a sixth with his head, after a brilliant cross by youngster Brad Smith. The Saints were vanquished, and a beaming Klopp would tell the waiting media, 'We may have to wait a long time to enjoy a football match again as much as we did tonight.'

Of course, we wouldn't wait too long for more evidence of his growing revolution, but this was a most enjoyable evening on the south coast. The final word is left to *The*

Guardian, which revelled in the display: 'It has taken Jürgen Klopp less than eight weeks to restore all the verve that, only two seasons ago, almost propelled Liverpool to the Premier League title. This was a scorching of Southampton, a display of counterattacking football so ruthless that it was hard not to feel for Ronald Koeman, shoulders hunched as he slumped on the sidelines, while the visitors plundered mercilessly.'

Klopp's Reds restore festive cheer with slender win over Foxes

By Boxing Day 2015, thrill memories of the 6-1 obliteration of Southampton in the fifth round of the League Cup had faded. What followed was a study in inconsistency that did much to highlight the task facing Liverpool's new boss.

The joy of that delightful display had been replaced by the all too familiar sense of 'here we go again' as Liverpool slumped to a 2-0 reverse to Newcastle, disappointing draws with Sion in the Europa League, and West Brom at Anfield, and a 3-0 defeat to Watford at Vicarage Road.

December had been a bust, so far. Two defeats, two draws and a solitary win had meant the last-minute leveller at home to the Baggies was greeted with all the fervour of a Champions League win and an unusual celebration from Jürgen Klopp and his players in front of the Kop. It would become a talking point for the media and a source of scorn from rival fans.

Our opponents on 26 December were Leicester City and my heart wasn't exactly filled with hope as I prepared to leave for the game. While we'd glimpsed the ghosts of Christmas future against Chelsea, Southampton and City earlier in the year, they had since been well and truly exorcised.

I've said it many times, and it remains as true today as any time in the past, going to the game is sometimes more about duty than anything else. Still, I wouldn't have wanted to be anywhere else. Boxing Day without football would be like Christmas without Brussels sprouts. It might be unpalatable and often leaves a terrible aftermath, but it's part of our culture and tradition.

Jürgen Klopp, in an interview on the BBC's *Football Focus* show, broadcast before the game, touched on the impact of England's tradition of putting its footballing heroes through the insane fixture congestion at Christmas time, as well as other subjects.

The exclusive interview had been another master-class from the boss.

Always the antithesis of modern football and routinely a challenge to the media's pre-conceived wisdom, he batted away their attempts to generate their preordained headlines, and instead chose to create his own.

The 'commentariat' had become consumed with Klopp's decision to lead his team towards the Kop end at full time, in the game against West Bromwich Albion. So, when granted exclusive access to the German's inner sanctum, the BBC couldn't wait to dredge up the 'incident' again.

Jürgen's response was both typical and brilliant.

'When people are so upset by this it tells me there's something wrong with football in this country. Why should we reserve these things for only the special moments? Don't the supporters celebrate every goal?'

As I contemplated the trip to Anfield, like some festive grinch, I could feel my heart grow two sizes too big with every word he uttered. However, this wasn't even his best line. He'd talked about football being about coming together as a family and being one, but the 'Liverpool family' line had become more of a marketing slogan in recent years and it did raise the hackles a little.

No, it was the eccentric and typically disarming way he addressed the 'controversial' celebration that struck me as so impressive. Klopp is the anti-cliché.

'It's like when people look at your Christmas tree and they criticise your multi-coloured lights. Why should we care what they think? It is only for us,' he said, with that twinkle in his eye which immediately took the sting out of the criticism.

There's nothing more Scouse than that for me, I thought. We'll climb the hill our own way. Well put Jürgen.

Klopp seemed to be repeating a pattern that went back to his time at Dortmund. The atmosphere there wasn't so good when he took over. Their supporters felt they had waited too long for the next success, but he changed all of that by creating a bond between the club and the fans.

It's just a shame that the BBC couldn't match Klopp's imaginative approach and instead immediately descended into cliché following the interview. So, is an atmosphere important, asked the show's anchor, with one pundit predictably responding that it was, while the other stated that really the game is all about results. Yawn.

Nevertheless, by the time I left the house I couldn't wait to get to the ground. Imagine what it must feel like in the dressing room if this is the effect it has on supporters in armchairs.

Mind you, I still harboured some lingering doubts, but they related more to festive traditions than the future under Jürgen Klopp. You see, in Britain our culture requires that we deny our colons even the merest sight of vegetables for 12 whole months, then on 25 December we launch an all-out assault on our digestive system, bombarding it with all manner of greens. Then we throw in an assortment of beers, wines and spirits and allow it all to ferment overnight.

The results are sometimes explosive and always noxious. If Jürgen truly wants the FA to consider a winter break, he should dispense with stats and logical arguments about player burnout. Instead he'd be better off getting them to take a seat in Block 109 on Boxing Day, without a gas mask.

Anyway, back to the football, and despite the team's inconsistency in the league, green shoots of recovery are all about, especially in terms of atmosphere. The ground was buoyant before, during and after the game.

The flags were back, after the ticket price protests in previous games, and the mood seemed remarkably transformed. This is not to be underestimated, especially in the context of recent results. Other parts of the ground joined in too. The Centenary Stand was bathed in the giant crowd surfer that usually adorns the Kop before kick-off, and during the match we could even hear the Main Standers singing too.

Liverpool dominated the first half with the crowd roaring on every tackle and applauding every attempt, even the wayward ones. Maybe it was the festive cheer but gone was the moaning and whining that usually accompanies the team not being 3-0 up after 20 minutes.

One lad behind me had decided to adopt Sakho during the game and was loudly cheering the player's every move. He was shouting, 'Go 'ed Sakho lad,' or 'Well in Sakho' every time the player went near the ball. He was drawing huge laughter with each shout. It reached crescendo when the player seemed to fall over, prompting this lad to shout, 'Yes Sakho, that's it come on!'

He was clearly doing it for effect, but it got everyone around him going and it was a great antidote to the usual carping that accompanies a skyward shot or poor pass. It also helped to raise the noise levels. Now songs that would usually start at the back of the Kop, only to fade away, were taking hold and everyone was joining in.

A Christmas miracle? The Klopp effect? Whatever it is, it warmed the soul.

As half-time approached the only source of angst was the fact that we hadn't taken full advantage of our dominance. Leicester had threatened little, but without a goal there was always the fear that Liverpool would be vulnerable when the Foxes inevitably rallied.

A succession of misses from Coutinho, Sakho, Lovren, Can, Lallana and Origi added to the feeling that this could be another one of those days. That was exacerbated by an injury to Origi, which saw one Belgian replace another due to a hamstring injury.

Back then it seemed like every time our players took a giant stride forward, momentum was robbed by knocks and strains. Christian Benteke took to the field to loud cheers and applause. The striker had been no stranger to the treatment room since his arrival from Villa himself.

Liverpool would then see out a goalless first half and left the terrace pundits to analyse why they weren't leading. In Block 109, I was surrounded by critics of Roberto Firmino. It seems almost comical to reflect on this now, especially given the haunting stanza the Kop have devoted to Bobby in recent time, but there were many who harboured doubts about the Brazilian back then.

It's probably a good job that supporters don't pick the team. Too many of us don't have an eye for player development, and we are increasingly impatient. Hopefully where Firmino is concerned, lessons will have been learned. I doubt it though.

I fully expected Leicester to come out fighting in the second half, but the Reds had other ideas. Klopp had sent the lads out early, which would become a feature of his management, along with his penchant for standing on the halfway line during the pre-match warm-up, studying the opposition routines.

As the Reds ran on to the pitch there was an air of purpose about them and the sense that this was a statement from the dressing room. Evidently it was, and instead of the anticipated attack from Leicester, it was Liverpool, attacking the Kop, who carried the game to the visitors.

Benteke caused problems from the off, heading narrowly over from the centre of the box on the hour mark. The noise levels rose and chants of 'we love you Liverpool we do' echoed around the stadium.

The players responded and just three minutes later Liverpool swept forward again. Firmino received the ball on the left and provided the Belgian striker with a gilt-edged opportunity he couldn't refuse. Benteke stroked the ball past a despairing Schmeichel and the keeper looked furious with himself. He could have done nothing to stop the goal though.

The scenes of raucous celebration belied the fact that this was just one goal and there was a long way to go. However, at Klopp's Liverpool it was okay to celebrate the moments; they're just for us and they're great.

The Reds saw the game out easily. They probably should have added to their tally. Firmino and Benteke were guilty of bad misses.

The latter probably had nightmares that night, tortured by a late, late squandered chance. It had seemed easier to score than miss.

The Kop watched on, incredulous, as the striker, with goal at his mercy, blew his chance. Schmeichel had advanced into Liverpool territory to try to snatch a late leveller from a Leicester corner. However, the Reds defended well and broke with pace. Firmino put Benteke through on goal, but instead of smashing his and Liverpool's second, he seemed beset with indecision. Great groans of frustration filled the air as the chance went begging.

Some in the crowd lost sight of the bigger picture and were still complaining about a missed opportunity to put the game to bed as they were leaving the ground. It seemed that drinking from a half empty glass is another festive tradition some among us struggle to let go of.

In truth, it only ever matters that the team wins. Doubt would of course be swept away by the Klopp juggernaut, eventually. However, in the Christmas period of 2015 that moment seemed a distant prospect.

Liverpool the knockout kings: Three epic Anfield nights send Reds to another final

We didn't realise it at the time. Perhaps some still don't realise it now. Others will point to a different moment, under Klopp, when the doubt evaporated, and belief came flooding in to take its place. For me – admittedly with the benefit of hindsight – it happened during three glorious months in 2016, between March and May.

Sure, the run of games that had Reds dreaming of silverware would ultimately end in pain and even despair. But for a time, we believed. And we hadn't experienced that for some time.

We certainly hadn't believed, with any great conviction at least, on the way down to Wembley to face Manchester City in the League Cup Final in February. When Philippe Coutinho took the game into extra time and penalties, I only detected nervousness in the seats around me. Then, as the players slumped to the turf in defeat, there was only resignation and thoughts of a tough journey home. It was no great shock.

However, even the vanquished of Basel had expected Liverpool to win that final. It was tough to take, because we knew we had a chance. We were believers once again. And who could blame us, especially after those three mesmerising Anfield nights that saw us defeat Manchester United, Dortmund and Villareal.

The momentum had started in the immediate aftermath of that Wembley defeat to City. The football fates would decree that Liverpool's first game would be against their cup final victors, just four days later. The Reds won comfortably – 3-0.

They then went to Selhurst Park and came from behind to win 2-1. The winning goal came at the death, courtesy of a Christian Benteke (remember him) penalty. As we come to realise, there's nothing quite like a last-gasp winner.

Then came a momentous tie against Manchester United in the last 16 of the Europa League. This was the first time the two rivals had met in European competition. The stakes were very high and being eliminated from Europe by that lot would have been agony.

As expected, Anfield rose to the occasion. People were in early and the place was rocking long before kick-off. This was the type of game that needed no hype, yet both managers would not shy away from stoking the fires.

Klopp called it 'the mother of all games' and Louis van Gaal would make the classic error of playing down the Anfield atmosphere. He would brag that he had already been there, earlier in the season, and won. It was the managerial equivalent of those scenes in comedies, where the protagonist utters the immortal line, 'What could possibly go wrong?' This is usually a prelude to disaster, and for United it would be.

A goal in each half saw off United. Sturridge converted a penalty on 20 minutes and, with 17 to go, Bobby Firmino sent Anfield wild with a goal at the Kop end. The noise that greeted that goal would have been heard for miles. It was simply deafening.

A *Guardian* match report agreed, 'Liverpool did everything their loud, appreciative crowd could have wanted and if it was not for David de Gea's goalkeeping they would have established an even more commanding lead to take into the second leg. Anfield has not sounded so good for a long while and, on this evidence, Jürgen Klopp's team will have to be strong favourites to finish the job at Old Trafford next Thursday.'

Old Trafford's attempt to match the fire and ferocity of Anfield was laughable. Liverpool fans almost felt sorry for them. Almost. A few tiny banners sprinkled in their 'singing section' and the playing of a John Denver song does not induce fear, only mirth.

An Anthony Martial penalty on the half-hour mark briefly threatened to inspire a United fightback. But, where they had wilted in the face of a barrage of noise in the first leg, Liverpool only grew in the benign surroundings of Old Trafford.

A moment of brilliance from Coutinho on the stroke of half-time put the away section into raptures and sent United packing. They had no reply. Liverpool strolled through the second half, safe in the knowledge that United needed three. And there was no way they were going to do that.

Liverpool were now in the quarter-final stage and a mouth-watering clash with Jürgen's old club, Borussia Dortmund, beckoned. For this there would be none of the bitterness and simmering hatred that accompanied the game against United. Here there was much respect on show.

Yellows and Reds mingled freely around the streets of Anfield, even swapping scarves and posing for selfies together. Anfield, to the Germans, was one of the great cathedrals of world football and Liverpool supporters were to be respected, even admired. The feeling was mutual.

The atmosphere created at the Westfalen Stadion in the first leg was awe inspiring and the famed 'Yellow Wall' a very worthy adversary for Liverpool's Kop. They would bring it with them to Merseyside and it was an incredible sight, occupying a corner of the Anfield Road end and attempting to go toe-to-toe with the red wall at the other end of the pitch.

This game represented everything Liverpool supporters love about European football. The chance to mingle with foreign fans, sample their culture, the mutual respect and absolute love of football and winning, while also having the time of our lives.

It's hard to explain what happened in that game. To put into words just how epic it was, in terms of the events on the field and the emotions off it. It was a game that had everything and took both sets of supporters through every conceivable emotion. From despair to determination and then on to euphoria, Liverpool and Dortmund did not disappoint. Though their supporters left in defeat, they can be proud of themselves and their team.

They did not fail as fans or players, they just succumbed to something akin to sorcery. There is no other way to explain how Liverpool took that place in the semi-final. It had to be a kind of magic.

Dortmund had plundered two away goals by half-time. The game looked to be won. Liverpool would have to score three without reply in the second half and given the attacking verve and clinical finishing on offer from the men in yellow, it seemed a tall order.

Divock Origi managed one just after the break and hope briefly flickered, before it was extinguished barely ten minutes later as Marco Reus made it 3-1 on the night. Then Anfield took over.

Philippe Coutinho made it 3-2 in the 66th minute, then Mamadou Sakho levelled the tie. It was 4-4 on aggregate and the old ground was rocking. Dortmund still had the edge, thanks to their three away goals, but they seemed to have read the script.

There are moments in these games where you just know. I don't know how, but you just do. A fourth Liverpool goal would arrive from somewhere, the Kop knew it and so did their players and supporters. It was only a matter of when.

As it happened, we would have to wait until the very end. In the 90th minute, Dejan Lovren would rise to head the winner in front of the Kop. In doing so he wrote his name into Anfield folklore and sent Liverpool into the semi-finals.

The *Liverpool Echo* front page screamed 'Klopp's Miracle' next to a picture of Lovren. Inside, the match report captured the majesty of Liverpool's feat, 'Anfield folklore has a new, glorious tale and it's one that promises to be told through the ages. Liverpool marched triumphantly into the semi-finals of the Europa League after the most thrilling of triumphs over Borussia Dortmund. Even for a club famed for its dramatic European comebacks against the odds, this was something truly miraculous. Trailing 3-1 on the night and 4-2 on aggregate with 24 minutes remaining, Jürgen Klopp's men looked doomed to a chastening defeat at the hands of his former club. But inspired by the deafening roar of the Kop, they produced a devastating riposte that left the high-flying Bundesliga outfit shell-shocked.'

Next up was Villareal and the first leg was away from home, just the way we like it. The atmosphere at the Estadio El Madrigal was lively, despite there being just 21,000 inside it. However, in a town with a population of just 51,000, the turnout was incredible.

Liverpool looked to be heading for a creditable goalless draw, when Adrián López stunned the visitors with a goal in the third minute of stoppage time. That said, the idea of taking a 1-0 deficit back to Anfield is not something that gave any Kopite sleepless nights. Nor should it have.

However, that didn't stop a seemingly disconsolate Jürgen Klopp saluting, almost apologetically, the away support. The players looked crestfallen too and perhaps that's a good thing. To lose a game in that manner should hurt, even if the tie wasn't over.

The final was still well and truly within Liverpool's grasp. It would be their second of the season and the smell of glory was strong. We wanted it badly. We needed it. It had been four years since that Dalglish-inspired League Cup win against Cardiff, and we were eager to taste victory again.

The game followed close on the heels of the verdicts handed down by the inquest into the Hillsborough disaster which unlawfully killed 96 Liverpool fans in 1989. The jury had exonerated Liverpool supporters on the day. The mood in the city was one of vindication and great pride at the long struggle for justice.

An emotional tribute took place before the game and supporters and officials of the Spanish outfit played their part with great respect. Then the game got under way.

Villareal had brought their 'Yellow Submarine' to the home of the Beatles and they were sunk almost the moment they set foot on the pitch. Anfield was in no mood to yield, to anyone.

Within seven minutes the visitors were behind, thanks to an own goal by Bruno Soriano. Their advantage cancelled out, they were in for a torrid time. However, we would have to wait until the 63rd minute for the Reds to take the lead courtesy of Daniel Sturridge. And oh, how he celebrated. This is how *The Independent* saw it: 'Daniel Sturridge's eyes were bulging, ecstasy seizing his face. His arms and fists were uncontrollable, driving through the night sky in unbridled celebration rather than cool, rehearsed dance.'

Liverpool almost gave away a penalty and Villareal would see a player sent off in a game of high drama and raw emotion. Adam Lallana, though, would seal victory and a place in the final with an 81st-minute strike, sending Anfield into new realms of ecstasy.

The *Daily Mirror* had this to say: 'There is always a sense of destiny surrounding Liverpool's triumphs in Europe. And at Anfield last night, the Reds produced another magical display to make you believe more history beckons. It was wonderful, as noisy as any of their great European nights and, on an emotionally charged occasion when the crowd paid a moving tribute to the Hillsborough victims, Liverpool produced a victory to live long in the memory. By the end, the supporters were chanting "Jürgen Klopp" over and over because, in just seven months, the Anfield manager has brought this club together and guided them to the Europa League Final.'

All of us felt that victory against Seville in Basel was inevitable, even destined. That run of three games had given us enormous belief. In the first half, our confidence seemed well-founded. Daniel Sturridge put the Reds 1-0 up and we could and should have scored more.

However, we somehow fell apart in the second half. Seville deserved their 3-1 win and Liverpool had been taught a lesson that they would eventually use to lift European football's biggest prize. For us as supporters, we had learned to believe again, and even though we had fallen in the final, that belief would prove to be our greatest weapon in the years that followed.

LIVERPOOL FC 2016/2017

Klopp and the long march back to Europe

Liverpool roar into new season and Henderson wonder-strike earns win at the Bridge

Liverpool opened the 2016/17 season with an explosive away win over Arsenal at the Emirates stadium. Some 60,000 watched stunned as the Reds raced into a 4-1 lead, cancelling out Theo Walcott's 33rd-minute opener.

The pace and power of Liverpool's attack was scintillating. Two goals from Coutinho and one each from Adam Lallana and Sadio Mané put the travelling Kop into dreamland. Jürgen Klopp could scarcely believe what he was seeing, even when his glasses were on his face.

When the fourth goal went in, a jubilant Mané, celebrating his debut goal, leapt on to his back in celebration and almost destroyed his manager's spectacles. It wasn't the first time that happened. Lallana had done similar after smashing a last-minute winner in a 5-4 thriller against Norwich City the previous season.

Sadly though, if Liverpool's attack was heavy metal, their defending wasn't. The Reds must have lost focus because within a minute future Anfield star Alex Oxlade-Chamberlain had pulled one back. Suddenly Liverpool looked nervy and a little over ten minutes later Callum Chambers had reduced the deficit to just one goal.

The Reds held on though, and three points would return with them to Anfield, but their Jekyll and Hyde qualities were once again on show in their next game against Burnley as they went down to a 2-0 defeat. By the time they faced Chelsea on Friday, 16 September at Stamford Bridge,

Liverpool had played four, won two, lost one and drawn one. It wasn't the best start, but it wasn't the worst either.

Chelsea were now managed by Antonio Conte. The Italian was about to lead the Londoners to the league title in his first season, but the Reds were about to give them a stern test.

This was a clash of cultures. North against south, the juxtaposition of heritage with the nouveau riche and the authentic versus the manufactured. There may have been no mass plastic flag show, but the silly light display before kick-off made the point just as well. It was the same on the pitch as Liverpool served up a first half that took us back to the glory days. The Reds were full of hard work, grit and class, while Chelsea sat back and did their nails.

Jordan Henderson might have had a good feeling before the game but, if we are honest, most of us would admit to a sense of trepidation. We needn't have worried.

Liverpool had already begun constructing their new era back on Merseyside. The new Main Stand a testament to the club's ambition off the field. However, that meant three tough away fixtures at the start of the campaign and two of them in the capital. The Reds had managed six points from a possible nine on their travels and the 4-1 mauling of champions Leicester at Anfield meant they were looking good on the pitch too.

The only blot on an otherwise splendid landscape was the 2-0 reverse away to Burnley on matchday two. To vanquish that from the memory, Liverpool would have to pull off a second win away to Chelsea in successive seasons. Thanks to a wonderstrike by Henderson, the team captain, they did just that.

None of us would have predicted that, except maybe the Chelsea manager. Conte had commented before the game that it was 'the wrong time to be facing Liverpool'. Apparently his expensively assembled players would have preferred a later appointment.

Whatever it was that inspired this inferiority complex, his comments would prove prophetic. It also influenced his tactics. Chelsea, sitting comfortably in second place and facing a Liverpool side still searching for consistency, chose to sit off Liverpool and invite them to attack.

The Reds took full advantage and went at the Londoners from the off. They may have been missing Firmino, playing a midfielder, James Milner, at left-back, and had two centre-backs in Dejan Lovren and Joël Matip who were still learning to live with each other but none of that mattered. Klopp's Liverpool were becoming a team who believe in the manager's plan. It doesn't matter where an individual is asked to play, that man would always put in a full-blooded shift. Never mind the Main Stand; this was the platform on which really big things would be built.

Chelsea on the other hand were almost anaemic by comparison during a first half that saw the Reds take the lead through Lovren. Diego Costa was anonymous and Branislav Ivanovic looked like he could walk into the referee's book at any moment. He was extremely lucky not get his marching orders for a cynical and deliberate stamp on Adam Lallana. The resultant free kick came to nothing but not so with his next infringement.

This time it was Wijnaldum he upended and again he was lucky to be on the pitch. Liverpool ensured they profited fully this time and worked in Coutinho, who floated in a delightful cross to the far post for Lovren to score. The away end, magnificent all night, was jubilant as the ball hit the net.

There were just 17 minutes on the clock. It was surely too early to get carried away, wasn't it? Chelsea would rally, wouldn't they? In reality Chelsea barely managed an attack in that first half and Liverpool handled everything they threw at them with distinction.

On 35 minutes things got even better. From a throw-in, deep in Chelsea territory, Lallana found himself in the box. Cahill's clearance was rushed and weak and Henderson intercepted. I expected him to take the ball on, maybe try to find a team-mate. Instead he controlled the ball sublimely, looked up and noted the keeper's position and in one flowing move stroked the ball into the top corner, past the outstretched hand of Thibaut Courtois from fully 20 yards.

The captain's celebration bore the hallmarks of a player as shocked as the rest of us that he'd pulled off such a wonderful finish. In the Liverpool dugout, substitute Marko Grujic leapt from his seat, his face full of wonder and elation.

The Reds were purring now, but this was only an early prototype of Klopp's Liverpool. They could be thunder and lightning up front, whipping up a storm as they broke teams down but terribly leaky at the back. The 4-3 victory away to Arsenal on the opening day had been testament to the fact.

Liverpool's defensive frailties have been a Sky Sports editor's dream for too long. It is true that successive managers have failed to recreate the defensive solidity created in the Houllier and Benitez eras. 'Where are the really tough gritty defenders these days?' debated Martin Tyler and Gary Neville in commentary.

Liverpool would find replacing the defensive discipline and solidity of players like Sami Hyypia and Jamie Carragher a very tall order. Time would eventually prove that as a partnership, Lovren and Matip were not going to cut it. However, the signs were there early on.

Chelsea's goal, which came in the 61st minute courtesy of Diego Costa, would ultimately prove to be a consolation for the home side. Nevertheless it was infuriating. Klopp rightly bemoaned the fact that three of his players were on their arses when the ball hit the net.

However, in football mistakes are made. Even the greatest of teams fall victim to lapses in concentration or poor decision making. This was true in the glory days and it's true today. Liverpool conceded daft goals under Shankly, Paisley, Fagan and all the rest. What was important then, and still important now, was their ability to stand tall afterwards and see the game out. Liverpool did that against Arsenal at the Emirates, they repeated it against Leicester at Anfield and here against Chelsea they had seemingly turned it into an art form.

Resilience is as important as flair. All the great teams have it. Their heads never go down. You can knock them to the ground but they just get up and keep coming at you. We saw glimpses of the previous season; the Dortmund game being the pinnacle. The 2016/17 Premier League season was showing signs that this particular trait was becoming a virtue.

The Guardian would get a little carried away by this result, especially given that this was only matchday four of a gruelling season. It wrote, 'Jürgen Klopp's wild celebrations on the final whistle reflected the psychological significance of this win. These teams are now level on points below Manchester City but, on this evidence, it is the side from Merseyside who have the more realistic aspirations to contend for the title.'

However, it wouldn't be until Klopp's alchemy could amalgamate true defensive solidity and attacking verve that Liverpool could return to their glorious best, but that's another story. We'll get there in good time.

Liverpool 2-1 West Bromwich Albion: A win is a win and any win will do

'If you go looking for problems lad, you'll always find them.' A throwaway line by a cabbie on the way to the match could be an epitaph for the culture of nitpicking that consumes the modern football. Sure he was actually talking about his vast array of medical problems – they were so bad I almost suggested pulling over and calling an ambulance – but his words are frankly an object lesson for anyone penning a post-match analysis or dialling a football phone-in.

We've arrived in October 2016 and the Reds are preparing to take on West Bromwich Albion at home. I'm in a taxi on my way to the game and indulging in the usual banter to pass the time.

Now, before you say it, I am aware of the irony of someone like me moaning about an over-analytical approach to the game. After all, I have devoted way too many hours of my life to doing just that. But even I can see that sometimes it's best to just enjoy the win and the accompanying drama, without agonising too much over the finer details.

In truth most of us expected this game to be a tough one. Our record against teams managed by Tony Pulis made grim reading back then. Liverpool had shown how they struggle against defensive teams, with a 0-0 draw to Manchester United just five days earlier.

Jose Mourinho's attempts to turn that back-to-the-wall draw into a moral victory aside, Monday night's game against United was turning into the perfect blue-print for any side looking to stifle the Reds' creativity. So, for me and the fella driving the cab to the ground that day, the consensus was that any kind of win would do.

The problem of course is that with this Reds team we were beginning to see that they were capable of so much more. There had already been many examples of their attacking prowess, that we were wondering why Klopp's team should struggle against anybody.

There was the 20-minute spell against Arsenal, on the opening day of the season. The Gunners barely knew what had hit them. In many ways it represented the pinnacle in terms of what this side may become. However, it was also the perfect cautionary tale. The Reds had looked unplayable at times, but ended up clinging on to a lead that should really have been unassailable. But, in the end it was a win, and any win will do.

As we weaved through the traffic on Utting Avenue, we could see the impact of the new Main Stand in the increased volume of cars and people heading to the match. Anfield's pubs were also struggling to come to terms with it too.

Inside the ground was a different story. The atmosphere had improved noticeably and the pre-match rendition of 'You'll Never Walk Alone' had rarely sounded as loud, possibly not since the 1970s. So noisy was the home crowd before kick-off, that the noise of the Midlanders singing about unemployment and libraries could barely be heard.

West Brom's tactics may be similar to those deployed by Manchester United, but they lacked the quality to keep the Reds at bay for long. Liverpool looked assured from the kick-off, with Coutinho and Milner both fashioning early chances.

On 20 minutes the Midlanders' resistance was broken with the kind of flowing move we saw routinely in the '70s and '80s. Coutinho's sublime dummy on the left of midfield completely flummoxed the visitors and Emre Can advanced on goal. The German was still finding his way after a lay off, though he looked less rusty than he had against United earlier in the week.

He bore down on the West Brom defence, who were now in full retreat and fed the ball wide to Firmino. The Brazilian had already begun to have the impact that would lead to him becoming a Kop hero. He took the ball in his stride and delivered a beautifully weighted ball to the foot of Mané, who dispatched it in one motion past Foster and into the net. The ground erupted, as much in relief as in celebration.

Liverpool had at last found a way to break down stubborn resistance. Pulis's men would have no choice but to abandon their game plan and come forward. This would mean more gaps opening up and they did. Can and Lallana both went close before Coutinho grabbed the second on 35 minutes.

This was long before the little magician began agitating for his 'dream move' to Barcelona that later became a nightmare. Back then he was adored and at times could be decisive in tight games.

Ben Foster, who would prove to be a proverbial thorn in Liverpool's side throughout the second half, gifted them a goal in the first. His scuffed clearance looped up in the air and instead of relieving the pressure on his defenders, he gifted possession back to the Reds. Can and Mané recovered the ball in midfield and released Coutinho. A shot seemed inevitable, but instead the little magician once more dummied, taking two defenders out of the game and fired in with his right foot.

A rout looked on the cards and all around me there was excited chatter about claiming top spot. Liverpool's position was nothing short of remarkable, especially given the unfavourable start they'd had. None of us would have bet on the Reds being anywhere near the summit at this stage of the season, but there they were.

Somehow West Brom made it to half-time without falling any further behind. A 2-0 scoreline at Anfield at the end of the first half now feels comfortable. Reflecting back on this game I realise just how far the Reds have come as a team. Back then, in the pre-van Dijk era, 2-0 didn't seem nearly enough to any of us.

The second half saw the Reds attacking their favoured Kop end. Despite our trepidation, hopes were high that the Reds were about to deliver a hammering. Chance after chance followed, with Lovren, Firmino and Can all denied. Foster pulled off a string of saves that drove the Kop mad. Frustration began to grow along with the sense that the longer this went on the Baggies would have opportunities.

Nacer Chadli and substitute James Morrison both went close, before an inevitable heart-stopping corner led to West Brom pulling one back in the 80th minute. Liverpool as a team has now become far more reliable at defending set pieces. However, in the early days of the Klopp era, an opposition corner or free kick near the box was enough to strike fear into our hearts.

From where I stood in Block 109, our defence seemed to lack any sort of plan to deal with the corner. They simply parted like the red sea, leaving Gareth McAuley unmarked to poke the ball past Loris Karius, who had seemed rooted to the spot. It was hard not to get angry in moments like this. I admit I joined in the momentary wailing and gnashing of teeth that followed. 'Another bleeding corner,' 'fucking typical' and 'don't they work on defending set-pieces anymore for fuck's sake,' were just some of the shouts emanating from all around me.

Anxious glances at wristwatches revealed there was still a full ten minutes to go. Fingernails were unlikely to survive. The Kop's response was magnificent though. Instead of descending into a baying mob, they raised their game once more and were fully deserving of the players' and manager's applause at full time.

Equally the team deserves praise, for not capitulating in the final stages. You sense that previous incarnations would have crumbled, but not Klopp's Liverpool. The growing strength of character and resilience has been a hallmark of the Klopp years. It flickered a little at times and almost vanished completely in some games, but its continuing growth has been a joy to see.

This had been a crucial win and it drew the Reds level on points with the team at the top of the table. There was nothing for Liverpool to whinge about, though many did. Most of us, though, continued to trust in the wisdom of that Scouse cabbie: you will always find problems if you look for them hard enough. Forget West Brom's poorly conceded consolation, a win is a win and any win will do.

Reds' new-found never-say-die attitude pays dividends as Palace defences are stormed in London

It's Saturday, 29 October 2016 and Liverpool have travelled to London to face Crystal Palace at Selhurst Park. Britain was preparing to turn back its clocks one hour, but this game again turned our minds back to 2014. Remember that season? The Reds were phenomenal going forward, but when it came to defending they were leakier than Hillary Clinton's e-mail servers.

It was a season that turned out to be a glorious but ultimately gut-wrenching thrill ride. So, when it comes to away-day victories, in which Liverpool need four goals to see off the opposition, it felt like a case of back to the future for me.

The life of a Red over the last 30 years has been all about surviving one false dawn after another. We've invested so much emotion and hope in the ascent that the come-downs left us on the floor. We'd be filled with anguish and wishing we could be more like that weird kid back in school, you know the one who didn't like footy. But then at the start of every season we'd pick ourselves back up and go again. A football team is for life after all, not just for Christmas.

So, you come to accept it, a little. Live in the moment as much as possible, because you know that sooner or later the wheels are going to come off the ride and send us hurtling into despair once more. That's how it used to be; then along came this German fella called Jürgen.

We'd been convinced for years that football was this really complex game, based on strategy and intricate tactics. Diamonds and Christmas trees replaced the 4-4-2, inside-rights and centre-halves we grew up with. Now there are flat back fours and fives as well as players who are tens, but really play like false nines. Whole news channels are now devoted to analysing the game in intricate detail, with the sort of gadgetry you'd normally see in a James Bond movie.

So, we all became convinced to look at possession statistics, passing accuracy and kilometres covered in a game. It's all fascinating stuff and I'm not saying it's completely irrelevant. Of course not. But in becoming consumed by this stuff, maybe we ignored one simple fact. While all this was going on, the best teams just bought good players, developed a plan, made everybody believe in that plan and then won titles.

Could it really be that simple? Well it used to be, but that was in the old days before football was invented by Sky TV. However, looking at the evolution of Liverpool under Klopp we see good players, playing with joyous freedom and utterly committed to their manager's blueprint. That doesn't sound very 'modern' does it?

This journey was taking us back to a time and place were a Liverpool team refused to crumble in the face of adversity. If they went a goal down, they wouldn't worry. They'd just stick to the plan and believe it will all be okay in the end. If they suffered a defensive calamity, they wouldn't waste time agonising over the complexities of zonal marking versus a man to man system; they'd just go right up the other end and bloody equalise.

Klopp's Liverpool was not the same team we'd been watching for the last 30 years. They were more like the ones from the previous three decades. They genuinely understand that football is a simple game. It's about the giving and receiving of passes and of making yourself available for a pass, but it's ultimately about winning even when you probably haven't covered yourself in glory.

Liverpool got the game underway in an appropriately named 'toxic' kit. It was the sort of high-viz garb that wouldn't look out of place on a motorway maintenance crew. Nevertheless they quickly established control and Coutinho fashioned the first effort of the game with a sliced shot that went over. It was a sign of things to come as the Brazilian was majestic for the whole game and very unlucky not to get on the scoresheet.

The opening 15 were all Liverpool, with Palace camped in their own half. I'm not sure what the possession stats were, but the Londoners could barely have managed double figures. The Reds were in irresistible form and the inevitable goal materialised on 16 minutes.

Coutinho and Alberto Moreno combined brilliantly on the left and the Spaniard whipped the ball to the waiting Emre Can who made no mistake. The move epitomised the fluidity of Liverpool's play this season.

What happened next, though, was the embodiment of what had become the Reds' obvious Achilles heel; conceding goals through unforced errors. Dejan Lovren had been showing signs of rebirth under Klopp but his role in Palace's equaliser drew much criticism.

It was route-one stuff from Alan Pardew's men. Steve Mandanda lumped the ball upfield and the ball found its way to Lovren. All he had to do was launch it back in the direction it had come from, but he somehow sliced his clearance. Karius rushed from his line and allowed James McArthur a simple header over his head. Palace could scarcely believe their luck, but Reds fans could definitely believe theirs.

Not to worry though, because back then it was just a case of, if they score one we have to score two. And that's exactly what happened. Liverpool immediately went on the attack and won successive corners. The first was typical fare and failed to clear the first man, but the second did that and more. Coutinho opted to lob the ball into the six-yard box and a decisive Lovren thumped the ball into the net on 21 minutes. Redemption? Well almost.

Remember, if you suffer a defensive calamity, don't worry. Just go right up the other end and score.

The Reds sensed the initiative had swung back in their favour and looked eager to put the tie to bed. Firmino went close before Moreno crashed an effort off the post from a tight angle. Yet once again our backline conspired to make life difficult for themselves.

This time Lovren failed to clear with his head in the centre of defence and Moreno was too passive in dealing with the second ball, allowing a cross into the box, which McArthur once again took full advantage of. The sense of déjà vu was palpable.

The game was turning into a thriller and you wouldn't have got good odds on a 5-5 at that point. Liverpool poured forward once more. Coutinho was somehow denied by the fingertips of Mandanda and shortly after Sadio Mané missed when it would have been far easier to score. Reds teams of old would be starting to grow frustrated by now; perhaps they'd lose concentration and concede again, but not this vintage.

With the half running out Liverpool won another corner on the right. Once again Coutinho shaped to take it. This time his delivery was immaculate and Matip met it sublimely to score his first for the club and Liverpool's third of the game. Such was the frantic nature of the encounter, the sight of the players going into the tunnel 3-2 up was a blessed relief.

We'd all expected Christian Benteke to prove a point in this game after he had been offloaded by Liverpool, and frankly he did. He was a nuisance in the second half and on a number of occasions seemed to have the Reds defence rattled. However, he failed to make the impact expected of him, which seemed like something of a metaphor for his career.

Liverpool continued to press, conscious that they needed another to stave off a devastating third equaliser. The Reds' saving grace was always that their forward line was forever capable of wreaking havoc on any defence in Europe. No longer were Liverpool dependent on the brilliance of a Luis Suárez. They now had an abundance of riches in Mané, Lallana, Coutinho and the absolutely superb Roberto Firmino.

The Brazilian's goal – Liverpool's fourth – was sublime, but the through-ball from Henderson was of equal brilliance. In the 70th minute the Reds captain found himself with the ball about 45 yards from goal in the middle of the Palace half. He looked up briefly before delivering what can only be described as a Gerrard-esque slide-rule pass to Firmino.

The number nine lifted the ball over the keeper with the deftest of chips. It looked so simple. It was anything but.

It was game over and once more Liverpool had seen the banana skin and sidestepped it. The victory over Palace owed as much to that stubborn belief that no matter what our opponents do, we will ultimately prevail, as it did to the brilliance of our attacking play. That would be a quality the Reds would find most rewarding, one day.

Troy Deeney loses the phoney war as Watford are destroyed

It's 6 November 2016, and Liverpool are preparing to host Watford. In the build-up to the clash, Watford striker Troy Deeney foolishly attempted to up the stakes by declaring he was ready to go to war.

There was just one problem with his futile attempts to psyche the Reds out; a war requires that at least two armies turn out on the field of battle. In truth, despite their late consolation, for long spells the Hornets may as well have stayed at home.

This was a consummate display from Klopp's men, breathless stuff at times. Liverpool were in complete control and toyed with the opposition in a way that bordered on cruelty. Belief in Klopp's Liverpool was not yet total, but there was a growing sense of trust in him and his charges and that was already starting to transform the atmosphere at Anfield.

It took Liverpool 27 minutes to break the deadlock. That's football. Rarely do the opposition turn up at Anfield, wave the white flag just after the kick-off and roll out the red carpet to the Liverpool strikers. Most teams come ready for a war of attrition and the task facing the Reds is to find a way past their stiff resistance.

As a veteran of the 1970s and '80s, watching the all-conquering Liverpool teams of Shankly, Paisley, Fagan and Dalglish, I always understood this. The Kop was famed for being the most knowledgeable group of supporters in the land, famed for their patience and unstinting support.

We never gave up until the final whistle back then. However, in recent years that patience was a vanishing virtue. Tension had begun to grow with every misplaced pass or scuffed shot. A corner that failed to clear the first man would be greeted with howls of derision. Thirty minutes without a goal would lead to unremitting tension that all too often spread to the team.

One of the early signs that Klopp's vision was starting to bear fruit at Anfield was the gradual erosion of that frustrated angst and its replacement with burgeoning optimism. In seasons gone by, supporters, who had stood in the pubs around the ground prior to kick-off, watching rival teams drop points, would have grown edgy with each passing minute.

Not anymore. On this day the Kop's transformation from doubters to believers was in full effect and the players thrived because of it. Of course, we would suffer relapses in the months and years that followed. The cure had not yet been administered, but the recovery was underway, nonetheless.

As the minutes ticked by, chance after chance was fashioned and spurned. But, instead of growing restless, all sides of the ground just seemed to lap it up. The noise levels rose with each missed opportunity and when the Reds won a corner in front of the away supporters a huge roar went up.

Milner stood over the ball and we all expected a delivery into the box. Instead, he opted for a short pass to Coutinho. The Brazilian, who had now been dubbed 'the little magician' by LFC TV's John Bradley and almost nobody else, whipped the ball into the box. The defence retreated and as they did, Sadio Mané leaned across his defender to glance the ball into the top corner. It was a finish of real quality, and to cap it all, Liverpool had scored from a corner.

The goal was celebrated with all the zeal of a last-minute winner. Fists punched thc air and there were high-fives all around. This was only the beginning though, and Watford and Deeney were in for a torrid time.

Liverpool's passing and movement was incessant for the full 90 minutes. It was relentless stuff and calling it 'poetry in motion' barely does it justice. One such move, just three minutes after the opener, saw Coutinho on the edge of the box. With defenders blocking his path, he somehow found the space to get off a shot that left Heurelho Gomes floundering. Thirty minutes gone, and the Reds were 2-0 up.

We were witnessing the sort of Coutinho skill that would later persuade Barcelona to part with more than £140m for his services. Liverpool were coasting and a rout was clearly on the cards.

With the half ebbing away, 2-0 looked like being a comfortable enough lead to take into the dressing room. Especially as the Hornets were forced into replacing their first-choice keeper due to injury. Costel Pantilimon must have cursed his luck as he donned the gloves. Liverpool were in imperious form.

With just a couple of minutes to the interval, Liverpool were about to ruin two goalkeepers' afternoons. They broke with pace and Watford retreated in panic. Adam Lallana, a man reborn under Klopp, swept a delightful ball on to the head of Emre Can, who rose to nod it into the net.

It was 3-0 now, and none of us wanted the half to end. Three points now seemed an inevitability, and they would be enough to carry the Reds to the top of the Premier League. The Kop basked in the moment. 'Liverpool, Liverpool, top of the league', they roared.

The Reds almost pinched a fourth on the stroke of half-time when Can flashed the ball across goal, but nobody was there to convert. This was joyous stuff and the second half would only mirror the first.

The fourth goal would arrive just 12 minutes after the restart. It was a goal of sublime simplicity and it had everyone in the ground purring. The Reds won a free kick to the right of the Watford goal and what followed took the breath away.

The ball was pinged around at pace and found its way yet again to Lallana, who slid it across goal to the waiting Roberto Firmino. The Brazilian dispatched it with ease. It was a thoroughly deserved goal.

Coutinho rightly drew praise at the time; he may be a sorcerer, but his fellow countryman is no apprentice. 'Bobby', as the Kop had already christened him, was everywhere against Watford. It was a feat he was beginning to repeat with ominous regularity. He was rapidly becoming an indispensable cog in a squad full of indispensables.

We had barely had time to draw breath, when he was at it again just a few minutes later. Liverpool were attacking with such speed now it was dizzying. The Brazilian raced on to a through-ball and beat the defender with ease. For his size he has incredible strength and he held the ball up long enough to size up his options. Mané's anticipation saw him ghost into the box and Firmino calmly handed him the fifth goal on a plate.

A 5-0 win is a magical scoreline. It conjures up memories of thrashings past and signals the complete destruction and humiliation of the opposition. That's why, when Watford grabbed a thoroughly undeserved consolation, Liverpool supporters greeted it with a collective sigh.

Watford had warranted nothing, not even this late goal. Thankfully though, the Reds regained their initiative and were soon back on the offensive. Sturridge, now on the pitch in place of Lallana, was at his rampaging best and created a hat-trick of opportunities.

The forward crashed two stunning efforts off the woodwork before fashioning Liverpool's final strike and sealing a thoroughly deserved 6-1 victory. It was Gini Wijnaldum, a player desperate for his first Liverpool goal, who would profit from Sturridge's attacking play.

In the 90th minute, the striker fired a shot that Pantilimon could only parry and the Dutchman was quick to react, firing home at the Kop end. His delight was obvious, and Liverpool had restored their five-goal lead.

Greater challenges lay in wait for this Liverpool team. However, such was the growing sense of belief on the Kop, that many of us were starting to believe that the glory days were on their way back. Following Liverpool in the Premier League era often tests the faith, but with every passing week it was becoming harder not to believe something special was happening at Anfield. Troy Deeney may have come prepared for war, but his Watford team-mates had lost this battle comprehensively. When will opposition strikers learn?

Klopp conducts the crowd, as Reds see off the Black Cats with patient display

November was giving way to December. As the feeble sun rose over the Mersey, fog enveloped the Liver Birds and a crisp frost bit the city streets. Yet in the chill of winter, the Jürgen Klopp juggernaut ploughed on.

Football in England doesn't whinge and take a break when the cold sets in. It just throws out an orange ball so you can see it a bit better. This is not a sport for the faint of heart and Liverpool now had a boss ready to lambaste anyone who shrinks from the fight.

Liverpool were now entering a crucial phase of the season. December would bring the footballing equivalent of trench warfare. The early season fire and optimism would turn to smoke and visiting teams would dig in, hoping their resolve coupled with the conditions would allow them to steal a point here or there. The season's early skirmishes would become a war of attrition.

In such circumstances no quarter can be given. Teams fighting for their managers' jobs, Premier League survival and sometimes both, set out to frustrate and grind out a draw where certain defeat had seemed inevitable. Championships are never won in the bleak midwinter, but they can be lost. Teams need to navigate this period with care, collecting precious points along the way and not giving in to despair.

A point away from home here and a late winner against inferior opposition there is the way to do it. Simply stay in the race until the spring comes and the fire returns. This is something Liverpool fans used to understand more than others. We prided ourselves on it. In fact we were famed for our patience and knowledge. It didn't matter if the Reds scored the winner in the first minute or the last, as long as they scored it.

Growing up I believed that, standing on the Kop, I was as much a part of the game as the players. I had a role to play. My job, along with thousands of others was to give our lads belief and scare the shit out of theirs. It wasn't complicated. So, when a Liverpool player scuffed a shot or misplaced a pass you didn't let out an audible groan. Instead you got behind them.

As much as we like to think of our past heroes as invincible, they were prone to gaffes also. Yes Shankly's men, even Paisley's too, made mistakes, dropped points and had off days. This is football. What separated them from latter-day teams and supporters was of course the quality of the players, but also sheer belief that all would come good; if we stuck together.

Before I'm accused of blurry-eyed nostalgia, I acknowledge that Kopites of the 1970s and '80s had their own whipping boys. Ask Ronnie Whelan, for example. However, despite a partial revival, their modern-day equivalents were still capable of a level of angst totally out of proportion with reality.

During the 2016/17 campaign Klopp's Liverpool had plenty of quality. Belief was growing but, on the evidence of the game against Sunderland on 26 November, it was still very fragile. No wonder then our manager decided to take matters into his own hands in the second half of a game where the frustration in the stands threatened to derail his game plan.

To Klopp, the atmosphere inside the ground is no minor detail. He puts it as high as 10 to 15 per cent in terms of its effect on the outcome of a game. Creating and harnessing that power has been a hallmark of his career. He did it at Mainz and Dortmund and he's trying to do it at Anfield. This is a man perfectly in sync with the history and personality of the club, asking its supporters to do no more than what they had done so often in the past. Yet, still, some seemed incapable of rising to the challenge.

David Moyes was now in charge of the Black Cats and he had immediately signalled his intent by parking the footballing equivalent of a double-decker bus in front of his team's goal. Patience would be a virtue, if Liverpool were to punch their way through.

The signs were positive at the start of the game, as the players took to the pitch engulfed in a huge wall of sound. The pre-kick-off rendition of 'You'll Never Walk Alone' was also at its slow, melodic and thunderous best. But throughout the first half the tension seemed to grow.

With each Sunderland foray forward, mutterings of 'they'll nick one here' grew.

Supporters plummeted new depths as they watched in despair the sight of Coutinho being stretchered off on the hour mark. The Brazilian had been so influential up to this point in the season.

He had been the foundation of Liverpool's early surge and the creative edge in their attack. The thought of him suffering a season-ending injury, coupled with two more dropped points at home seemed almost too much to bear for many.

Suddenly phones were chiming and reports from home were suggesting first a snapped ankle, then a fractured toe and finally the whole limb was broken. Behind me someone sneered, 'I bet it's just his bloody toenail', and laughter punctured the gloom for a brief moment.

Liverpool weren't bad in the opening half. Sure they were a bit slow in their approach play and indecisive in the final third at times. At least that's how it felt inside the ground. Having watched the highlights later, I realised that my assessment had been a little unfair.

So much of your perception is coloured by the mood around you. The truth is Sunderland mounted a huge roadblock and what was required to get round it was a tactical patience; a quality many of us struggle with. Thankfully Liverpool's players and Jürgen Klopp didn't. The German would deliver a masterclass on the touchline that day.

Bill Shankly once quipped that he had kicked every ball from the dugout. He claimed he had scored a few and that he'd saved a few on the line too. Nobody could deny the man had a huge influence from the touchline.

On the evidence of this game, so too does Klopp.

Jürgen has been tactically brilliant since his arrival. Sure, he's made errors. All managers do. The key is making fewer than your rivals. In that sense, Klopp is one of the best in the business. For that reason, we are blessed to have him. In addition, it's difficult to think of a Liverpool manager, since the days of the boot room, more in tune with the zeitgeist of Liverpool Football Club than this one.

As the second half rolled on, Liverpool supporters were given a glorious illustration of this fact. From my vantage point there was a sudden and inexplicable change in mood. The noise levels inside the ground seemed to grow enormously. The Kop was once more in full fury. Sometimes their rage was aimed at Sunderland, often with the match officials and occasionally with our own players. Nevertheless, the sound was immense.

I was immediately caught up in it but was blissfully unaware that the ringleader of this mighty uproar wasn't sat in the singing section at the back of the Kop. Instead he was marching up and down the touchline, teeth snarling and fists pumping the air. It was our manager issuing the clarion call and scolding us for our impatience and ordering us into battle alongside his men.

The supporters in the Main Stand responded magnificently and those in the Kop picked up the baton. As if by magic, so did the players. It should come as no surprise that the players grow in stature when the crowd weaves its spell.

As Klopp says, in games like this, you must be ready to take full advantage in the moments. You need to create the atmosphere in which the players can enjoy the challenge, not run scared from it. Fear leads to doubt and indecision. But when the players feel the force of 50,000 people at their backs, they fear nothing.

Divock Origi, on for the injured Coutinho, was the embodiment of this. Wave after wave of Liverpool attack had failed to yield a goal. Sunderland had survived through a mixture of luck and packing the 18-yard box to bursting point. When Henderson put a free kick over the bar, after Mané had been upended just outside the penalty area, despair threatened to engulf us once more. However, the young Belgian, brilliant from the moment he came on, simply kept going.

Just three minutes after the captain's effort had buzzed the crossbar, Origi found himself with the ball at his feet, on the right side of the Sunderland goal. He tormented his defender then manufactured himself the most meagre of opportunities. Given the angle, the obstacles in his way and the distance from goal, disappointment seemed inevitable. Not so.

His effort was sublime and as it hit the net the ground exploded. A wave of sound crashed down on to the pitch, an outpouring of relief and unadulterated joy. The dam had burst and the flood was irresistible. Pandemonium broke loose all around me. A few fell backwards, others hugged and fists punched the air.

It was like we were celebrating a cup final goal, instead it was a potential winner in a home game against a bottom-of -the-table side from the north-east. That's how much football has always meant to us in Liverpool. That's how much winning means.

With 15 minutes left, though, there was still time for a Sunderland side, who had shown no ambition so far, to spoil the party. If we had given them an inch, they'd have stolen a yard and our celebrations would have been for nothing. But the belief was back and nothing would deny the Reds.

In the final moments Sadio Mané burst into the box, holding off the attentions of the Sunderland rearguard. The only way they could stop him from scoring was to foul him and Ndong dutifully obliged. Up stepped James Milner. Just as he would do in the years ahead, James had delivered a pivotal performance. He had been a workhorse when needed and a craftsman when the moment called for it. From 12 yards out, in the big pressure moments, well you wouldn't swap him for anybody would you? He didn't disappoint in this one either.

It was 2-0 and game over. As Klopp led his players towards the Kop in thanks, it was us who owed a debt of gratitude to him. Just like Bill before him Jürgen had scored those goals and he'd also kept out the rare efforts from the opposition. His intervention in the second half turned the game. When some of us had lost patience, he didn't and thankfully neither did the players.

It was a lesson for all of us.

Liverpool surrender on the south coast as defensive problems resurface at Bournemouth

Liverpool travelled to Bournemouth early in December 2016. They were riding high and performances had won the admiration of many neutrals. However, what should have been a routine victory became a humiliating capitulation.

Gut-wrenching, nauseating, head-wrecking, humiliating and totally infuriating! Somehow, I don't think I've found the words to describe how I felt in the aftermath of Liverpool's surrender to Bournemouth on 4 December 2016. Heaven knows how the poor Reds who faced the epic journey back to Liverpool must have felt.

The game served as a painful reminder that Klopp's Liverpool were still a work in progress. For all their attacking prowess, their vulnerability at the back was a persistent thorn in the side.

There's simply no way to rationalise a defeat like the one Liverpool suffered on the south coast. It remains as inexplicable to me today as it was back then. How could a team as in control as Liverpool were in that first half, surrender the way they did in the second.

The Reds were on the front foot from the beginning. Their passing and movement were a joy to watch, just as they had been all season. They were closing down space and had the Cherries penned in.

After ten minutes Divock Origi squandered a golden opportunity to open the scoring for Liverpool. Henderson, who had been a colossus in that first half found Clyne on the right, who delivered a perfect ball for the Belgian. All that was required was a decent contact and the ball would have been in the net. Somehow, though, he managed to fluff his lines, when it seemed easier to score.

He might have missed, but at least he was getting into decent scoring positions and with Liverpool crawling all over

Bournemouth a goal still seemed inevitable. The Reds won one corner after another and the Cherries' defence appeared to be creaking under the relentless pressure.

They would eventually succumb after 20 minutes, when a brilliant cross by Emre Can found Sadio Mané. The Senegalese was through on goal and managed to shrug off his marker, Nathan Aké, before slipping the ball past the onrushing Artur Boruc.

It was no more than Liverpool deserved and, in that moment, I could only imagine all three points returning to Anfield at the end of the game. As if to rub Bournemouth's noses in it the Reds went two up just a couple of minutes later. The Reds won the ball in the middle of the park and Henderson's pass was inch perfect. Boruc again gambled and lost, as Origi's pace left him red-faced. Divock clipped the ball around him, but momentarily looked to have squandered the opportunity.

Defenders rushed back and the angle looked way too acute for him to capitalise, but he simply shrugged off his earlier miss and slammed the ball into the net. This all seemed too easy. Liverpool had been brilliant up to this point and saw out the rest of the half, despite a let off as Firmino appeared to foul a Bournemouth player in the box.

Nobody realised it, but this was a portent of things to come.

Liverpool could and should have put the game beyond Bournemouth. Instead, though they walked off the pitch, two goals to the good and with nearly all the possession, you couldn't help but agree with Alan Smith in commentary; 2-0 is a dangerous scoreline.

And so it proved to be. Eddie Howe's men were always going to improve. They were after all the home side and their supporters were never going to let them roll over. They'd also given Arsenal a tough test a week earlier. So, Liverpool could and should have been switched on to the dangers.

The Cherries' manager made a change, bringing on former Red Jordon Ibe and I must admit to feeling a pang of nerves. Ibe had seemingly had huge potential at Liverpool and when Liverpool let a young talent go there's always the fear that it will come back to haunt us. However, it would be Howe's other substitution, Ryan Fraser, who did the damage as far as the Reds were concerned.

He was only on the pitch two minutes and he had won his team a penalty. Having been solid for the last three games, Liverpool's defence just crumbled. Milner's lunge upended Fraser and he could have no complaints as the referee pointed to the spot. Up stepped Callum Wilson to send Loris Karius the wrong way and suddenly it was game on at 2-1.

The Reds had of course suffered setbacks before under Klopp. They had justifiably been praised for their resilience. So when in the 64th minute they restored their two-goal advantage it looked like normal service had been resumed.

Mané, who simply refused to give up the fight, made his way into the home side's penalty area. Facing a wall of defenders, he passed it to Can who was 20 yards from goal. The German then unleashed a right-footed shot that sent the away support into fits of ecstasy. That should have been it. However, the Reds' resolve simply evaporated from that point on.

Following their early-season defeat to Burnley, Liverpool had been relentless. They weren't always without flaws, but they had never been outfought until this game. Klopp had instilled a mental strength into his charges. It had seen them through games where they were perhaps a little sub-par, until this game. In Bournemouth, in spectacular fashion that toughness deserted them at a time when they were seemingly in complete control.

Maybe that was the problem. Maybe they had come to believe their own hype. Maybe Bournemouth just wanted it more. Whatever it was, Liverpool were about to learn a very important lesson. The game is never won until it is over, and the points are in the bag, and you must fight until the very end. It would come too late in this game, but it would serve them well in the games to come.

Talk of Liverpool's 'defensive woes' had become a cliché since the days of Brendan Rodgers. They had done well to silence such chatter. However, after this game it would be all the press could talk about.

It could all have been different had Liverpool added a fourth, and they nearly did when a Milner corner looked to have been carried over the line by Boruc. Sadly, the referee thought differently.

From that moment on, the Liverpool defence seemed to go missing for the rest of the game. An injury to Matip was a factor but that wasn't enough to excuse what followed. The Cherries' fightback began in the 76th minute. Bournemouth once more halved the deficit and it was the substitute Fraser again, finishing brilliantly from the edge of the box. Karius should have done better though.

With 15 minutes to go, the game could have gone either way, but it would be the home side, who clearly smelled blood, who continued to press. Liverpool's backline appeared to be made of straw and it became hard to dispel the nagging sense that an equaliser was inevitable.

It came as a result of Liverpool's inability to deal with a free kick, and Jack Wilshere, anonymous in the first half, whipped the ball into the box. Steve Cook, a centre-back, controlled it with all the guile of a seasoned forward and volleyed it into the back of the net. It was a disaster.

Liverpool almost went back in front through first Origi and then Lallana, but both squandered their chances. Dropping two points from a winning position is always hard to bear. To drop three would have been unforgivable. But, that's exactly what Liverpool did.

With the game seemingly over the fourth official somehow found five minutes of additional time. Klopp looked flummoxed, but not as perplexed as he would do three minutes later. Cook, now a constant menace, unleashed a fierce drive straight at the Reds' keeper. Karius spilled the ball and Nathan Aké couldn't believe his luck as he tapped home the winner.

Liverpool, having made a mess of their clean sheets, were now facing an almighty walk of shame back to the dressing room. The travelling Kop were looking at a miserable journey back to Liverpool and all of us faced an awful wait for the next game.

They had followed their previous defeat to Burnley with a 15-game unbeaten run. They would follow this one with a shorter streak of seven matches without defeat. It would include a memorable victory over the Blues in the Merseyside derby that would see Liverpool fans ironically singing 'Merry Christmas, Everton.' Well, it was the season of love and understanding, after all.

Henderson's rallying cry leads Liverpool and Sadio Mané to gun down Spurs

We've arrived in February 2017. It's Saturday, it's 5.30pm and Liverpool are hosting Tottenham Hotspur. Despite a grim start to the year, just over 53,000 people have braved the winter to see the game.

January is a two-faced month. Apparently, it was named after the Roman god, Janus, who had two faces; one looking forward to new beginnings while the other says farewell to the past. Most of us were glad to see the back of a month that saw the Reds win just one game out of nine, fall out of two cup competitions and surrender a genuine championship challenge in the process.

Apparently, February originates from the Latin for 'month of purification'. Well that was all well and good, but there had been nothing pure about the 2-0 reverse to Hull City a week earlier. Mind you, although we didn't know it at the time, at least we'd managed to get a glimpse of a future Champions League-winning left-back. Andrew Robertson had lined up for Hull that day and turned in a display that would catch the Liverpool manager's eye.

In Liverpool, assuming you believe the commentary dished out to tourists on the Mersey ferry, our mythology is a little less poetic and much more rooted in the here and now. Ours relates to the iron birds that sit atop our waterfront and have come to symbolise our city. Apparently one bird looks out to sea, eyeing whether the sailors are coming home, the other inland, to see if the pubs are open.

Of course they're always open and as they once more welcomed customers from far and wide for the visit of Spurs, they would have found those decked in Red looking back fondly on 2016 and asking themselves what the hell happened to us. To say the mood was sombre was putting it mildly, and not many of us were all that keen on looking forward.

Tottenham were already a good side and ahead of Liverpool in their development. They had players who were more than capable of hurting Liverpool, who seemed locked in an inescapable personality crisis. Prior to the game Spurs sat in second place, while the Reds were clinging on to fourth.

It was now so tight around the top four that failure held up the spectre of Liverpool falling out of the race, allowing Manchester United in. Unthinkable. In the pub, conversations turned to debate. Where had it all gone wrong? With little appetite to question Klopp, the club's owners took the brunt of the criticism.

Some pointed out that FSG had rode in on their white steeds to buy the club, preventing Tom Hicks and George Gillett from flushing one of the 'most storied franchises' (their words) down the drain. However, many remained deeply sceptical of them.

The 2017 version of Liverpool FC was a more financially stable operation than the 2010 incarnation. The club was happily climbing football's financial rankings. The problem in February 2017 was that most Liverpool supporters could care less about Forbes's top ten and worried more about league titles.

Seven years on from the takeover by Fenway Sports Group, pre-match bar conversations were perpetually consumed with talk of owners and ambition. It wasn't supposed to be this way.

I was never in the 'FSG out' crowd. I just didn't see the point. However, I remained a sceptic for some time. So, as we debated the cause of the Reds' slump, one inescapable reality kept coming to the fore. Heading into the new year, Liverpool were desperately in need of reinforcements that never arrived.

Matip, Henderson, Milner, Coutinho, Clyne, Lovren and Mané had all missed a significant number of games. It seemed obvious to us that the squad would struggle. A hectic festive period followed by nine games in 31 days came as a hammer blow to a team already out on its feet. We could all see it, hoped Klopp could see it, but the club somehow failed to do the right thing, at least in our eyes.

It was hard to escape the sense that all the major decisions at the club were being based on finance and not footballing considerations. That may well have been the prudent thing to do. It turned out to be the root to the club's economic stability and eventual resurgence. However, I was impatient. Many of us were. In a sport that thrived on romance and mystique and on heroes and villains, we argued, surely there's a place for a few calculated gambles.

In the end it would be the players themselves, the ones still at the club, who would drag themselves from the malaise they had found themselves in. In particular, the much-maligned Jordan Henderson would rise to the occasion. Though none of us knew about it until after the game.

The Liverpool sides of the glory days prided themselves on being able to sort out their own problems. Paisley and Shankly before him placed game intelligence high on the list of desirable qualities, whenever they scouted new talent. John Barnes once told me that if a player asked for guidance from Ronnie Moran or Joe Fagan, the reply would come back smartly, 'Sort it out yourself.'

It may seem to devotees of the modern game to be an abdication of duty, but the all-conquering Reds sides of old depended on players with skill and brains. It was a potent combination and delivered unparalleled success.

This would become a hallmark of the Klopp years too. The ability of the manager to create an atmosphere and ethos in which the players could dream up solutions for themselves during a game, and execute them on the pitch, would deliver hugely significant results later on down the line. More of that later.

In 2017, the seeds of that revolution were already in place. *The Times* explained, 'The moment everything fell back into place for Liverpool came, for some, when Adam Lallana and Roberto Firmino emerged from the shadows to wrest possession from Tottenham Hotspur and recreate the swarming, attacking motions of the autumn. Others pointed to the creativity provided by Georginio Wijnaldum's threaded through-ball for the opening goal, or cited Sadio Mané's clinical finishing. Yet the players themselves departed Anfield convinced that the catalyst had actually come in the sterile confines of a dressing room at Melwood 48 hours earlier. It was on Thursday afternoon when the Liverpool captain, Jordan Henderson, called an impromptu, players-only meeting, demanded a response to the insipid defeat by Hull City the previous week and then offered the floor to his team-mates to air their own thoughts on a worrying malaise.'

As we spent the hours before the match whining about missed opportunities in the transfer market, the players, egged on by their manager, were dreaming up solutions of their own. What did we know?

Eventually the team sheet arrived though, and with it some hope that our injury headaches were beginning to ease. Only in defence was there cause for a little nervousness. I was a big fan of Lucas, but he was not a centre-back. The thought of him going toe to toe against Harry Kane and Dele Alli didn't inspire confidence. However, we were all buoyed by the sight of a midfield trio of Lallana, Henderson and Wijnaldum, behind the restored triumvirate of Coutinho, Firmino and Mané.

So, filled with grog and with hope in our hearts we left for the ground. We found the Kop in defiant mood and resplendent with banners and flags. By way of contrast the sizeable Spurs following looked depressingly monochrome.

Henderson won the toss and as the last flames of 'You'll Never Walk Alone' flickered, Liverpool prepared to attack the Anfield Road end. That would mean a second half of running into the Kop and despite our pre-game misgivings, hope once again sprang eternal.

As it happened, we had every right to be hopeful. In a blistering first half, under the noses of the travelling Tottenham contingent, Liverpool tore the visitors apart. It was a performance that left the away end with nothing to do but once again sing about the plight of the unemployed and search for famous atmospheres.

The Reds' attacking play in the opening 45 minutes was devastating, reminiscent of happier times. I was reminded of the days of Sterling, Sturridge and Suárez ripping Arsenal and Everton apart for fun, during that magnificent spell under Brendan Rodgers. All over the park Liverpool were first to the ball and broke with unrelenting pace.

The difference appeared to be Sadio Mané coupled with some great performances from Henderson, Wijnaldum and Firmino. Even Coutinho looked to have rediscovered some of his sharpness, after struggling with injuries. Though he did tire later. For his part Lucas also put in an assured performance.

Quite how the Brazilian won a header in the middle of the pitch against Harry Kane who towered above him was beyond most of us, but it would lead to the attack that saw Liverpool take the lead in the 16th minute.

Wijnaldum collected the second ball and sent Mané, who seemed to create pandemonium every time he went near the Spurs defence, clean through. He left defenders in his wake and rounded the move off with a glorious finish. How we had missed him.

Just two minutes later he would end the game as a contest. Firstly, he set Lallana up for what looked like a certain goal, but the keeper saved. Then the ball fell to Firmino, who again drew a great stop. Sadly, for Spurs and Lloris the rebound fell to the Senegalese hitman. Sadio made no mistake and gave the keeper no chance as he thumped the ball into the roof of the net.

Jubilation and celebration broke out everywhere. Liverpool were back it seemed. Was a rout possible? Maybe the Reds played within themselves after that. Perhaps Spurs were too good a side to allow themselves to be thoroughly humiliated. Whatever the reason Jürgen's men opted to shut the game down after that. It was familiar and comfortable and it was a joy to see the old swagger return.

The autopsy that followed the January from hell was now forgotten, at least for the time being. Liverpool may have been a little reliant on a player who seemed to be able to bring those around him back to life, in Sadio Mané. They may have been two or three players away from a title tilt, but they showed against Spurs that they had the quality to stay in that top four.

In the end that would do. Liverpool were fighting their way back after a difficult period, with a new manager who was getting to grips with a different league. They had players who were starting to think for themselves and a boss who let them do it. The penny hadn't quite dropped during the frosty early months of 2017, but we would eventually see that patience was a virtue. And of course, we would be rewarded in spectacular style.

Supporters ensure Reds' legends never walk alone

It's a scene that has been played out many times during Liverpool's illustrious history. A player enters the arena to a crescendo of applause and cheers. Two of his team-mates rush to greet him. They embrace and 'You'll Never Walk Alone' fills the air. The sights and sounds are so familiar. The passion is not dulled though time moves inexorably on.

These were not scenes from Rome or Wembley though. This was not a halcyon Anfield, built by Shankly in the 1960s and decorated by Paisley in the '70s and '80s. This was instead the Devonshire Hotel, Liverpool, on an ice-cold evening in January; the scene of a 'Scouse Tribute Night' organised entirely by supporters of the club, in aid of their heroes.

That night Tommy Smith, Chris Lawler and Tommy Lawrence, men who had been the very foundations of the club we love today, embraced again and once more soaked up the admiration they so richly deserved. In another event Ian St John and Willie Stevenson had been similarly honoured.

Liverpool supporters have always prided themselves on the bond they have with their heroes. The days when fans and players got the bus home together after the game may have passed into history, but the sense of belonging to a 'great society, where people all around you are loyal and passionate', as Shanks put it, has never left us.

The Kop invented individual songs for these legends in their playing days and serenaded them before kick-off, one after the other. Now they have hung up their boots, the admiration and respect is mutual.

Ian Golder, one of the organisers of the events, explained how the former players and legends felt when first approached. 'They were so humbled to be recognised by the fans individually,' he said. 'Willie Stevenson in particular was almost moved to tears, because he thought the fans had forgotten about him.'

As someone lucky enough to attend Stevenson's night, I can testify to the fact that it meant the world to him. In truth it's the least the man deserves. This is a guy who helped us to our first FA Cup. Along with his team-mates, he lit up Anfield for so many years.

It's fitting then that the atmosphere at these tribute nights can be as raucous and passionate as any game under the Anfield floodlights. The event held in honour of Chris Lawler turned Liverpool Town Hall into the Kop for one night only.

Ian recalls the night that still gives him goosebumps. 'We had this young lad, known as Irish Luke, who Peter Hooton of The Farm had brought along. He got up at the end and sang every verse of "Liver Bird Upon My Chest", a tribute to Shankly's great teams of the '60s. Everyone was clapping and stamping their feet.

'Chris was then led down the red carpet to a waiting taxi as Mike Dean, of the Hat, Scarf and Badge store, started singing "There's only one Chris Lawler". It went on for 15 minutes and a video of it went viral.'

Despite the grandeur of the venue, Ian says the event had a raw feel about it. This was no corporate affair. Instead it was a uniquely Scouse tribute, with supporters and players coming together as one.

'The idea was borne from the fact that we didn't believe the club was doing enough to look after these lads. They are the very foundations. They are the Shankly boys,' Ian added.

Liverpool would go on to recognise the contribution of their heroes more formally. As we will see, club CEO Peter Moore would be integral to the creation of an ex-players association and finally those who built the foundations of the club would be honoured as they should be. However the club itself deals with these legends, as far as the supporters are concerned, they have never walked alone.

Anfield mourns the loss of 'Mr Liverpool' with the passing of Ronnie Moran

Ronnie Moran will always be known by Reds supporters as a key member of the legendary Anfield Boot Room, and for his stints as Liverpool caretaker manager. His career at Liverpool spanned 50 years and his death on 22 March 2017 came as a huge blow to everyone associated with the club.

The Crosby-born left-back captained his hometown club in the 1959/60 season, played in a European Cup semi-final and was part of a championship-winning side under the legendary Bill Shankly. In an astonishing career there simply isn't a job Ronnie didn't do for the club. Nor is there a post-war achievement he wasn't somehow involved in, a fact that earned him the honorific 'Mr Liverpool'.

Moran was born on 28 February 1934. At the age of 15 he was awarded a scholarship at the technical college in Bootle, where he studied as an apprentice electrician.

In his spare time he played for the Crosby Boys team. This is where the universe would intervene, and begin a chain of events that would ultimately lead to Ronnie playing a key role in the Reds' decades-long domination of European football.

Watching him play amateur football was the postman who delivered mail to the Liverpool chairman, Samuel Williams. A recommendation was made and soon Williams, accompanied by Reds manager Don Welsh, was literally knocking on the door of Ronnie's family home.

How remarkable it is that the actions of that Royal Mail carrier, so seemingly insignificant at the time, could set in motion a career that lasted almost 50 years.

In that time, Moran would carry out almost every role at the club, from player, to physio, coach and manager, and oversee the club becoming the most successful team on the planet.

Ronnie would play as an amateur in Liverpool's 'C' team, before signing professional papers in 1952. Shortly afterwards Everton began to show an interest in him, but they were too late – he'd become a Red.

The early days of his playing career were tough, and Moran would taste defeat on his debut and see his team relegated in the 1953/54 season. Eventually, the man who Ronnie credits most with his career, Don Welsh, would leave the hot seat and Phil Taylor took over.

Ronnie would become an almost ever-present at left-back under Taylor, missing just six games in five years as Liverpool pushed to get out of the Second Division.

His service and consistency earned him the captaincy in 1959/60, which meant he would be taking the armband from his older and more experienced cousin, Johnny Wheeler.

Taylor would eventually be replaced by Shankly, but tragedy soon struck for Moran. He picked up a serious injury in the October of Shanks's first full season and was out for over a year.

However, he fought his way back and would play enough fixtures in the 1961/62 promotion campaign and was a key member of the 1964 First Division championship team.

His playing career seems to be one filled with both agony and ecstasy in equal measure.

For example, Moran had earned himself a reputation for his prowess from the penalty spot as early as 1960. With an 80 per cent success rate from the spot, Ronnie then went on to miss four in a row.

The last penalty he took was in an FA Cup quarter-final against Swansea City at Anfield in 1964. Liverpool were losing 2-1 in what was described as the most one-sided tie ever witnessed. The Reds had held the Welsh defence under almost constant siege, but could not break through.

Jack Rowe, a football writer, offered in his report, 'I have never seen a team attack so much and for so long, for so little.'

Shankly would comment that Liverpool should have had 14 goals, such was their dominance, while the Swansea view was understandably that the Reds only had themselves to blame. Nevertheless, Liverpool eventually forced the Welshmen's defence into an error and won a penalty late in the game.

There were just ten minutes left and the ball was on the spot. Another heroic Reds comeback was on the cards. Despite having missed his last three Moran was the designated penalty taker, but he looked anything but confident.

Ron Yeats approached him and asked him to take it. Then suddenly the Kop began to chant 'Moran, Moran, Moran'.

Their vote of confidence in him stiffened his resolve and he walked up to take it, but he clearly didn't fancy it.

As the ball ballooned way over the crossbar, Ian St John clasped his hands behind his head and fell to his knees. The Kop fell silent and Ronnie found himself to be the loneliest man on planet earth, praying for an earthquake to swallow him whole.

The game ended with the Reds out of the cup and a desperate Moran brushed aside the reporters, saying, 'I missed the pen, what else is there to say.'

Yeats could simply bark, 'With luck like what we've had today, we'll be lucky to avoid relegation, never mind win the championship.'

Such bitter disappointment would prove to be a mere footnote in what was to be a glorious future.

The Reds did indeed win the championship, and they add the elusive FA Cup the following season. Sadly Ronnie would miss that, losing his place in the team to Chris Lawler.

His playing career was coming to an end. He'd put in 379 appearances for the Reds and scored 17 times. He'd won the Second and First Division championships and steered the club as captain.

Ronnie was there during Liverpool's formative years in European competition, playing in the very first continental encounters at home and away, but even all of that would pale by comparison with what was to follow.

As the team was warming up for the 1966/67 season, Shankly called Ronnie into his office.

Having been out of the side for a while, and knowing that other teams were showing an interest in him, Moran thought that his time at Anfield was finally over. Shanks, he thought, was about to tell him that he had been sold.

Instead, he was offered a seat at the very top table and membership of the most exclusive and elite club in European football: the Boot Room. Amazingly, Ronnie asked Shanks if he could think about it first.

Neither he nor his wife had any desire to leave the city in which they were born, but he had to consult with her before accepting such a momentous offer. She agreed and the next day Ronnie walked into Shankly's office and accepted.

He would go on to be the 'sergeant major' of Melwood. No player, no matter how big their reputation, was allowed to rest on their laurels.

Every season would start with the same ritual. Players would line up to collect their medals from a cardboard box, Moran's words ringing in their ears, 'Take one, if you think you've earned it.'

Last year was dead and gone to Ronnie, consigned to history, and if anyone dared to dwell on past glories Ronnie would say, 'You've won nothing yet this year lad.'

Many ex-Reds say that this mentality was responsible for Liverpool becoming the relentless, unstoppable force they were in the 1970s and '80s. You were never allowed to pat yourself on the back while there was more silverware to be plundered.

There was great humour also, as Jan Molby would attest.

After joining the club from Ajax the Great Dane was preparing for a game against Norwich City at Carrow Road. The rest of his team-mates decided to play a trick on him, and encouraged him to ask Ronnie for a massage before the game, which he foolishly did.

The result was predictable but nonetheless hilarious, Ronnie roared, 'Fuck off! You earn the fucking right to have a massage. Go out and play some games and then I might consider it.'

The rest of the dressing room struggled to contain their laughter, and Jan had been introduced to one of the greats, in fine style.

Ronnie was a footballing maestro. He understood the game and knew what made a Liverpool player. There was nothing he couldn't do on the training pitch, or in the dressing room.

However, his unease with the media and the player recruitment side would see him pass up the chance to become perManént Liverpool manager, and his brief caretaker role would come to an end with the appointment of Graeme Souness in 1992.

Ronnie sadly passed away in 2017, at the age of 83. He was still a regular at Melwood and regularly patrolled the perimeter walls, overseeing training until his passing.

He left behind a treasure trove of sporting memories, accumulated by the great Anfield dynasty of which he was such an integral part.

Football may have changed, but the lessons dished out by Ronnie Moran over decades at Anfield are as valid today as they ever were.

Yesterday's success counts for nothing in today's battles, you have to earn your way in football every day and tomorrow's glory is built on the back of humility, hard work and togetherness.

Liverpool clinch top four and say emotional farewell to Lucas Leiva

Lucas Leiva has always divided opinion. His early Reds career was blighted by unfair comparisons with a midfield described by most Reds as the best in the world. As a youngster arriving from a different continent, Lucas had to deal with many challenges.

Adapting to a new culture and language was the obvious one. However, trying to make your way in a midfield made up of the likes of Gerrard, Alonso and Mascherano was nothing short of a Herculean challenge. Add that to the task of convincing a sceptical Kop that you deserve to wear the shirt, and nobody would have forgiven him from shrinking away and ending up on loan.

Hindsight tells us that would have been a disaster. That successive managers could see what so many fans couldn't, suggests that our treatment of him in his early Anfield career fell way short of our finest hour.

Rafa Benitez had scouted the young midfielder, who had begun his career at Gremio as a box-to-box goalscoring midfielder. He looked an exciting prospect. He had already played at international level and had become the youngest ever player to win the prestigious Golden Ball award. Previous winners of this accolade included Zico and Falcao.

His new manager spoke of his goalscoring ability, but also his character and tenacity. While we saw few goals, Lucas displayed character and tenacity in spades.

He put in an impressive 39 appearances in his first season (19 coming from the subs bench). Like many young players, particularly those desperate to make an impression, he was prone to errors and lunging into tackles recklessly. This saw him booked five times and sent off once. A certain Steven Gerrard, no stranger to this in his early career, would have doubtless sympathised with him.

However, fans and pundits quickly grew impatient with him. Not many of us, myself included, fully understood the tactical adjustments being asked of him.

In his second full season, 2008/09, those frustrations boiled over during a terrible 0-0 draw against Fulham. In what was to my mind an unprecedented step, a section of Liverpool fans actually booed Lucas as he waited to join the game as a sub.

Lucas would later say, with typical honesty, that this was a low point in his Liverpool career. He thought seriously about leaving. Thankfully, though, he would display the qualities that first brought him to the club, held his head up and fought for his place in Reds history. There's nothing more Scouse than that in my view.

His struggle would earn him the respect of his team-mates and eventually the admiration of the Kop. He would pick up the 'Golden Samba' award from supporters in the final home game of the 2011 season. This Adidas training shoe, beloved by fans in the 1980s, sprayed with gold paint and mounted on a wooden plinth, is the Kop's highest accolade.

The following season we were given a graphic illustration of his importance to the team. Under his new manager, Kenny Dalglish, Lucas started in his now familiar position in front of the back four. This was a transitional year with Kenny still picking up the pieces from Roy Hodgson's ill-fated spell at the club.

Just as he was getting into his stride, Lucas sustained a season-ending knee injury in a League Cup game against Chelsea at the end of November. He had been one of the best players on the pitch in a game the Reds won 2-0. The injury would prove to be a huge blow to Liverpool's league campaign.

Prior to losing Lucas, Liverpool lost only 11 per cent of their matches, conceding 0.88 goals per game. Following his injury, they were defeated in 37 per cent of the remaining fixtures, conceding 1.15 goals per game. In the first half of the season Liverpool consistently hovered around the European places. By the end they were a dismal eighth.

He of course battled back from this setback, but the arrival of Brendan Rodgers coupled with further injuries meant that he would fall further down the midfield pecking order.

He would take his final curtain call in the 79th minute of a three-nil victory over Middlesbrough at Anfield. He replaced Roberto Firmino. Goals from Georginio Wijnaldum, Philippe Coutinho and Adam Lallana had already ensured that Liverpool were guaranteed Champions League football for the following season, and Lucas's new manager, the fifth of his Liverpool career, would allow him to leave in the summer.

Not before an emotional farewell in front of his army of adoring fans on the Kop. He had climbed his own hill and every time he lost his footing he got back up and continued that ascent. There's nothing a Liverpool supporter admires more in a player than perseverance and sheer bloody-mindedness.

These were the qualities that saw Lucas Leiva play 346 games for the Reds, under five managers. It's what earned him our respect and his Golden Samba. Of course, it also earned him his song:

Whoa, whoa, whaoooo
Whoa, whoa, whaoooo
His first name is Lucas,
Is Lucas,
Is Lucas,
His second name is Leiva
Is Leiva
Is Leiva
And that is why we like him

We like him
We like him
In fact, we fucking love him
We love him
We love him
Whoa, whoa, whaoooo
Whoa, whoa, whaoooo

With his children born in Liverpool and after ten years living and playing football on Merseyside, Lucas Leiva considers his family to be Scouse. He will always enjoy a warm welcome should he ever return to the city.

LIVERPOOL FC 2017/2018

The African Kings, the Samba Señor and the road to Kiev

Reds strikers run riot as 'disastrous' Gunners destroyed at Anfield

The 2017/18 season exploded into life at Anfield on 27 August, with Arsenal the sacrificial lambs. It would end with tears of disappointment, but a new-found sense of pride.

Along the way there would be great days and nights, magical moments and the Kop would find a whole host of new heroes.

This was a season of song, with many new anthems created. It would fuel nostalgia in people like me, who were reminded of the culture of the 1970s and '80s. It would also ignite a new generation of Liverpool supporters who no longer had to listen to people like me. They would have their own songs to sing and stories to tell.

The season may have ended without a trophy, but it would mark the rebirth of Liverpool FC. The team would stride around the cities of Europe, chests pumped out and declaring we are Liverpool. Europe didn't quite submit in the end. But we left them in no doubt that the sleeping giant had awoken.

Off the field, Liverpool made great steps forward in terms of squad development. The addition of Mohamed Salah would prove pivotal. The capture of Andrew Robertson from relegated Hull City for just £8m was nothing short of inspired. However, the signing of Alex Oxlade-Chamberlain raised a few eyebrows among Liverpool supporters.

He would turn out to be a great signing, if an unlucky one. His injury during the Champions League semi-final with Roma would rule him out of a starting place in not one, but two European Cup finals.

The squad was looking strong and, in Salah, Liverpool had found a potent goal machine, although most of us thought Klopp had bought another winger. How wrong we were. Mo would spearhead one of the most lethal front threes in the history of the club.

The Egyptian would grab 44 goals in his first season, and another 27 in the second, bagging the Golden Boot in both. Liverpool fans adore him and penned several songs in his honour. One of them drew attention from the national media because it talked of their respect for him as a Muslim.

In a post-Brexit Britain dogged by rising racism and Islamophobia, this was nothing short of remarkable, at least to the broadcast news. Later a study by academics would show that the 'Egyptian King's' arrival would correlate with a 20 per cent fall in incidents of Islamophobia in the city. We didn't care what his religion was, we loved Mo and if he was sitting in a mosque, that's where we wanted to be.

The Reds had eased past TSG Hoffenheim, guaranteeing their place in the group stages of the Champions League. And, after a disappointing 3-3 draw away to Watford on the opening day, in which they had conceded a late equaliser, Liverpool had won their other league game against Crystal Palace 1-0.

The mood around Anfield was bright as the Reds got ready to welcome the Gunners. Arsenal on the other hand looked like a pale imitation of the sides who had troubled

Liverpool in the past. *The Times* would refer to the away side as a disgrace. Wenger would later call their performance disastrous.

Liverpool pressed their opponent relentlessly and Arsenal had no answer as they were simply ripped apart. *The Times*'s match report drooled, 'Arsenal had no answer to Roberto Firmino's positioning and invention, to Sadio Mané's acceleration and trickery or the strength and ambition of Emre Can, Georginio Wijnaldum and Jordan Henderson in midfield. Arsenal's players deserve all the opprobrium for their lack of effort, their failure to track back.'

Firmino opened the scoring after just 17 minutes and Anfield could sense blood. So too could Liverpool and Klopp. The Reds hunted in packs, snuffing out any Arsenal move before it could get started, winning the ball high up the pitch and mounting attack after attack.

The away end was in meltdown and couldn't comprehend the way in which the home side were humiliating their heroes. In desperation they sang about 'famous atmospheres' and asked why the Kop wasn't singing. It was all they had to offer. Their players were giving them nothing else to shout about. In the Gunners' dugout, Wenger looked nonplussed.

So too did Rob Holding, the young Arsenal defender. He looked completely outclassed and out of his depth, allowing Mané to grab the second in the 40th minute. At this point it was clear that Liverpool could score as many goals as they wanted. A rout was on the cards.

Then, in the second half, Hector Bellerin failed to control the ball properly and Mohamed Salah stole in to bag Liverpool's third just before the hour mark. It was already the fourth goal of his Liverpool career, in just five games.

Klopp had seen enough in the 74th minute, when he decided to give Sadio Mané a rest and an ovation. The Senegalese striker clapped the Kop as he walked slowly to the bench, before greeting Daniel Sturridge on the touchline.

Sturridge was in what would prove to be his penultimate season at Anfield. He has been one of the most gifted finishers in the history of the club. But for injury, he would surely have gone on to become one of its most prolific. It took him just four minutes to score the Reds' fourth with a powerful header. The rout was complete, and the Kop showed its appreciation.

Under the headline 'Liverpool run four past pitiful Arsenal, *The Independent* summed up the fourth and final nail in the Gunners' coffin with these words, 'The final blow followed in the closing stages, when again the excellent Can carried the ball through midfield unopposed. He found Salah on the left and the Egyptian, not known for his crossing ability, sent a sublime, arching ball to the back post where Sturridge was on hand to head home.'

Arsenal had not managed a single shot on target all game. Liverpool by contrast were lethal. However, there would be many ups and downs in that first half of the season. The low points would be a 5-0 hammering by Manchester City at the

Etihad, and a 4-1 defeat away to Spurs. The latter would prove the catalyst for a revival though.

They would go on a 14-game unbeaten run that included an incredible 4-3 victory over Manchester City at Anfield. The Reds were starting to show they could more than match their much wealthier rivals on the domestic front.

Later in the season we would begin to see that they were more than capable of taking them on in European competition. Oh, what a night that was.

Anfield's new colossus makes history against the Blues

It's 5 January 2018 and Liverpool's brand-new centre-back is about to dump Everton out of the FA Cup, on his debut. Of course, Virgil van Dijk is now a firm Kop favourite after transforming the club's backline into one of the stingiest defences in European football.

He has his own song, to the tune of Ewan MacColl's folk song 'Dirty Old Town'. It goes like this:

He's our centre-half
He's our number four
Watch him defend
And we watch him score
He'll pass the ball
Calm as you like
He's Virgil van Dijk
He's Virgil van Dijk

In the weeks before he arrived, Liverpool had enjoyed a prolific December, scoring 27 goals in eight games. The Reds had demolished Brighton 5-1, smashed seven past Spartak Moscow, beat Bournemouth 4-0 and swatted Swansea City aside with a five-goal drubbing. However, a chaotic 3-3 draw on Boxing day made the case for defensive reinforcements.

The eventual arrival of van Dijk in a deal worth £75m – a world record for a defender – on 1 January 2018 was greeted with euphoria by Liverpool supporters across the globe. It had brought to an end a pursuit that pre-dated the 2017/18 season, and which looked to have collapsed in spectacular fashion on 8 June 2017.

Liverpool's interest in the player had been well publicised and when identical stories began appearing in the press stating that van Dijk's preferred destination was Liverpool, fans began to believe that the club's defensive woes would soon come to an end. Their glee would be short-lived though.

Southampton were infuriated by Liverpool's apparent hubris and were convinced that the Anfield club had 'tapped up' their prized asset. Stories began to circulate that van Dijk had met with Jürgen Klopp in Blackpool, something that would constitute an illegal approach for a player under contract.

Faced with the prospect of a complaint to the football authorities and the possibility of severe punishment, if found guilty, Liverpool sensationally ended their interest. To add insult to injury, at least as far as Reds supporters were concerned, they issued an apology to Southampton. A statement on the club's official website read, 'Liverpool Football Club would like to put on record our regret over recent media speculation regarding Southampton Football Club and player transfers between the two clubs.

'We apologise to the owner, board of directors and fans of Southampton for any misunderstanding regarding Virgil van Dijk.

'We respect Southampton's position and can confirm we have ended any interest in the player.'

It represented a bitter blow to Klopp's transfer plans. The club had an obvious issue in defence and while Liverpool's strikers were doing the business, their tendency to leak goals at the back represented a significant handicap to their aspirations.

To Liverpool supporters, it felt like a humiliation and many took to social media to decry the club, Southampton and anyone else they could implicate in the failed deal. The player himself took a different stance, posting a photograph on his Instagram feed, which showed him in a chilled-out pose, with his feet up, staring wistfully out the window of a private jet.

Was he sending a message? What did it mean? Some saw it as a sign that Klopp would eventually get his man, but as the transfer deadline approached, their anxiety reached fever pitch and the growing realisation that Liverpool would enter the 2017/18 season without signing a commanding centre-back set in.

The Reds had signed Mohamed Salah, Dominic Solanke, Andrew Robertson and Alex Oxlade-Chamberlain for over £80m. It was a clear display of ambition and three out of the four players would go on to become integral members of the squad. One of them would win the Golden Boot and would shatter club records for fun, but that's another story.

For all the progress being made at the club, many Liverpool supporters saw their glasses as half empty, such was the despair at the collapse of the van Dijk deal. In truth, it would be a simple case of delayed gratification, because in the January of 2018, Liverpool sensationally announced that they had finally got their man.

They had stumped up a significant premium and it had taken a personal intervention from Liverpool owner, John Henry, but on 1 January the Reds welcomed a new colossus for the colossal fee of £75m. A transfer record had been shattered, but another would be established within days, when Everton visited Anfield for the third round of the FA Cup.

Virgil van Dijk became the first Liverpool player to score a debut goal in a Merseyside derby since 1901.

A total of 93 players have scored on their debut for Liverpool. The first five men to achieve this feat did so in an 8-0 thrashing of Higher Walton in 1892.

The first to grab a goal on his debut against our neighbours across Stanley Park was Bill White, in a 2-2 draw at Anfield, in front of 30,000 people. He had opened the scoring inside two minutes. Everton would race into the lead before half-time, before Sam Raybould grabbed an equaliser within three minutes of the restart.

White, a Scotsman, would only play six times for Liverpool. His goal against Everton in his first start would be his last. He left the club for Dundee in 1902. Van Dijk's Liverpool career would take a different path of course.

It was an evening kick-off under the floodlights and I, along with 52,000 others, watched the big Dutchman make his debut. It was obvious from the start that Virgil was set to make a huge impact and his ability to organise was apparent. We could hear him barking orders to his defensive partners from the stands.

Just as in 1901, the atmosphere was fierce and the rivalry intense. Liverpool's team was packed with stars, but whereas the crowd of 1901 worshipped Raisbeck, Raybould and Cox, the class of 2018 idolised Mané, Salah and Firmino.

James Milner opened the scoring for Liverpool in the 35th minute, but Gylfi Sigurdsson brought the tie level on 67 minutes. With the Reds a vastly superior team to their neighbours from across Stanley Park, failure was unthinkable. Less than a month earlier Everton had snatched an unlikely point in one of the most one-sided derbies ever witnessed on Merseyside.

Sam Allardyce had been brought in to ensure that the Blues would avoid relegation and he would achieve his task by marshalling an Everton side who seemed pathologically averse to crossing the halfway line. Yet somehow his charges had left Anfield with a point, courtesy of a disputed penalty in front of their own supporters who celebrated like they had just won the league.

The Reds seemed determined not to give Allardyce any more reasons to gloat and the prospect of not settling the tie in the regulation 90 minutes was unbearable. With time running out, the Kop braying for victory and Blue fingernails chewed down to the bone, van Dijk got ready to write himself into the Anfield record books.

There were just six minutes left on the clock when Liverpool won a corner at the Kop end. An almighty roar filled the night sky, as the ball sailed into the box. The Kop held its breath as forwards and defenders leapt into the air. One man rose above them all though. That man was Liverpool's £75m defender, who powered a sublime header into the net, before running down the goal line, arms outstretched in front of a delirious Kop.

The noise was thunderous as supporters all around the ground indulged in tumultuous celebration. Arms flailing and lungs bursting they revelled in the late winner. In the away end scowls and expletives were the order of the day.

Another derby was won, and Everton were out of yet another cup. They hadn't won a trophy since 1995 and the Kop was only too happy to remind them of the fact.

Once more the glory was Liverpool's and the night belonged to van Dijk. F.A.B. Virgil.

Liverpool say farewell to a Reds legend and goalkeeping pioneer, Tommy Lawrence

On 10 January 2018 Tommy Lawrence passed away at the age of 77. He was of course Bill Shankly's fearless goalkeeper during an era when a resurgent Liverpool emerged from the shadows and grew into one of the most feared teams in Europe. His name will live on in the hearts of Reds fans everywhere.

Lawrence played 390 games for Liverpool, winning two league titles and the club's first FA Cup, in 1965. He was the man Shankly trusted between the sticks for eight years, and he would miss just four games during the club's meteoric rise to the top of the English game.

He eventually gave way to the man he mentored, Ray Clemence, who had waited two years to break into the first team such was Lawrence's consistency. However, the man the Kop christened the 'flying pig' – because of his unlikely agility and stout physique – wasn't always in Shanks's good books.

After one game early in his career, he had to hide from the great man after a calamitous goalkeeping howler.

The Reds were playing Arsenal away at Highbury and were a goal up with time running out. This would have been a great result in the capital.

However, with just 20 minutes left on the clock, Gunners striker Joe Baker hit a tame shot from distance that trickled slowly along the turf. It looked for all the world like the easiest of saves for Tommy, but for some unknown reason he opened his legs as he bent to collect the ball.

It rolled through them and into the net. His team-mates couldn't believe it, and on the bench the boss smouldered.

The Reds survived a late bombardment from the Londoners and the game ended 1-1. However, Lawrence knew he was in for a roasting from Shankly. So, as soon as the whistle blew, he ran straight down the tunnel and into the bath, where he hid behind his team-mates.

Shankly, who ruled the club with a rod of iron, burst into the dressing room full of fire and brimstone, and booming, 'Where is he?' Tommy knew what was coming and realising it was better to front up, raised his hand in the air, saying, 'Before you say anything boss, can I just apologise to you and the lads for opening my legs to that ball.'

Shanks glowered, 'Oh it's not you I blame son, it's your mother, for opening *her* legs!'

This is a story Tommy and the rest of the Shankly boys continued to tell with much laughter for years after, and it has now passed into folklore. Perhaps it also serves as a lesson to us all, that even the very best make mistakes.

For Lawrence though, the damage was far from perManént. The boss would keep faith in a player who would go on to become a goalkeeping pioneer.

Lawrence was the first 'sweeper-keeper', often rushing out of his area to break up play – a tactic he and the team worked on tirelessly at Melwood. Before Lawrence, keepers focused on commanding the six-yard box and often stuck rigidly to their goal line.

However, Tommy's instructions were to come out more and frustrate the opposition attack. If the opponents were on the halfway line, he would be on his 18-yard line. If they broke through the Reds defence, his orders were to rush out and smash them.

Lawrence later revealed that, as a strategy, it didn't sit comfortably with him at first. He recalled, 'At first I was frightened to death. We did it at Melwood a few times, then we tried at Anfield. Well, I'm standing there, and the Kop is giving me some stick. "Get back on your line!" they're all yelling. No goalkeeper did that in those days. I thought, "Oh my God." But it worked. I'd come out and do like they do today. You didn't get sent off in those days either. So, I used to bring them down. If they pushed it past me, I'd just hit them.'

Modern Liverpool was built by players like Tommy Lawrence: fierce, brave, loyal and humble. Everything we love about the club today, the history, the cups that sit in the museum, the very ethos that makes it unique and special to all of us, we owe to people like him.

He played in the first European game to be contested at Anfield, a tie the Reds won 11-1 on aggregate. Of course, he was also between the sticks when Liverpool won their first FA Cup, defeating Leeds United at Wembley in 1965.

What joy he must have experienced on the balcony of the Town Hall as hundreds of thousands beneath him swayed and sang, basking in the pride he and his team-mates had brought to the Red half of the city.

His will have been but a fraction of the pleasure he gave to Liverpudlians in every corner of the city. A great hoodoo had been lifted. No longer could our blue neighbours laud their FA Cup triumphs over us, and many Reds proudly proclaimed that they could die happy, knowing Liverpool had finally won the cup.

Tommy was one of the men responsible for that.

This will have been the greatest moment he experienced in a Liverpool shirt, greater than winning the title, more akin to winning the Champions League than a domestic trophy to 1960s Reds.

It is an achievement that will live on in the hearts of Liverpool supporters for as long as the club exists, and so too will Tommy Lawrence.

Rest in peace Tommy, Liverpool's number one. You'll never walk alone.

Welcome to Hell: Manchester City feel the full force of Anfield's tumultuous atmosphere

Urchins atop gate posts, Reds perched on rooftops, streets bathed in flare light and smoke filling a golden sky; it may have seemed like Dante's Inferno to the City team bus as it weaved its way past the Arkles pub and on to Anfield Road, but to Liverpool supporters this was paradise – and it was still more than an hour to kick-off.

Of course, this was a European night. It was 4 April 2018. The visitors were Manchester City. On paper, a much superior foe, but fortunately football is played on grass. And, the grass in L4 would be scorched before the night was out, such was the ferocity of Liverpool's attack.

The crowds had gathered early, filling the pavements and side streets. Every vantage point was occupied and the air on Anfield Road crackled and fizzed, as supporters waited to greet both team buses. They sang 'Allez, Allez, Allez', a new anthem born in the pubs around Liverpool and transported on to the Kop and away grounds alike.

It owed its true origins to an Italian pop song about lost love, but it had been commandeered by Liverpool's travelling support. Soon its haunting melody would fill all four corners of the old stadium on Walton Breck Road, as even Reds in the posh seats belted out its chorus.

This was Anfield. Gut-churning, blood-curdling, heart-pounding, spine-tingling, voice-shredding, fist-pumping Anfield, in all its wonderful glory. City's supporters and some of their players made a huge miscalculation when they tried to play it down in the run-up to the game.

To be fair to them, others have made the same mistake and suffered in the same way. Remember the Madrid press declaring, with their banner headline 'This is Anfield, So What?' just before their gladiators were mauled 4-0?

It's as if City's fate was sealed the moment Leroy Sané, City's exciting young attacker, shrugged off playing in such noise. His comments only served to stoke the fire burning beneath the tie and every Red who arrived early for the game felt they had a point to prove.

The City team bus arrived first and the noise along Utting Avenue was thunderous. I was stood near the fan-zone on Anfield Road, facing the stadium. Both sides of the road were lined with supporters, straining their necks to catch a first glimpse of the bus as it weaved its way into the ground. Flags and banners wafted in the air. This was a pageant of terror designed to intimidate the visitors and lift our heroes.

There was 'pyro' everywhere and red smoke filled the air and drifted along the streets. I had seen it on the walk up to the ground. It had turned the sky crimson and the smell of cordite was everywhere. This felt more like a battlefield after a huge conflagration than the precursor to a football match.

There are those who decry the intimidating nature of the spectacle. Especially in light of the rough treatment meted out to the visiting team bus, played *ad nauseam* on social media afterwards. I was there, and I saw bottles and cans hit the side of the vehicle carrying the City team. I didn't see the damage. I felt at the time it was regrettable and unnecessary, but I won't join in the hysteria surrounding the incident.

The actions of a minority among a crowd of 54,000 couldn't possibly detract from what was an incredible atmosphere and spectacle. Football is, after all, just a game played on a field, until tens of thousands of screaming, swaying, mad bastards pitch up and transform it into an event.

What an event this was, and if the journey to the ground was hellish for Guardiola and his men, the game would prove even more tortuous for them. Liverpool blew City away in a 19-minute first-half spell that saw Mohamed Salah, Alex

Oxlade-Chamberlain and Sadio Mané smash goals past a hapless Ederson in the visitors' goal. They then calmly shut their opponent out in the second half.

The Guardian singled out Oxlade-Chamberlain's goal for particularly high praise, writing: 'Oxlade-Chamberlain certainly chose a good night to produce the outstanding moment of his Liverpool career to date. He struck his shot with the kind of power that might have reminded Liverpool fans about the way Terry McDermott used to drive through the middle and let fly from 25 yards.'

As glowing as they are, those words don't seem to do justice to power of the former Arsenal man's shot. It was a thunderbolt struck with lightning pace and it lit up the Kop in an explosion of noise and raw emotion. Many of us could scarcely believe what we were seeing, and neither, it seemed, could the City fans.

The Times captured the mood perfectly, saying: 'Manchester City ran into a wall of noise and a swarm of red last night. Liverpool were magnificent, attacking devastatingly in the first half and defending maturely in the second.'

And of any potential excuses City may offer for their humiliation, the paper had this to say: 'When City conduct the inquest into events in the opening half-hour, they may talk of the psychological damage wrought on Guardiola's players when their coach was ambushed on the approaches to Anfield. They can talk of that, if they like, and it was undeniably distressing, but the focus should be more on

Guardiola's surprisingly cautious tactics and line-up that sent out the wrong message.'

The Manchester City boss had been outwitted by Jürgen Klopp, not for the first time. His players had been outfought and outclassed. Meanwhile, in the stands, his supporters had been out-sung. They had foolishly enquired as to the location of our 'famous atmosphere', and Anfield did not disappoint.

The Liverpool crowd are always original, always authentic and still as powerful as ever when it matters, just as they did after St Etienne, Chelsea and Dortmund. Auld arses like me will wax lyrical for years to come about the night City came to Anfield, and we left them feeling blue.

I'll recount endlessly about how their players tried to talk the atmosphere down, branding it as hype and myth.

We'll all laugh as we remember the Main Stand rocking and red smoke billowing from the Kop when Salah grabbed the first. Tears will fill our eyes when we recall the colour and the noise, how the earth beneath our feet shook when Oxlade-Chamberlain smashed his shot into the roof of the net, and how we danced when Mané headed home the third.

I will never forget the Kop throng leaving the ground, screaming at the top of their lungs, their vocal chords already in tatters, and merging with the crowd leaving the King Kenny Stand and spontaneously bursting into a rendition of 'Allez, Allez, Allez'. I can still smell the cordite in the air and I love it.

We all left proud that though the battle was not yet over, there was a second leg at the Etihad to come the name of

Anfield was once again on the lips of the footballing world. The legend of its power, majesty and passion endures in the minds of a whole new generation.

The second leg would see Liverpool reach even greater heights. With Guardiola sent to the stands, they would respond to an early setback by winning the game 2-1 and the tie 5-1 on aggregate. City had burst out of the traps and were a goal up, thanks to a van Dijk error, inside two minutes.

The signs were ominous and wave after wave of City attacks threatened to sweep aside Liverpool's first-leg advantage. There was even a disallowed goal for the home side, but the Reds held out. By the end of the half an Oxlade-Chamberlain effort suggested that Liverpool had not only weathered the storm but may even get back in the game.

The second half brought goals from Mo Salah (56) and Firmino (77) and amazingly, magnificently, the tie was over, City were out and the resultant noise from the away end could be heard in the streets far beyond the Etihad. Liverpool were improbably in the semi-final and what a memorable tie that would be.

A forgotten hero returns: Johnny Wheeler, Liverpool's oldest living captain, is honoured by the club

It's Saturday, 28 April 2018, the streets around Anfield echo with the footsteps of Kopites and Reds from all over the world. Just as they have for over a century, Liverpool's loyal supporters chat excitedly about their team, before taking their places in all four corners of the ground.

Stoke City are the visitors, but all the chatter was about the momentous Champions League semi-final against Roma just four days earlier. The Reds had raced into a five-goal lead only to see two late goals take the shine off an epic European encounter. More drama lay ahead, but before that there was a small matter of a Premier League fixture and a quest for a top-four place to contend with.

As the players took to the field, treading a path carved out by the boots of truly great men down the years, one of those past heroes was watching from the Boardroom in the Main Stand above. That man was none other than Johnny Wheeler, Liverpool's oldest living captain.

Johnny Wheeler, the cousin of club legend Ronnie Moran, was born in Crosby in 1928 and would grow up to captain the Reds during the 1958/59 season. Moran would take the armband from him the following year before going on to become a member of the famed Boot Room that plotted Liverpool's conquest of Europe.

Wheeler's journey to the captaincy was a long one. He arrived at Liverpool in 1956 from Bolton Wanderers, at the age of 28. He had started his career at Tranmere Rovers in 1944 and was snapped up by Bolton in 1951, who reportedly paid £15,000 for him.

Johnny was a right-sided midfielder who Liverpool had scouted while he was playing at Prenton Park. However, Bolton manager Bill Ridding, an ex-Reds trainer, was well aware of his talent and swooped before the Anfield outfit could make their move.

He played 200 First Division games for the Burnden Park club but the highlight of his spell at Wanderers was his appearance in the 1953 FA Cup Final against Blackpool. This game became known as the Matthews Final, after the famous Stanley Matthews inspired an incredible fightback by Blackpool to snatch the cup from Bolton's grasp.

Wheeler must have thought all his birthdays had come at once as Wanderers raced into a 3-1 lead with 35 minutes left on the clock. Then the game turned on its head, and the Wembley crowd of 100,000 watched in amazement as Matthews took the game by the scruff of the neck and inspired an astonishing turnaround.

Blackpool drew the tie level in the 89th minute thanks to Stan Mortensen's hat-trick. Then, with Wheeler and his team-mates out on their feet, Bill Perry hit the winner in injury time. Despite this crushing blow, his performances for Wanderers continued to catch the eye of the Reds scouts.

The following year Johnny received his one and only England cap, playing in a British Home Championship game against Northern Ireland at Windsor Park. England won the game 2-0 thanks to goals from Johnnie Haynes and Don Revie.

Around this time, Phil Taylor took over the Anfield hot seat from Don Welsh, and soon earmarked Wheeler to reinforce a Liverpool side fighting to get out of the Second Division. Taylor was a big admirer and saw Johnny as a utility player, telling the *Daily Mail*, after he had signed him, 'I played against Johnny a number of times and was always impressed by his forceful personality and fine club spirit. He is a man who will play anywhere.'

The transfer came about in interesting circumstances. Wheeler had suddenly decided to move back to Liverpool, while still a Bolton player, and sought permission from his manager to look at houses in the city. The Reds got wind of this, or maybe they were tipped off, and immediately inquired about his availability.

In 1956 a deal was struck to bring him home to Merseyside and he became Taylor's first big signing. The fee is often quoted as £9,000, but some sources state it was £12,000. Given his big game experience and the fact that Bolton had paid £15,000 to get him from Tranmere, the Reds thought they'd picked up a bargain.

The *Coventry Evening Telegraph* reported, on 8 September 1956, 'Liverpool took a big step towards strengthening their defence yesterday when they paid Bolton Wanderers a "very substantial" sum for Johnny Wheeler, the England right-half. Wheeler joined Bolton from Tranmere Rovers in February 1951, and thus returns to Merseyside where he is now living. The transfer fee is understood to be about £12,000. This is £3,000 less than Bolton paid to Tranmere.'

In truth it was something of a gamble, as Johnny had been out all season with an ankle injury. However, he would be cleared to play in the Reds' next game, just seven days later, a 2-0 home defeat to Stoke City.

He scored his first goal for Liverpool, an equaliser against Bristol City in a 2-2 draw, on 13 October 1956. However, the best was yet to come.

In the November, Wheeler enjoyed the most remarkable game of his Liverpool career. Playing as an inside-forward, he lined up at Anfield against a Port Vale side famed for their rock-solid defensive line. The game would end with an unlikely Liverpool victory and Johnny Wheeler entering the record books.

The final score was 4-1 to Liverpool, but the gentlemen of the press felt it flattered the Reds. Only one man had made this scoreline possible, Johnny Wheeler. This is how Leslie Edwards, writing for the *Liverpool Daily Post*, saw it: 'Liverpool's win was nothing like as emphatic as it sounds, and the visitors must have left Anfield wondering how they lost by such a margin. The answer is contained largely in two words – Johnny Wheeler.'

Port Vale had weathered Liverpool's early storm and had gone a goal up in the first half. At half-time, Anfield and the Kop was a brooding and sullen place. The attendance was far from impressive, with just 33,000 turning out, but somehow the supporters rallied themselves for the second half.

The *Daily Post* noted how the Kop's performance transformed the Reds' intensity, 'The Spion Kop roar must take much of the credit for the improvement in Liverpool's front line in the second half. Although there were plenty of open spaces in its mighty terrace, there was no appreciable difference in its usual volume of sound.'

The noise must have terrified Vale, because their usually reliable defence crumbled. It took just eight minutes for Billy Liddell to level, then something truly magical took place.

With the game heading for a draw, and just ten minutes left on the clock, up stepped Johnny Wheeler, with the then-fastest hat-trick in English football history. His goals came in the 81st, 82nd and 85th minutes.

In the space of just five minutes, a breathless Anfield could only look on in amazement as Wheeler plundered three goals to win it for the Reds. According to the *Post*, the feat left Port Vale 'gasping with its speed and devastating efficiency'.

In 1959 Phil Taylor made way for Bill Shankly, and although Johnny stayed on a couple more years, he would leave for New Brighton in 1961, where he played as an amateur. In 1963 he was offered the post of player-manager but left to take up an assistant trainer role at Bury, where he stayed until 1969.

Johnny Wheeler played 177 times for Liverpool, scoring 23 times. Sadly, his career didn't produce any silverware, but he gave Kopites of the 1950s many happy memories and in one unbelievable five-minute spell, he single-handedly dragged the Reds to victory against one of the toughest defences in the country, just as he had watched Stanley Matthews do to his Bolton side back in 1953.

In 2018 Johnny would witness an Anfield transformed from the decaying and crumbling ground he once graced. However, as the Kop roared into life, and the referee signalled the start of hostilities, he would be transported back to a time when football was undeniably the people's game.

Johnny's daughter, Sue Taylor, had been determined to give her dad the opportunity to return to Anfield. Sadly, he had developed dementia, and although recognising family members was a struggle at times, the memories of his footballing career are deeply imprinted. This was a chance for him to relive those days, said Sue.

'For me it's about creating some special memories of my own too,' she said.

The club had begun taking strides to formally recognise the contribution of their former stars. Chief executive Peter Moore had become very keen to develop an ex-players association after taking up his position at the club.

Sue had contacted the club herself, making an impassioned appeal to the public relations department, who immediately agreed to sort something out. She explained, 'I think it's important because men like my dad represent the foundations, the beginnings of the club we see today. He is part of the history and we are very fortunate that he is still alive at the age of 90. I am very proud of his achievements. We all are.'

Sue was brought up on football and was acutely aware of her dad's importance to Liverpool and the importance of the club to him. He would often regale her with tales from his playing days, and one had stuck in her mind.

'Dad told me that on matchdays he would travel to the ground on the bus, with my granddad and my brother. Then, at the end of the game, tired from his exertions, he would run over to where they were in the stands and take them down to the dressing room.'

Johnny's memories of growing up remain clear. As do his boyhood allegiances. 'I was a Red. I'm a Liverpool lad,' he recalls. He also remembers the man who granted him his dream move with affection.

'He was a good manager, a nice man. Very calm when he spoke to you,' he says.

There are also memories of the greatest player he had ever seen, Billy Liddell. Wheeler and Liddell share an unusual distinction, in that both have Liverpool streets named in their honour. Wheeler Drive and Liddell Avenue are situated within yards of each other, in the Melling area of the city.

This tells us everything we need to know, in terms of the esteem in which Wheeler was held by the club and his hometown. However, Johnny was a hero to two sets of supporters.

Reds fans of the 1950s and '60s will have recalled with joy his devastating five-minute hat trick against Port Vale. While fans of Bolton Wanderers will recall his duel with Stanley Matthews at Wembley.

At Anfield, on Saturday, 28 April 2018, Johnny was afforded a hero's welcome at the club he had served with distinction. He was greeted by Kenny Dalglish, Robbie Fowler and CEO Peter Moore.

However, the family were deeply moved by a presentation from Jürgen Klopp. It was a framed photograph of Johnny in his prime, stood on the Anfield turf and wearing his Liverpool kit. On it, the Reds boss had written, 'LFC is only the club it is today thanks to players like YOU. YNWA, Jürgen Klopp.'

Thank you, Johnny Wheeler.

Rampant Reds plunder five against Roma, but late horror show gives Italians hope

We have reached 24 April 2018; I am stood on the corner of Anfield Road and Utting Avenue. The Arkles pub looms large and beneath it a throng of delirious supporters fill the pavements and take over the highway.

Yellow police vans enveloped in red smoke peer out from the haze, like apparitions among the joyous chaos. Kopites dance and sing on their rooftops and the men and women inside pay them no attention. It's a full hour before kick-off and the streets are packed to bursting.

Almost three weeks earlier we'd all been here to 'welcome' our English foe, Manchester City. They had been vanquished in a hail of song and banners; and a few bottles. Tonight it was the turn of the Romans to face Anfield's might. They didn't stand a chance. Few sides can live with Liverpool on a night like this.

I joined what felt like a torchlight procession down Anfield Road. The torches were of course flares, spewing crimson smoke into the night air. Around me the crowd break into song as we walk slowly along. 'Allez, Allez, Allez' and 'Fields of Anfield Road' waft into my ears, their strains sound haunting and they fill my belly with butterflies. To my left, kids are clinging to the Shankly Gates and clambering on railings and posts.

I lift my phone above my head, the camera setting activated. What I capture is a sea of red humanity. It stretches all the way down the road and beyond the Main Stand. Pillars of red smoke are dotted among the crowd. They funnel towards the sky and the whole scene resembles an oilfield, set ablaze.

The mist temporarily clears. I see a Reds supporter perched on the shoulders of his mate; he's leading the singing, with arms waving as he urges those around him to turn up the volume. It's a raucous and chaotic mix of sights, sounds and smells. It's all cordite and choruses; visions of football's joyous abandon and I felt the power of Anfield in my bones.

These mere words are but a fragment of the experience. They can never do justice to the real thing. When you're there, you feel it all around you. It makes your skin come alive with goosebumps. The air itself fizzes with electricity and it makes the hairs on your arms stand to attention.

As I walk, I'm transported through the ages, I'm walking in the footsteps of my forbears, their hopes and dreams are now one with my own. This is a shared experience that transcends time. I've never been religious or had a religious experience, but I can only imagine it would feel something like this.

Nights like this are why I love football and adore my team. That feeling of being part of something bigger and greater than myself, of being connected through time with long-lost ancestors and of sharing in age-old quests. That night, on Anfield Road, I felt as much a part of Shankly's great community as I have ever felt before; yet the game itself hadn't even begun.

Little did any of us realise at the time that a very different drama was unfolding yards from us on Walton Breck Road. Just as they do before every Liverpool game, scores of home supporters were gathered outside the Albert Pub in the shadow of the Kop.

Among them was Sean Cox, an Irish fan who had journeyed over to watch his beloved team. In an act of sheer cowardice a small group of Roma supporters attacked Liverpool followers and the unsuspecting Sean received an awful head injury. It would prove to be an instant of madness that would change both his and his family's life forever.

Reds supporters and the players would rally to their aid. However, surely nothing could compensate this innocent family for the trauma they have endured.

Inside the stadium, the atmosphere was spellbinding. I will maintain that there is no greater sight or sound than the Kop in full bloom. Other supporters around the world create incredible atmospheres, of course they do. However, their rhythmic and often choreographed displays carry but a fraction of the power of the Kop's raucous and spontaneous majesty.

There is a 'homemade' quality to the atmosphere at Anfield. It feels organic and though the songs are honed in pubs around the city and on coaches travelling to away days, there is nothing stage-managed in their renditions. I believe that's what sets us apart, and that's what lifts our players and stifles theirs. That is the magic of Anfield on a European night. It's not 11 versus 11; it's 50,000 versus 11.

St Etienne felt it, Olympiakos did too. Chelsea withered and City crumbled amid the furore and ferment of an Anfield European night. Roma would too.

The feeling in the crowd at kick-off was one of exhilaration. The adrenaline kept fatigue at bay, and those who had been singing for an hour by the time the referee signalled the onset of battle would push themselves still further during the game. Our hearts pounded and sinews strained as we let out a deafening chorus of boos each time a Roma player touched the ball.

The Italian giants gave it their best, and for just over half an hour they managed to go toe-to-toe with Liverpool. The game had the feel of a titanic encounter between evenly matched opponents. Then, in a moment of brilliance, Mo Salah decided he'd had enough and proceeded to sack Rome, all on his own.

His first goal was an act of sublime finishing. From the right-hand corner of the box he chipped the ball exquisitely past the outstretched arm of future Reds' keeper Alisson Becker at the Anfield Road end. The Egyptian, who had signed for Liverpool from Roma, refused to celebrate the goal. The same could not be said for his team-mates or supporters as the ground erupted and almost lifted out of its foundations.

However, those celebrations paled into insignificance compared to what followed for his second. With Anfield boiling in a white-hot atmosphere, Bobby Firmino broke through middle. Salah angled his run and his Brazilian team-mate threaded a perfect pass leaving him one-on-one with the on-rushing Alisson. Salah made no mistake and calmly chipped the ball over the stopper to make it 2-0.

It was the stroke of half-time, the perfect moment to score and the sense that something magical was once again on the cards was everywhere. None of us wanted the interval. If Liverpool had been allowed to play on at that point they'd have been in double figures by full time. Such was their belief and the ferocity of their play; such was the cauldron that was Anfield.

Instead we all had to take a breather and none of us could quite believe what we were witnessing. However, as we would soon learn, the second half was about to deliver something truly incredible for both the right and the wrong reasons.

In a spell that lasted less than 15 minutes, Liverpool shook Roma to their foundations. First came a goal from Sadio Mané on 56 minutes followed by a brace from Firmino. All three were at the Kop end, which melted into a sea of chaotic bodies churned by sheer joy. None of us could comprehend what was happening before our eyes.

The players themselves could not have dreamed they could be five goals up against a team of Roma's quality. For their part, the visitors looked out on their feet, shoulders slumped and fearing a rout of epic proportions. Then Liverpool offered them a route back into the game.

Nobody can blame Klopp for his substitution of Salah on 74 minutes. The Reds were 5-0 up, at home, and he had every right to believe that his team would see the game out without incident. However, in a foreboding premonition of the final in May, Liverpool were about to see what can happen when they lose their star man.

Roma seemed to gain an extra yard after the substitution. Where they had been filled with self-doubt, vanquished before the battle was over, they ventured forth once more. In the 81st minute they were rewarded when Edin Džeko grabbed one back.

Most of us were irritated by what we felt was a thoroughly undeserved consolation, none of us were prepared for what happened four minutes later. With the Reds defence seemingly in panic mode, Roma won a penalty. James Milner was adjudged to have deliberately handled a Radja Nainggolan shot from close range. To say it was harsh was an understatement. Nevertheless, Perotti made it 5-2 and suddenly Roma had two away goals and the Italian press could dream of miracles.

Perspective is a peculiar thing. Had anyone told me before kick-off that the Reds would end up 5-2 victors, I'd have been ecstatic. However, as I trudged out of the ground that night I felt anything but. That late Roma salvo may have flattered them, but it cast doubt over an outcome that should have been beyond question.

What none of us would realise was that we were witnessing one of the most epic Champions League semi-finals of all time, and it was about to get a whole lot more dramatic in Rome. We weren't worried though; we always win in Rome – well, sort of.

The sacking of Rome: The Reds are Kiev-bound despite second-leg drama

The game in the Italian capital was a classic. Roma, buoyed by their late, and somewhat undeserved salvo at Anfield, put up a fierce fight. Liverpool never really looked in danger though. The damage had already been done in that breathtaking 13-minute second-half blitz, just eight days earlier.

The game would end with an emotional tribute to Liverpool supporter Sean Cox, who had been viciously assaulted outside Anfield before the first leg. In a move that symbolised the growing bond between players and fans, the Reds paraded a banner in honour of the Irishman on the pitch. Seeing such a potent symbol of the symbiosis that exists between players and supporters was a fitting way to celebrate another dramatic chapter in the Reds' glorious history and Liverpool reaching their eighth European Cup final.

Before kick-off, with the Stadio Olimpico packed to the rafters, the noise was deafening. The Italians fancied a miracle, but the men from Anfield had other ideas. For Liverpool, European conquest feels like a birthright. Time and again they have found themselves at the continental top table. Even when their domestic form suggests they don't belong, they somehow crash the party anyway.

Despite not winning the league title for three decades, in that same period the Reds had featured in three UEFA Cup finals and were heading for their third Champions League final. We trace the roots of our love affair with Europe all the way back to 1959.

On the eve of the 1960s, the great Scotsman had arrived at Anfield with a dream. He would turn Liverpool into a 'bastion of invincibility'. All of Europe would have no choice but to submit, he promised. It would have seemed like a pipe dream to many, especially those used to watching Liverpool labour in the second tier of English football. Yet, here we were, in 2018, and still the scourge of an entire continent; feared and respected in equal measure by the biggest teams in the game.

For all their bluff and bluster, Roma looked uncharacteristically fragile on home soil. Like gladiators facing a crowd baying for blood, Liverpool came out of the traps fighting and after just nine minutes Sadio Mané had put the visitors in front. Gini Wijnaldum added a second, and equally priceless, away goal after 26 minutes, but not before a James Milner own goal had inflicted an unnecessary wound and granted hope to the Romans.

The Guardian would praise the fearlessness of Klopp's men, pointing to the febrile atmosphere and Roma's air of invincibility at home in European competition: 'Of all the places Liverpool have been in this competition, all the stories they have accumulated over the years, have they ever experienced such a febrile din? That, however, was probably the most impressive part of Liverpool's performance: their fearlessness. Roma's record of having not conceded a single home goal in this competition –some achievement when their opponents have included Barcelona, Chelsea and Atlético Madrid – was gone within eight minutes.'

The half-time scoreline of 2-1 was far from disastrous though, and the Reds looked to have planted their flag in the Ukraine already. However, this is Liverpool, and we never do things the easy way. There must always be drama. It's as much a part of our DNA as that lust for conquest on foreign soil.

It is little wonder that the *Mirror* would proclaim at full time: 'Even by Liverpool's own incredible standards, this will go down as one of their most dramatic European nights. A night never to be forgotten, a night to go down in Liverpool folklore.'

Three second half goals by the home team would prompt those words. The history books will suggest that Jürgen's Reds were rattled by Roma. The 4-2 scoreline paints a distorted image of the tie and Liverpool's 7-6 aggregate victory flatters their opponents considerably.

Had Edin Džeko's 52nd-minute equaliser been the final word on the game, even that would have been unfair, given Liverpool's level of control in the tie. That it wasn't became a source of frustration for Reds everywhere and of worry to those looking ahead to a final against far superior opponents.

David Maddock, writing in the *Mirror*, agreed that the final score did not accurately reflect proceedings: 'The scoreline is misleading because Liverpool never really came close to blowing it even if Roma got to within a goal of completing the most remarkable fightback. Liverpool never do it the easy way.'

He was right. Liverpool had been heading towards a very creditable 2-2 away draw that would see them reach the final in style. Only four minutes remained on the clock and the celebrations had started in the stands. Those who hadn't done so already were booking their flights and accommodation for the final, when Roma snatched a third.

The Italians looked tired and when Radja Nainggolan found himself 25 yards from goal, all he could do was swing his boot at it. The shot should have hit a Liverpool defender or sailed hopelessly wide of the mark, but of course it went in off the post and past the flapping grasp of Loris Karius. Surely it was a consolation, merely granting the home side some dignity. Though they had lost the tie, they had at least won the home game. That would have been drama enough for any other side, but we are Liverpool.

With barely any time left, the referee decided that Ragnar Klavan had handled in the penalty area. It seemed harsh in the extreme, but Nainggolan did not waste the opportunity to set Red nerves jangling. In the end it was not enough though, and Liverpool would emerge victorious.

These words, written in *The Times* captured the mood at full time perfectly. They would also neatly outline the task facing Liverpool against Madrid in Kiev: 'When the final whistle blew here, shortly after Radja Nainggolan's penalty had incredibly put Roma within a goal of extra time, Liverpool players sunk to their knees in joy and relief and exhaustion. They'd given everything, been exposed defensively, but had still reached the Champions League final in Kiev. Liverpool love Europe's elite trophy, old Big Ears, and their fans, whose emotions were put through the wringer, celebrated wildly. They now face Real Madrid, a repeat of the 1981 final, knowing that they will need to defend better, far better than this against a far superior strike force in Kiev.'

Of course, they would not. Kiev would prove to be a disappointment on the pitch. But, as we will learn, it proved to be just another staging post on the road from doubt to belief. Liverpool's tale has always been as much about the journey as it is about the destination and as the road to Kiev proved, it's not worth setting off at all, unless there is going to be some drama along the way.

Supporters rock Shevchenko Park and doubters become believers, despite defeat in Kiev

On 26 May 2018, Liverpool and their vast army of supporters turned the city of Kiev red. The team would eventually succumb on the pitch, but off it they had transformed legions of fans from doubters to believers. The legacy of that final defeat to Real Madrid would prove far more significant than any trophy ever could. Here's why.

Long after the pain of Kiev had subsided, I sat in a restaurant opposite Jamie Carragher. I was interviewing him for a book idea that ended up on the back-burner. We were discussing what Europe means to Liverpool; the club and its supporters and the conversation strayed back to that night in the Ukraine.

We marvel at how that defeat to Madrid felt different to the one a year earlier, to Seville. The aftertaste had been different to the one we endured after the final in Basel, in which Seville's three second-half goals had cancelled out Daniel Sturridge's first-half opener and broke the hearts of Reds everywhere.

Of course, unbeknown to all of us, Jürgen Klopp hadn't waited long before he had begun to use the pain of that setback to stir his players and put them back on the path to another assault on the citadels of Europe.

The sun had not even set on that defeat and the German had risen to his feet to deliver an emotional rallying cry. But, for the rest of us the journey back to belief would take much longer.

After Kiev though, well, most of us felt strangely buoyant. Carra, who had borne witness to the 2018 Champions League Final as a supporter with his son, captured the mood of most Reds, as he reflected on the aftermath of the defeat to Madrid.

'Don't get me wrong,' he said, 'I was devastated that we lost the final. But I spoke to my son about the night we had, and I said, "You won't get many of them you know" – everyone together and enjoying themselves. It doesn't come around all that often.'

For Jamie, Kiev was as much about the spectacular highs experienced by supporters, who had travelled the continent writing their own chapters in the club's history of European adventure, as it was about any trophy.

I asked him if some of the euphoria among supporters stems from the fact that Kiev never felt like the end of something, but more like a beginning. After Basel it had felt like the Reds had run into a solid brick wall, but, despite the defeat, Kiev felt like a staging post to something more.

Carragher agreed and added that there was a bonus. The undimmed joy of Reds everywhere had apparently become a running sore for rival supporters. They just couldn't understand why Liverpool fans were still crowing despite seeing their team lose the final.

'In some ways I think it's pissing a lot of people off that we're actually enjoying ourselves,' Carragher explained. 'Because they're all saying, "Oh, you didn't win it." But we're having the time of our lives going home and abroad and watching Liverpool.

'We're loving Klopp, loving the football we play. Okay, we haven't won the trophies yet, but we're having a great time, and I just think it needles people a little bit.'

To understand this, you have to get beneath the psyche of Liverpool, the city and the club. We love fighters. We hate defeat, but we can tolerate, even celebrate it, so long as we feel we've gone down fighting. The capitulation in Basel felt like a surrender. In Kiev, the team had given their all, only to succumb to a mixture of brilliance, industrial levels of cheating and, sadly, calamitous goalkeeping. None of that could take away the belief that Liverpool had gone toe-to-toe with the best and more than looked the part.

It may have been a case of close, but no cigar, but we were close for sure. We were beaten, but we could hold our heads up high, because we had given it a good go and had a fucking ball in the process. That is as much the Liverpool way as anything else.

Neil Poole, editor of the popular fanzine *We Are Liverpool*, was one of those who witnessed the rarefied atmosphere that surrounded the trip to Kiev and his experience illustrates just why the smile will never fade from Kopite faces, after that amazing run to the final.

Nothing was going to keep Neil from the final and he had resorted to selling his season ticket to raise the necessary funds for the trip. He remembers the irresistible drive to get there at all costs: 'This was my first real opportunity to attend a European Cup final. I was too unborn in 1977, too newborn in '78, too young in '81, '84, '85, too on the other side of the world in 2005 and too skint in 2007. We tried everything we could to get to Kiev, but it looked doomed to failure. Then, through sheer good fortune, everything turned at around 2pm on the Wednesday, just three days before the final.

'I somehow managed to spawn tickets and direct return flights to Kiev. I won't say how much it cost because I've tried to pretend it didn't really happen, but I had to sell my season ticket for 2018/19 to fund the trip. I sacrificed 19 games for one and I still think it was worth it. Even knowing what I know now, I would do it all again.'

For Neil and many other supporters, the defeat could never come close to matching the unbridled joy of reaching the final and experiencing the scenes in the Ukrainian capital first-hand. Mingling with tens of thousands of fellow Reds, enjoying the sunshine and spotting famous faces were just some of the highlights.

'We got to Kiev nice and early so had a good chance to have a look around,' explains Neil. 'I think as Liverpool fans, we were definitely a curious but welcomed oddity, and they seemed intrigued by us and were filming us on their phones as we marched to the stadium. We were singing "Allez, Allez, Allez" and the sense of camaraderie, high spirits and optimism walking down to the ground filled me with pride.

'The whole trip and experience made the result far, far more palatable. After the game we discussed how far more gut-wrenching it would have been to watch on the telly at home because the game would be the be all and the end all. At least we had the build-up to the trip and the trip itself. You enjoy those aspects in the moment. And, once you get over the initial disappointment you can reflect on all the rest and realise how buzzing you were at the time and how great the whole thing was.'

For Tony Zeverona, a lifelong Liverpudlian who, at the age of 57, has seen it all, Kiev was a magical experience. Tony went to his first match in 1967, a 1-0 victory over Sheffield Wednesday courtesy of a Chris Lawler goal. Since then he has attended six European Cup finals. Though he will always rank the 1977 final against Borussua Mönchengladbach, the club's first victory in the competition, as the greatest, he now claims that Kiev is 'right up there with it'.

Rival supporters may struggle to understand it, but following Liverpool can be a joy, whatever the result. Tony explains why, 'It's about the build-up to the final really. The qualifying games and the euphoria around the whole run to the final made it magical. As a Liverpool supporter I was spoilt as a young lad, and it was a tremendous buzz for me to see the young lads experience the atmosphere and the build-up to the final.'

Tony, his mates and his son all booked their trip long before Liverpool had even secured their place in the final. The 3-0 home drubbing of Manchester City had convinced them that the Reds would do it. And, despite the result, Tony still feels that the £390 spent getting there was the best money he ever spent.

Like many Reds, their journey was a complicated one, as they tried to mitigate the price fixing and supporter gouging of the tour operators and airlines. They would take in Oslo and Vilnius en route to Kiev and perhaps this in part explains why European competition is so appealing to Reds. It represents a chance to explore and sample other cultures. It's about more than the game. It's about being part of the world's biggest touring party, full of colour, humour, songs and adventure. That's why Liverpool supporters crave European football. Yes, we want to win. The five European Cups the club had won by 2018 were a tremendous source of pride. However, so too were the many stories that have woven themselves into our banners and songs down the years.

Tony and his mates would land in Kiev at around 10am and made their way to Shevchenko Park. The venue, named after the player whose penalty miss delivered Liverpool's fifth European Cup in Istanbul in 2005, will forever live in the minds of all supporters who experienced it. Its name will resonate even with those who didn't. It is now part of Reds folklore.

The beer, just £1.30 a pint, was flowing and music and song filled the air. Tony recalls the madness, as Jamie Webster, a rising star of the Boss Night movement, rubbed shoulders on stage with Peter Hooton, lead singer of The Farm, and John Power, frontman for Cast.

All three men would reflect later, when speaking to LFC TV, on how that fan park experience cemented a bond between everyone in attendance. For Webster, it was about the belief such a communal atmosphere engenders. For those like Peter Hooton and Tony Zeverona, veterans of past conquests, it was about passing the torch.

Hooton would comment, with a tear in his eye, that he almost felt like an intruder when looking at the faces of a new generation of Reds, baptised in European revelry. This was their time, he had thought, and he filled up as he reflected on how proud Liverpool's iconic former manager, Shankly, would have been, had he witnessed the culmination of his vision writ large on the faces of children who had never known His Liverpool.

'We conquered all of Europe,' they sang. Almost 60 years on from the arrival of the great man, those words rang true in a park on the far side of Europe. Though the team would leave Kiev empty-handed, the supporters' soaring belief remained a 'bastion of invincibility'.

It was a scene replicated across the globe; in bars, living rooms and even at Anfield itself, Liverpool supporters were connected in pain and pride. Like those who had journeyed across a continent to watch their idols, I had made my pilgrimage to our historic home ground to watch the Reds on giant screens that lined the pitch. But, for me, just like them, it was about more than the game. It was about wanting to be part of that great journey, somehow. And, it was about sharing the experience of it all with other like-minded people.

And, as I walked out of Anfield that night, head bowed and heart heavy, I felt connected in spirit with tens of thousands of people across the globe. Liverpool was everywhere that night, in the hearts and minds of millions.

There would be Reds supporters in New York, Africa, the Far East, Australia and of course Kiev, who felt exactly as I did. Following Liverpool is a communal experience greater than the sum of its component moments. It's bigger than all of us. In defeat or victory, we share the experience as one community. That's our strength.

So, I'll leave the final word on this cup final to Tony Zeverona who so eloquently captures the legacy of Kiev: 'After the game we sat broken-hearted on the steps outside the ground, the turnstiles at our backs.

'We all agreed that this had been a great trip, a fantastic tournament and all of us had memories that would live with us forever. The red machine was well and truly back, and we were already looking forward to our next exciting adventure.'

They were believers once more. As supporters, they'd conquered all of Europe and they were never going to stop. For the team, they had formed an important beachhead in their quest to rule over a continent.

The pain of Basel had been replaced with a grit and determination. They had tasted defeat and were battle-hardened. On the morning after, at 6am, in his Formby home, Klopp and his friends were captured singing defiantly about returning to avenge their defeat. It went like this:

'Madrid had all the fucking luck
We swear we'll keep on being cool
And bring it back to Liverpool.'

And that was one promise Jürgen would keep.

Arise Sir Kenny, but in Liverpool you will always be King

As the injustices of the final in Kiev were slowly being put to bed, another lingering gripe of many Liverpool fans were finally laid to rest. Their hero, club legend and icon,

Kenny Dalglish, had never been honoured by the nation. Manchester United's Alex Ferguson had been made a knight of the realm, but not Kenny. However, all that was about to change.

On 8 June 2018, it was announced that Kenneth Mathieson Dalglish, a man the Kop had anointed King four decades earlier, would become a knight. The honorific 'Sir' would now forever preface his name.

It may surprise some to know that the award divided opinion among Reds, particularly those on Merseyside. While many Liverpool fans had looked at the granting of similar honours to men like Alex Ferguson and argued that overlooking Kenny was an affront, others would point out that, in Liverpool, we have no time for such trinkets.

The appreciation of his people is honour enough, surely.

For the record, had he never been knighted, Kenny would have been more than happy with his status among the Liverpool faithful. However, some felt he was a more than worthy recipient, given his contribution to the club and city, on and off the field.

I admit to feeling conflicted about the subject myself. I'm no royalist, and while I can accept that a nation should honour its finest citizens, I associate such things with an establishment complicit in many of my city's problems. In wrestling with the issue, I reflected on how for most of my life, Kenny Dalglish has been a significant figure, and not just in a purely footballing sense.

I wrote the following for *This is Anfield* on 10 June 2018, and I think it encapsulates my feelings on the subject perfectly.

Kenny Dalglish: In Liverpool we call him King

It's the summer of 1977, August. The sun is blazing and there's Union Jack bunting still hanging from some of the telephone wires in my road.

The silver jubilee celebrations and street parties are behind us, but some can't be bothered taking all the flags down.

We didn't mind displaying the nation's emblem in Liverpool, back then.

It had been a great summer already. The weather was great and memories of the '77 European Cup victory parade were fresh in my mind. They easily eclipsed the pain of losing to United in the FA Cup, and besides, who wanted to be kings of England when you could rule over an entire continent?

I'm on my way to the shop with my mum. I'm annoyed for two reasons: number one, she's dragged me away from playing football in the street with my mate Dave. I'm still carrying the ball under my arm. It was a 'Casey' and, at the time, my pride and joy. Number two, Dave had just told me he won't be supporting Liverpool anymore. We'd had a furious row.

My mother notices I'm not happy and asks me, 'What's up with your face?' So, I blame it all on Dave. I wasn't going to argue with her about going shopping. That was never going to end well.

My mum can't believe what she's hearing. 'What's the matter with him?' she asks, her face dripping with scorn, as if he had some kind of infectious disease.

Now, to be fair to my mate, we were just kids. I'd have been nine years old. Still, such a declaration amounted to blasphemy in my eyes, and clearly to my mum too.

'He says we'll be nothing without Kevin Keegan,' I explained.

Her reaction is swift and dismissive. 'Keegan! He's just a money-grabber anyway. Your dad says he's a mercenary you know.'

I did, but I didn't want to believe it. I was gutted we had lost Keegan. He had been my idol. An all-action hero who scored goals. What's not to love?

My bedroom wall was covered in posters of the Liverpool squad, but the pictures of King Kevin were the biggest. This was a genuine superstar. He did adverts and even had a song in charts and everything.

My mum continues, 'They've got that Scottish lad now anyway, haven't they,' she says. 'Is he any good?'

'Yeah, Mum. Kenny Dalglish.' Like most Liverpudlians, I pronounce it Dagleesh. 'I dunno. Supposed to be.' I replied.

There's no social media, no YouTube and only three channels on the telly, and I wasn't allowed to read newspapers.

The only way I knew about a player was if he was playing in the First Division and I saw him on *Match of the Day.* I had no idea if Kenny from Celtic could ever replace Kevin, who'd gone to Hamburg.

'Well you tell Dave Liverpool Football Club was here before Kevin Keegan and it will be here long after he's gone,' she told me. That was it. Case closed.

Dave and I got our answer almost a year later, at Wembley. A ball from Souness and a sublime dink from Dalglish brought the European Cup back to Anfield for the second year in a row.

Kenny's coronation was complete and where once there were pictures of Keegan on my bedroom wall, there would now be images of his replacement. I can still see those posters now, clinging with the hospital tape that found its way into my mum's uniform pocket, to the woodchip wallpaper next to my bed. His kit is a blaze of red, the ball is at his feet, the faded crowd in the background roars him on still, in my mind's eye.

As a player, from that moment on, Kenny Dalglish had no rival for my affections. He could simply do no wrong.

Now it's May 1978. I'm stood trembling in my junior school assembly hall. This is Monksdown County Primary School, Norris Green, Liverpool. I'm getting ready to read out an essay I had written. I say essay, it was one side of A4 paper and written in colour pencil.

It was a piece I'd written on the morning after the European Cup Final, which Liverpool had won in London. The teacher had employed what I continue to believe was a stroke of genius.

Realising that she was going to get no sense out of half the class, after such a momentous night, she decided to set us an assignment that would keep us quiet.

'I want you to imagine you're on the team bus as it returns home to Liverpool after the cup final,' she says.

The grin on my face is as broad as Kenny's was when he jumped over those advertising boards. In my head it was already written. 'You should describe what you see, hear and how you feel.'

With that, the class went to work. You could hear a pin drop. Amazingly, I wrote that I was Emlyn Hughes, not our number seven. But the work was all about Kenny and what he was doing and saying.

The teacher, her name was Miss Ash, by the way, seemed to like it and she chose mine and a few others to be read out in front of the whole school.

I was terrified, but as I stammered my way to the end of it my confidence grew. Finally, I reached the last line, I paused, took a deep breath and confidently declared, 'Kenny Dalglish is cooler than the Fonz!'

In my head there was huge applause, confetti fell from the ceiling and I was carried shoulder-high from the hall. In reality, there was polite and sporadic clapping and a few giggles.

I'd robbed the line from a Kop chant, but I didn't care. It was true. He was. He still is.

Move forward to 1985. Kenny Dalglish has three European Cups under his belt, a slew of league titles and other assorted accolades and trophies. We all love him so much that we'd happily walk a million miles for one of his goals.

The man has become so lethal in front of goal, that people joke that while Jesus might save, Kenny would always score the rebound.

However, the club's reputation on the continent and at home is in ruins. Thirty-nine football supporters, mostly Italian, lay dead in a crumbling Belgian stadium, after a group of Liverpool fans led a charge that caused a wall to collapse under the weight of fleeing Juventus supporters, crushing them underneath.

I'm watching the scenes on a television screen in my parents' living room. I'm filled with horror and the sense that things will never be the same again.

I see Kenny, he's wearing that grey tracksuit top with the red and white stripes on it, and his face is grim and etched with worry.

In the aftermath of that terrible night, Liverpool Football Club was at its lowest point of any time in its history. It faced the loss of a great manager, in Joe Fagan, and along with all English clubs, was banned from European competition.

Our status as kings of Europe was over.

Into the breach stepped Dalglish, guided from above by Bob Paisley. He led the club to new highs on the domestic front, as the Reds' first-ever player-manager.

In 1986 his team would clinch a historic first league and cup double.

I was at Wembley to see that. The nation's stadium had been our second home throughout my childhood. It's now a red-and-blue carnival of football. Liverpool and Everton fans have converged on the capital to show the city their true colours. Chants of Merseyside, Merseyside erupt outside and inside the stadium.

On Wembley Way, campaigners for the 47 Labour councillors, who were battling Thatcher back home, were handing out stickers. Support Liverpool City Council, they declared. You could have one in red or blue, depending on your allegiance.

In Liverpool, there are no more Union Jacks flying. The city has declared itself Scouse, not English.

Inside the national stadium, Kenny and Howard Kendall lead out their teams, their faces brimming with pride.

In the stands, a city stands united, but ready for the footballing equivalent of civil war. Brothers and sisters all year round, but mortal enemies for 90 minutes, give or take extra time and the possibility of penalties.

When the battle is finally won, Kenny, dressed in his footballer's kit but every inch the manager and leader, parades the FA Cup in front of his screaming and jubilant supporters.

He had shown the world how to rise from your darkest moments. How, in the face of righteous rage and almost universal doubt, you can fight for, and earn, the right to be respected again.

Under his leadership, Liverpool showed the world who we really are and what we are about.

If anyone underestimates the scale of that achievement, it's because they have forgotten or weren't around to experience the soul-crushing grip of Heysel and the resultant conquest of football's innocent joy.

Now I find myself in 1989. Liverpool and Everton are back at Wembley. The Reds are about to win another FA Cup, but I'm not there.

It's been an exhausting season, filled with the all-consuming horror of Hillsborough. I couldn't face travelling. I didn't want to be involved in another thrilling chase for tickets, pretending to be happy while my heart was breaking.

Earlier in the year, 96 Liverpool supporters had their lives cruelly taken from them at Hillsborough. Football had seemed irrelevant after that. It was. Like many, in the immediate aftermath, I went to Anfield. It was the obvious place to be.

The pitch is covered all the way to the halfway line. The Kop adorned with scarves and flowers.

My friend and I make our way to the terrace and climb on to the steps. Our eyes are filled with tears and we are choked as we read poetry written on pieces of paper and fixed to the crash barriers. On some of those steel posts, the names of victims have been scratched into the paint.

It's hard to describe the pain, to do justice to the hurt and the anguish. We were literally on our knees, in need of help and support. We knew we could rely on each other; we didn't expect the attacks that would come. But come they did.

Many people did heroic, selfless things in the wake of the disaster. The supporters themselves fought to save their mates and offered comfort and support to each other in the days and weeks that followed.

The players and the manager went to funerals. They visited survivors in hospital and doubled as grief counsellors along with their wives and girlfriends. Everton supporters rallied in solidarity, as did their club.

Most of all though, while all around us the lies and vitriol flew, when the risk of self-doubt was high and our community could have easily fractured, we had a leader. A man who understood us and our city. Someone who knew that his job now was to rise above football and hold together a shattered city.

Years later, while reading his autobiography, *My Liverpool Home*, I would be moved to tears by these words: 'I knew too, that I had to stand up and take a more public role and speak to the press, something I was uncomfortable with. I acted spontaneously, honestly and straightforwardly, dropping my guard and talking as a parent, not as a manager under scrutiny for his tactics. The reason for the way I responded was because the people of Liverpool were, and always will be, part of my family.'

Kenny was there when Kelvin Mackenzie asked him to assuage the city's anger at the infamous and diabolical front page he personally had ordered.

Dalglish told him he would have to print another one saying the evil rag had lied, otherwise there was nothing Kenny could do to help.

When inmates at Walton prison became unsettled by Mackenzie's headline, the governor of the jail called Kenny for help. Dalglish went in there and spoke to them, calming them down and assuring them he was there for the city and all its people.

This was a man in transition from footballer and manager, to leader of a community, and he was doing it all at great personal cost to himself.

By the time the club found it within themselves to play football again, the game had lost some of its appeal to me.

We reached another final though, so I watch it on TV. The windows of our house are plastered in newspaper posters and pictures of the players. My mum has made sure we showed our support for the lads, in the same way we had for every final in the past.

Outside, in the street, you can tell family allegiances by the colour of the decorations in their windows. Some even have red windows on the ground floor and blue ones above.

As the action unfolds, I start to feel it again. That desire to win is finding its way back. I want Liverpool to triumph, for the 96, for the survivors and for all of us.

It's a titanic struggle and Everton do themselves proud, as they fight for every inch, twice equalising. We never expected or wanted them to lay down and they didn't. Liverpool edge it 3-2.

In the end though, it's the sight of Kenny that fills my heart to bursting. His thick padded jacket and that beaming smile. Football was back. We had the fight of our lives on our hands. It would take decades to win, but we could do it. We were on the march with Kenny's army.

Two years later, in 1991, the Reds are battling it out on a number of fronts. None of us realised the inner turmoil our manager was enduring.

A gruelling 4-4 draw with Everton at Goodison Park is seemingly the catalyst for his shock resignation. In truth, Kenny had been carrying the scars of much earlier battles for too long.

I am walking from work to the bus stop with some mates. The news had reached us earlier via a supervisor who had taken a call from her friend. She had announced to a shocked office that 'Dalglish has resigned', and we were still reeling.

It's hard to believe now, but some have already begun to question Kenny's tactics, team selections and signings.

In particular, the arrival of David Speedie raised eyebrows. Still the shock and upset at the thought of a Liverpool without Dalglish is palpable.

In many ways, the club took a long time to recover from the loss of Dalglish. That is testament to how he, through force of will, talent and personality, had held it together in the aftermath of Hillsborough.

Many, including Alan Hansen, felt that the team that entered the 1990s was the most limited they had played in, but Kenny still led it to a title and on the day that he resigned, that same team was in the midst of another championship fight.

Things were very different after that though, and Liverpool would struggle to replace him.

Now I'm in 2012. I am at Wembley with my son, who wasn't even born in 1991. Liverpool are in the League Cup final and once again Kenny is our manager. He is there once more, to answer a cry for help from the club.

We've been through a torrid few years and even flirted with administration. All around the club there had been frowns. In the stands, in the dressing room and the boardroom.

The Anfield hierarchy would finally realise that the man in the dugout, Roy Hodgson, wasn't fit to be there and they had brought back a King to rescue us from mediocrity.

Suddenly we were all smiling again. There was someone at the top who understood us, who knew what the club was all about and would fight our corner. It was an inspired move.

Within months Kenny had taken us to a cup final. He would get us to another before the season was out too.

It was a risk for him, but the much bigger risk in his mind was not being there, not helping and seeing his people suffer yet more heartache. So, he took the risk because we have always been part of his family.

He gave my son his first and second cup finals. He also gave him a glorious day at Wembley to witness the Reds beat Everton in a semi-final.

Thanks to Kenny, the man whose image adorned my bedroom wall as a kid, my own child would see a fraction of the glory my eyes had witnessed.

Throughout my years of supporting this club, Kenny has been there. In glory and in failure. At our highest points and in our lowest, often dragging us up off the floor and leading us once more to new heights.

I can't heap enough praise on the man.

In the history of this club, he is a Tom Watson, an Elisha Scott or a Billy Liddell. Kenny transcends the club and the game and embodies the spirit of an entire city; two cities actually.

His contribution over such a long period of time has shaped and defined the history of Liverpool Football Club, just as the great Bill Shankly and the superb Bob Paisley did before him.

So now, we arrive finally in 2018. The establishment have finally seen fit to recognise what we have known since the moment he first kicked a ball in a red shirt.

They have knighted a man who we declared was our King many years ago.

It is right and proper that a nation should honour its most exceptional citizens. Kenny Dalglish is certainly that. There can be few, if any, more deserving of this country's highest accolade.

Whatever my feelings about the system that has belatedly bestowed this award on my hero, I am pleased for him and his family. Kenny Dalglish deserves all the recognition he gets.

So, I'm happy for the English to call him Sir. So they should.

In Liverpool though, we call him King.

LIVERPOOL FC
FROM 2018–2019

Who wants to be kings of England, when you can rule over an entire continent?

Another pivotal summer as Klopp solves Liverpool's glaring problem and Reds say farewell to Coutinho

Liverpool supporters marched into the summer 2018 transfer window with hope in their hearts and a smile on their faces. It may have puzzled rival supporters, disappointed not to see us weighed down with despair, but the Red half of Merseyside was buoyant. We'd enjoyed a memorable season, watched our team march across Europe and, thanks to a fourth-place finish back in August, we were about to do it all again.

As ever the window would be dominated by at least one transfer saga. That was of course Philippe Coutinho's move to Barcelona. Despite the club's efforts to keep him, the want-away Brazilian was adamant that he would swap Anfield for the Camp Nou. Apparently, he wanted to win the Champions League, but just like Michael Owen before him he would find the grass in Spain was no better than in Liverpool.

In truth, the moment the first murmurings of discontent surfaced, Klopp had started to plan for life without the player. For the club and its owners, it was a point of principle. After selling one star player in Luis Suárez, they were not going to give in without a fight. That would lead to an eye-watering £142m fee and restrictions on the Catalan giants' ability to plunder Liverpool resources in the future. So onerous was the deal from Barcelona's point of view, that some Liverpool supporters were calling for a statue to be erected in honour of the club's sporting director, Michael Edwards.

Liverpool didn't waste time reinforcing, bringing in Brazilian Fabinho from AS Monaco. The reported fee was anywhere between £39m and £43.7m and although he would take some time to settle – one tough encounter against Arsenal would have some questioning his ability – he would become one of many players whose contributions brought glory back to Anfield at the end of the season.

Another was of course Alisson Becker. Liverpool briefly set the record for a fee paid for a goalkeeper, shelling out £65m for him on 19 July. That would be usurped less than a month later when Chelsea paid £71.6m for Athletic Bilbao's Kepa.

Alisson may have conceded five goals in front of the Kop while wearing Roma colours, but Liverpool supporters had no doubts about his quality. He had also caught the eye of Jürgen Klopp.

The goalkeeping position was the club's obvious weak point. While nobody could question Simon Mignolet's attitude, he had failed to give the necessary leadership and confidence to his back four.

Sadly, for poor Loris Karius, far from instilling belief, he had actually struck terror into Liverpool's defensive line on occasion.

So, with the arrival of Naby Keita for £52.75m – this deal had been sealed in the previous summer – Klopp looked to have addressed all but one of his team's weaknesses. He'd shored up a defence that had proved too leaky during his time and added some flare and bite to the middle of the park.

However, he hadn't replaced the creativity of Coutinho, or so we thought.

The Reds would try to do that with the capture of Nabil Fekir from Lyon. In a saga that will go down in legend, the clubs appeared to have agreed a fee, the player agreed terms and even went as far as making an official video talking about his joy at coming to Liverpool, only for the deal to collapse at the last moment.

Stories about his medical surfaced and his troublesome knee was used to explain why Liverpool seemed to have snatched defeat from the jaws of victory. Some supporters had celebrated his capture prematurely only to find themselves in despair. It all seemed familiar and for many it left the sour taste of failure. Just when we thought the club had turned it around in the transfer market, this happens, was a familiar refrain.

We should have all just shut up and trusted the club. Liverpool is now a far cry from the days of Rick Parry, a CEO branded 'Coco the Clown' by many supporters. Parry had almost managed to lose the club's most prized asset in the aftermath of the 2005 Champions League Final victory, only for Steven Gerrard to have a change of heart. Parry's perceived dithering over a contract extension had almost convinced the player that his future lay elsewhere.

The Liverpool hierarchy of 2018 was a much savvier operation than the one that ordered the club shops to close the day after they became the biggest merchandising draw in the world. Liverpool moved on after the collapse of the

Fekir transfer and simply made do with a former Champions League winner, Xherdan Shakiri. The Yugoslavia-born Swiss International had won Europe's highest honour at Bayern Munich and was plying his trade at relegated Stoke City in 2018. The fee of £13.5m seemed prudent, and after one heady December day at Anfield against Manchester United it would feel like the deal of the century.

With the pieces of Klopp's jigsaw coming together nicely, Liverpool fans would be in for one of the most memorable seasons in the club's history. It would involve a much more pragmatic Liverpool than the one they had come to love. One possessed of a dogged determination, persistence and character. It would have flair from its full-backs, just like in the days of old, would go agonisingly close to ending that 30-year wait for the league title, but it would scale the highest echelons of European football and return with the greatest of treasures. Just like Klopp promised.

A trio of debuts as the Reds smash the Hammers and rack up 500 Premier League wins

The 2018/19 season began on 12 August 2018 with an overwhelming sense of optimism. The pain of Kiev had long since evaporated and only the residue of expectancy remained. This was a world away from the way we felt after defeat to Seville in Basel, back in 2017. The loss of a potential sixth European Cup may be greater than a fourth Europa League trophy, but the feeling was utterly different.

Sure, it hurt. The manner of the defeat was hard to take, and an error-strewn performance by Loris Karius in the Reds' goal ended his Liverpool career. Seemingly legitimate claims that he was concussed after a clash with Sergio Ramos cut no ice, and Klopp would make a huge decision in the summer.

The capture of Alisson Becker, for a world record £65m, gave everyone faith that the boss had acted quickly and decisively to solve a glaring gap in the squad. In addition, the capture of Fabinho, Naby Keita and Xherdan Shaqiri for a combined £110m was a real statement of ambition.

Liverpool had cruised through pre-season and the optimism was palpable. So much so that the loss of Coutinho barely caused a ripple of concern, particularly as the Reds had managed to hold on to the devastating trio of Mané, Salah and Firmino.

Klopp's attempts to frame Liverpool as plucky underdogs, saying they were more akin to 'Rocky Balboa not Ivan Drago', caused a few laughs and as I clutched my match programme, a determined-looking Salah staring back at me from the cover, I wanted to remind everyone that Rocky smashed Drago by the end of the film.

Over 53,000 people would hear George Sephton, the match DJ who is always tuned into the subplot to any match, play 'Eye of the Tiger' before kick-off. It caused a few puzzled expressions but those who'd heard Jürgen's comments allowed themselves a wry smile.

Liverpool clearly had a superior squad and although West Ham now had a Premier League-winning manager in

Manuel Pellegrini, the team he brought to Anfield was no match for the Reds. As the game got underway the noise was immense, a point picked up by James Pearce in the *Liverpool Echo*: 'Roared on by an expectant crowd, Liverpool flew out of the traps and dominated from the start. The midfield was a mismatch with the Reds having far too much athleticism and guile for Mark Noble and Declan Rice to handle.'

Liverpool swept forward across the sun-soaked pitch and in the stands the crowd lapped it up as first Firmino and then Sadio Mané went close to opening the scoring. There was no sign of the more pragmatic approach that would become a hallmark of Liverpool's tactics during the remainder of the season and the Reds simply picked up where they had left off a season earlier.

The Hammers defence was creaking at the seams and in the 19th minute it collapsed. Naby Keita, who was putting in a man-of-the-match performance, picked up the ball and surged through the middle before laying it off to Andy Robertson.

The Scottish left-back was on the cusp of a career-defining season, and his low pass into the box was met by Salah who had surged into the box and slotted it away with consummate ease. Suddenly it was like the Champions League Final had never happened, and the Reds were off and running again.

Not to be outdone by his counterpart on the left, Trent Alexander-Arnold was rampaging down the right. This was sumptuous stuff. The young Scouser then had the Liverpool supporters on their feet as he crashed a 25-yard free kick off the bar. Then another mesmerising run by Keita set up Wijnaldum, who missed narrowly.

Liverpool were in cruise control and looked like they could score with every attack. Only the referee, Anthony Taylor, looked a threat for the Hammers. A series of strange decisions had the Kop in uproar and when he seemed to block Wijnaldum as he made his way forward, their ire almost erupted. In truth, these kinds of moments only galvanise the crowd and the resultant furore drives the players on.

It worked and the Reds kept pressing. Firmino set up Salah for another chance but his shot was saved. My only concern at this stage was that West Ham would make it to the interval only a goal down. Such a scoreline would have been scant reward for Liverpool's dominance.

My fears were unfounded though, as just on the stroke of half-time Sadio Mané smashed home a James Milner cross. Mané was wearing the number ten shirt after the departure of Phillipe Coutinho. His influence in this game and the rest of the season would eclipse that of the Brazilian.

The Senegalese striker would seal victory just eight minutes after the restart. He may have looked offside when he picked up a pass from Firmino and put it past Lukasz Fabianski, but the 3-0 scoreline was thoroughly deserved.

Firmino was then taken off with more than 20 minutes of the game remaining. He deservedly received thunderous applause. The decision by Klopp to give him an early bath was a testament to the Reds dominance and the quality Liverpool now had on the bench.

With the arrival of Henderson and then Shaqiri and Sturridge, the Reds hardly missed a step. Sturridge's addition had an instant impact as he ran off the bench and scored with his first touch. It was a fitting end to a game Liverpool had thoroughly dominated.

Talk in the media spoke of statements being made and warnings delivered to rivals. What could not be played down was the sheer ease with which Liverpool had dismissed the opposition. They would strangely go on to make hard work of many games as the season unfolded, but as we left Anfield on a sunny August afternoon, we were in no doubt that the Reds had got off to a perfect start.

In a season that would see records tumble faster than Theresa May's Brexit red lines, this was Anfield's biggest opening day win since 1932.

Pellegrini may have thought the margin of victory flattered the Reds, but he was on his own. Andy Hunter, writing in *The Guardian*, disagreed: 'West Ham United were swatted aside as Liverpool recorded their biggest opening day win at Anfield for 86 years. With four goals on the board, and Mohamed Salah and Sadio Mané on the scoresheet, Klopp's team slipped back into the old routine seamlessly.'

Klopp was typically cautious, cautioning supporters who may have been forgiven for getting a little carried away. 'We know about our expectations and we know there is a really positive atmosphere around us. That is good,' he said, before adding, 'but this season will be unbelievably hard. We didn't win anything since I was in so we have to invest more, we have to fight more and then we will see where it leads.'

He was right. This was going to be an arduous season. It would test the resolve of manager, players and supporters alike. However, nothing that is worth fighting for is ever won without a little pain along the way.

Red redemption at Wembley as Liverpool beat Spurs

Liverpool's opening four games of the 2018/19 season saw them climb into top spot with four victories. They'd followed up the opening-day hammering of West Ham with a series of slightly less impressive wins over Crystal Palace, Brighton and Leicester City.

In the latter game, Alisson had come under severe scrutiny after he messed up an attempted Cruyff-turn on his byline allowing himself to be dispossessed. What followed was a desperate scramble across the face of the goal, which ultimately failed to prevent the Foxes from grabbing an undeserved entry on the scoresheet. With the score then 2-1 to Liverpool, the Reds faced an unnecessarily anxious final 27 minutes.

Naturally some began to question the fee paid for the Brazilian and one Jordon Pickford of Everton would foolishly join in. More of how his comments came back to haunt him later. All of this of course was less than ideal as the Reds prepared for the trip to Wembley to meet Spurs on 15 September.

Tottenham's move into their new stadium had suffered another delay and some of us felt they had manufactured the set back to avoid a thrashing at the hands of Liverpool marring their house-warming. That was a bit of a stretch, not least because none of us were that convinced that we could dish out a hiding away to Spurs anyway.

Of course, it was us who were on the receiving end of a rout the previous season. In front of a crowd of 80,000, Liverpool had suffered a 4-1 defeat that had sparked something of a revival. The Reds responded magnificently and went on 18-game unbeaten run.

Still, the ghosts of that humiliation lingered and the last thing we needed were doubts about our keeper. I caught up with former Reds defender Jamie Carragher in the week before the game, to do an interview for a feature on *This is Anfield*. Inevitably we got chatting about Alisson.

I'd heard several theories put forward to explain his apparent moment of madness. Some said Alisson was struggling with the pace of the Premier League or that he can't handle the ball played to him under pressure, while some conclude that he's just too cocky, maybe even arrogant.

As usual Carra is forthright in his opinion and absolutely clear that it's the latter. Her argues that we'd seen the warning signs in the game against Brighton. Does that mean that his team-mates or even Klopp will have pulled him to one side and read him the riot act then?

'Well to be honest, I think there's no point telling him after Leicester. I always think there's no point having a go at someone after they've made a mistake. Have a go at them before the mistake happens, when they're looking like they've got a mistake in them. Once he's done it, he knows what he's done. You see Klopp on the side saying, "Kick it!" He knows that. I hope Klopp is telling him when he does that at Brighton, before the mistake happens.'

Of course, Alisson is known as a ball-playing goalkeeper. Surely Klopp, all of us for that matter, knew what we were getting into?

Carragher continued, 'Actually, someone showed me something on Twitter. He does it all the time for Roma, the Cruyff turn all the time, and I saw that. But listen, he's brilliant on the ball, and I'm not advocating, you know if you're saying he's got to kick it all the time. But, even if you're a great player on the ball and you're getting put under pressure right by your goal, you don't do a Cruyff turn.

'I always say it's the risk to the reward. There's no point taking the risk. Now if he's not under pressure he gets it, he switches play, fine, brilliant. You don't need to take on a man. That's not just for a goalkeeper, that's for anyone.'

The worry for us was surely that opposition teams looking at the two games, against Brighton and Leicester, are going to look to put Alisson under pressure, fans are going to have a go. After the experience of seeing Karius go to pieces under the spotlight, surely this was the last thing we needed but Carra had no doubt about the player's overall quality.

'I think the brilliant thing about him is, number one, his reaction after it, in the game. Didn't look flustered. But, also his comments after the game. He said, "I'm not going to be arrogant enough to say I'm going to do it [again]." You get some cocky people who go, "Well that's just the way I play, deal with it." Besides that, he played really well at Leicester.'

It was true. The one thing I'd noticed after both errors was that the Brazilian had shown not a sliver of mental fragility. The same could not be said for me though, and when Sunday came around, so too did the pre-match tension.

Within a minute of the game starting the anxiety vanished. The Reds were out of the traps quickly and Firmino set up Mané to score an easy tap-in, but the linesman adjudged the Senegalese to be offside. It was frustrating but as a signal of intent it was very welcome.

Liverpool were on fire and they would eventually get their way in the 39th minute. With all the talk of the Reds' goalkeeping uncertainties we had overlooked the fact that Spurs were playing with stand-in keeper Michel Vorm.

The Dutch stopper would contribute to the Reds' opener, failing to clear properly from a Milner corner and putting Eric Dier in all sorts of difficulties. His attempted headed clearance only found Wijnaldum, who joyously looped his header beyond Vorm, whose desperate attempts to claw it out of the net were in vain.

It was 1-0 to Liverpool at half-time and in truth it could and should have been more. The same was true in the second half, and when Firmino tapped in the second after another error by Vorm, who had failed to handle a Mané shot effectively.

Spurs were not devoid of opportunities and Lucas Moura and Eriksen had the best of them before Erik Lamela induced unnecessary nerves among the away support with a 90th-minute consolation.

The score line flattered Spurs, whose error-strewn performance hadn't been punished nearly as much as it deserved to be. After the debacle in the corresponding fixture in 2017/18, any victory would have done. However, the confidence and swagger of the Reds' display had us all asking whether Liverpool could actually mount a serious challenge this time round.

The press certainly thought so. James Pearce, in the *Liverpool Echo*, wrote that Liverpool had proven their title credentials, pointing out, 'A fifth straight win extended the Reds' best start to a season since 1990 as they continue to set the pace in the Premier League. This triumph will serve to fuel the belief that they can stay there.'

That was five wins in five, and it was becoming increasingly difficult to suppress that growing sense of belief that maybe, just maybe, this might be our year at last.

Bobby's last-gasp winner against PSG sends Reds on the road to Madrid

Liverpool opened the 2018/19 season with an impressive five straight wins. They had scored 11 goals and conceded just two. It was now time to return to Champions League football and begin the long road to redemption, after their final heartache against Madrid in Kiev.

The Reds will always have an affinity with European football. Those games under the Anfield lights are the stuff of legend and they have helped to write the folklore and mythology of Liverpool Football Club. But this season, the competition was fighting alongside the Premier League for supporters' affections.

The wait for our first league title since 1990 had become a monkey on our backs, and this season we felt we had a genuine chance of winning it. We would go agonisingly close, but we would once again breathe the rarefied air at the summit of European competition. However, the climb to the top began with a momentous clash against Paris St Germain at Anfield, and a wonderful last-gasp winner from the boot of Bobby Firmino.

The Brazilian would cement his place in the hearts of Liverpool fans during the season. During the last, Jürgen Klopp had ordered a song for Bobby from the Kop. They dutifully obliged. It went:

There's something that the Kop wants you to know
The best in the world is Bobby Firmino
Our number nine
Give him the ball and he'll score every time
Si Señor
Give the ball to Bobby he will score

The atmosphere around the ground on 18 September was joyous. The sense of optimism was everywhere. The Paris team possessed a great threat, with the likes of Neymar, Mbappe, Cavani to name a few. However, Liverpool had Salah, Mané and of course Firmino. Though the latter would take his place on the bench, with Daniel Sturridge starting instead. Klopp was just keeping Bobby hungry.

It proved an inspired decision as Sturridge would score Liverpool's first from an Andy Robertson assist. The left-back's contribution to Liverpool's attack would become a feature of the season. Bobby hit their third and winning goal. When it comes to managerial decision-making, you can't really get much better than that.

Before kick-off, a huge banner in the Kop read 'ALLEZ LES ROUGES', a throwback to the halcyon days when St Etienne had come to Liverpool dreaming of glory only to leave with nothing more than hangovers and memories.

Buoyed by yet another incredible atmosphere, Liverpool raced into a two-goal lead. James Pearce, writing in the *Liverpool Echo*, described the cauldron-like nature of the game: 'The atmosphere was more akin to a high-stakes knockout tie than a group stage opener. Klopp's men fed off that energy from the stands during a frenetic opening spell. PSG couldn't handle the Reds' tempo and intensity.'

In a frenzied six-minute spell in the first half, Sturridge put the Reds in front and James Milner added a second from the spot, after Gini Wijnaldum was felled in the box. PSG were struggling to live with Liverpool.

Thomas Tuchel, in 2016, had been a victim of Anfield's penchant for serving up legacy-defining moments for

Liverpool managers. Then he had been representing Borussia Dortmund in the dugout. Little wonder he would simply shrug his shoulders at full time when asked to explain his side throwing away a valuable point, simply saying, 'This is Anfield. It's what they do.'

Even after his expensively assembled side had restored parity in the game, he must have been unable to relax. At Anfield, it's never over until that final whistle. PSG struck in the 40th minute through Thomas Meunier and then again when Kylian Mbappe netted an equaliser, with just seven minutes to go.

Liverpool looked furious and, in the Kop, we were 'spitting feathers'. The cheek of them, coming to our place and mounting the type of fightback we were famed for. If anything, the noise from the home crowd intensified at the insult Paris had just inflicted.

The Reds were far from done with this game. Daniel Sturridge had made way for Firmino in the 72nd minute and with time almost up, he produced a moment of pure magic to win the game for Liverpool.

From my vantage point in the Kop, it looked impossible for him to score. Yet somehow, he danced his way through the PSG defence, leaving his pursuers on their backside, before unleashing a shot which arrowed into the corner of the Anfield Road net.

It was almost the last kick of the game, and as he wheeled away in celebration the Parisian defence collapsed to the ground in defeat. Their supporters could barely believe what they had seen, though should have. Their manager knew only too well. This is Anfield after all. It's what we do.

The Guardian saw it like this: 'It was the second minute of stoppage time when the ball left Roberto Firmino's foot, when Jürgen Klopp set off on his victory run amid a crescendo of noise inside Anfield.

'And in that moment, even though these are only the early stages of the Champions League, perhaps we learned some more about last season's beaten finalists.'

Kiev was now in the past. The Reds were on the road to Madrid.

Origi breaks Everton hearts and ignites the Kop in laughter

Supporters of Everton Football Club have long cast envious eyes across Stanley Park. Once the most successful team on Merseyside, they are now perpetually looking up to their neighbours. There hasn't been parity between the great rivals since the days of the 1980s, when Howard Kendall's Blues regularly competed for English football's top honours.

In 2019, Everton fans would spend an anxious nine months worrying about Liverpool winning the league and praying that they could at least throw a spanner in the Klopp machine. They would do so, later in the season, at Goodison Park, but at Anfield they would fail in comical circumstances.

The Blues seemed confident going into the game. They often are, and my phone is regularly full of hostages to fortune in the form of text messages and memes in the run-up to a derby match. They arrive in large numbers as they always do, pockets bulging with blue smoke bombs that looked more purple in the winter sunshine.

Their plan would be to let off their pyro in the event of a victory or even a draw, which these days amounts to the same thing in Everton eyes. After the game Liverpool fans joked that they let off purple flares, because that's what Everton fans wore the last time they won at Anfield.

In truth, this was not a great game. Neither side set the world on fire with their performance. However, they did at least give Liverpool a game. It was arguably the closest they had come to pulling off a result against the Reds in almost two decades.

Not close enough though.

Liverpool went through the motions on the pitch and, in the stands, supporters did the same. The Kop sarcastically wished their neighbours merry Christmas by reminding them of an earlier defeat at the hands of Sadio Mané.

Mané scoring
All around us
Kopites singing, having fun
It's the season of love and understanding
Merry Christmas Everton

And of course, it wouldn't be a derby if we didn't remind the Blues that they haven't won a trophy since 1995. For their part, Everton fans sang about Steven Gerrard.

It was all typical stuff and as the game headed to the finish line the Blues could sense a famous draw was on the cards. If they could take points off Liverpool and potentially derail their title challenge, they could sleep easier and dispense with the nervous glances at the league table.

Then the fourth official lifted his board and indicated five minutes of stoppage time. A frustrated Kop roared into life. Was there time for a late winner? We had no idea. Some Everton fans may have dreamed the same, but most will have been content to take a point. The huge plumes of purple smoke that filled the Anfield Road end as the game entered the sixth minute of injury time was ample evidence of that.

Then it happened. It made no sense. It was a moment of pure comedic brilliance and it had Kopites unsure whether to laugh or scream for joy. In the end we did both.

The game was all but over when the ball fell at the feet of Virgil van Dijk. Supporters groaned in frustration as his looping shot seemed destined for row Z. Then incredibly it dropped out of the air and seemed to be dipping over Jordan Pickford in the Everton goal.

The keeper made a hash of an attempted save, and replays suggested the ball would have bounced out had he not attempted to reach it. Instead of catching it or knocking it out for a corner, he only managed to roll it along the crossbar.

The moment seemed to last an eternity, as it bounced once then twice off the woodwork, before the waiting Divock Origi pounced and headed it into the net. There was a moment's silence, as all of us waited for the linesman to flag. He didn't. The goal stood.

Anfield exploded and scenes of mayhem were all around. In the away end, there was a collective wail and the great gnashing of teeth. Their rage at the goalkeeper's ineptitude was quickly redirected towards the Liverpool manager.

Pickford tried to blame everybody but himself. He would come to rue his earlier comments about how he would never make mistakes, like Alisson had against Leicester earlier in the season, and we'd never let him forget it.

In a moment that was quintessentially Jürgen, the boss lost his head. Then, he was on the pitch and running towards the Everton end and into the arms of Alisson. The pair danced, then seemingly realising his faux pas, Klopp ran back into the dugout.

Judging by my text messages, Everton supporters regarded Klopp's infraction as a capital offence. To Reds, we had come to expect no less. We have a manager who wants victory every bit as much as we do, and we love it.

The *Liverpool Echo*'s James Pearce captured the wonderfully farcical nature of Liverpool's winner better than most, 'Anfield folklore has a new chapter after the most dramatic of finales to the 232nd Merseyside derby. Liverpool have inflicted plenty of body blows to Everton over the years but few quite as devastating as this one. There just isn't a better way to beat the Blues. The defining moment in the sixth minute of stoppage time was glorious and farcical in equal measure.'

The game would inspire another tune, which will be used for years to come, to mock the Blue half of the city. The game is now part of derby folklore. Poor Jordan Pickford. The song goes like this:

He couldn't reach the crossbar
He couldn't reach the crossbar
He couldn't reach the crossbar
He's only got little arms.

I love the Merseyside derby.

That's amore: Liverpool hold off Napoli to enter the knockout phase of the Champions League

The early optimism of the opening game of the group stage had quickly turned to frustration. By the time Liverpool faced their last game against Napoli, they were facing a must-win game. The mathematicians had quickly calculated that the Reds needed to win 1-0 or, if the Italians scored, by two clear goals. That would set up a heart-stopping finale and scenes of celebration at full time.

The game took place on 11 December. Liverpool were in the midst of a purple patch domestically. They sat at the top of the table and were unbeaten in the league. However, their Champions League form had been dire, especially on the road.

They'd lost away to Napoli, succumbing to a last-gasp goal after a tepid and tortuous display. They would then lose away to Red Star Belgrade and PSG. Only fortress Anfield had kept them in the race for the knockout stages, with wins over Paris and Red Star on home soil. In the process, they had managed 15 shutouts in 19 games at home. They would need her mesmeric powers one more time.

With everyone connected to the club knowing exactly what was at stake, Liverpool supporters would ensure that the team went into battle knowing they had an army of reserves in the stands. The welcome for the team bus would become one of the most iconic moments of the season and was every bit as passionate as the ones that greeted City and Roma the season before, minus the odd bottle of Kopparberg.

The heat of the reception was the perfect contrast to the chill in the December air. Winter was in full bloom and Liverpool and Napoli fans were bundled in thick coats and scarves as they made their way into the ground.

The game will be forever remembered for two decisive moments of brilliance. The first was a Mohamed Salah goal in the 34th minute. It would be the only goal of the game, thanks to the second. That was a save of an almost impossible nature by Alisson Becker.

Describing the goal, Daniel Taylor, writing in *The Guardian*, marvelled at the guile on display from the Egyptian: 'Suddenly, Salah was picking up pace, gliding away from the next opponent, Kalidou Koulibaly, into a position where he could take aim. As he continued this diagonal run, it was his sideways look that fooled David Ospina into thinking a cross was coming, rather than a shot. The scam was brilliant and as the former Arsenal goalkeeper moved off his line the ball was directed through the gap in his legs. It was the eighth time this season Salah had opened the scoring for his team.'

We celebrated like crazy when the ball hit the net, but all of us believed that if we were going to progress in the competition, we would need another couple of goals. We were wrong. All we needed was Alisson.

Two minutes into stoppage time, Arkadiusz Milik found himself in the six-yard box with the ball at his feet. Anfield held its breath and I closed my eyes. I didn't want to see the net bulge or the scenes of wild celebration in the Napoli end.

If I'd have kept them open, I would have witnessed one of the greatest saves ever made by a Liverpool keeper. We celebrated it as much as any goal. This may have been one of many down payments made by the Brazilian stopper as he looked to repay his sky-high fee, but it was one of the most crucial.

Jason Burt in *The Telegraph* agreed: 'The only summer signing in the starting line-up was Alisson. But what a difference he makes. The Brazilian is a world-class goalkeeper and that one save alone underlined his importance.'

Klopp would laugh off talk of his keeper's fee, saying with a huge grin, 'I have no idea how he makes a save like this. If I knew Alisson was this good, I would have paid double for him.'

Ian Ladyman, in the *Daily Mail*, pointed out that future generations of Reds will now be able to add a goalkeeper to their list of heroic players: 'The great European nights of

Anfield folklore have usually had a goalscorer's name written in lights next to them. David Fairclough against St Etienne in 1977. Steven Gerrard against Olympiakos in 2004 and Luis Garcia against Chelsea four months later. And there are others. Now, after another breathtaking night of Champions League football on Merseyside, there is a goalkeeper to talk about too. If Liverpool's last Champions League campaign ended in goalkeeping calamity for Loris Karius in Kiev, this one was given the kiss of life by his replacement.'

Liverpool were now through the group stage, finishing in second place to Paris St Germain. They had struggled and at times were unimpressive. All of that was about to change though. When it comes to the knockout stages, two-legged ties, and do-or-die nights at Anfield, nobody does it better than the Reds.

Liverpool 3-1 United: Shaq attack steals the show and Mourinho exits stage door left

Sunday, 16 of December 2018 was the day Liverpool inflicted a defeat so comprehensive and so damaging to Manchester United that the bookies would mark them as a miserable 100/1 to win the league.

It had been decades since the Reds of Anfield had been so far ahead of those from Old Trafford. Such was Liverpool's dominance – Andrew Robertson and Trent Alexander-Arnold would have Mourinho dizzy in the dugout – the ladies and gentlemen of the press went to town on the United manager. The board of Manchester United were in despair, their supporters were in revolt and Jose was sacked in short order.

'We couldn't cope, Mourinho's stark admission after United crash at Anfield' screamed a headline in *The Guardian*. *The Express* dubbed Liverpool's performance 'Shaq and Awe', a reference to the devastating impact of substitute Xherdan Shaquiri who had plundered two of Liverpool's three goals. The *Mirror* would accuse Jose of 'RUNNING SCARED' as the Portuguese manager would attempt to blame everyone but himself for United's inability to live with the Reds.

This was perhaps the most confident I had felt going into a game against Manchester United. I kept having to tell myself to get a grip, in case I jinxed it by getting ahead of myself. I could be forgiven for my optimism though. The league table held ample evidence of a gulf in terms of points, with Liverpool at the summit and United languishing in mid-table, 19 points behind the men from Anfield. The field of play would show there was also a gulf in class.

The win didn't come without a scare though. The Reds, who took the lead in the 24th minute thanks to a finish by Sadio Mané, saw their advantage cancelled out in the 33rd minute by Jesse Lingard and, it has to be said, a rare blunder by Alisson Becker. Lingard's celebration in front of the Kop was as premature as it was foolhardy.

Had United escaped Anfield with a point it would have been a travesty. In fact, so was the 1-1 half-time scoreline. Liverpool were streets ahead of their rivals. Fortunately, that wouldn't happen, thanks to a genius substitution by Klopp in the 70th minute, and a wonderful cameo from Xherdan Shaqiri.

Jason Burt, writing in *The Telegraph* gave a glorious description of United's ineptitude and Liverpool's brilliance: 'Mourinho later marvelled at Liverpool's "200 miles per hour" approach and also made some usual barbed comments, suggesting that United had not recruited as smartly as their opponents and, well, what can he do after inheriting a bunch of injury-prone crocks? But this really does not wash. His team, meanwhile, were rinsed. "They are a better team than us," Mourinho concluded. He is not wrong. If Liverpool were 200 miles per hour, then all Mourinho appeared to want to do was slow it down. Instead, United stalled. Outrun, outplayed, outfought, out-thought. United brought on Marouane Fellaini – whose most noticeable contribution was to shoot so waywardly he took out a steward on the other side of the pitch – instead of Paul Pogba who stayed on the substitutes bench, while Liverpool turned to Shaqiri.'

It would take the Swiss international just three minutes to put United to the sword and cause Anfield to explode. So much for Mourinho's much-vaunted defensive solidity. This was to be his first defeat at Anfield since 2007 and his expression bore all the hallmarks of the busted flush he was.

Liverpool were still unbeaten and enjoying their best start to a domestic season in the club's entire top-flight history. United were a team in terminal decline.

His goal had taken a massive deflection, but we didn't care and neither did he. Shaqiri raced towards the Kop, which was a mess of dancing and cheering supporters, mouths wide open and eyes bulging. The noise was deafening and the outpouring of joy and relief incredible.

I almost fell over the seats in front of me, locked in an embrace with another supporter and laughing and cheering as we struggled to stay upright. Eight minutes later Shaqiri was at it again, cannoning a shot off a United defender and wrong-footing de Gea, in the United goal. Cue pandemonium and delirium. More falling more screaming.

The substitute had ruined United and cost their manager his job. There were nine minutes left, not time for the team from the other end of the East Lancashire Road to mount a comeback though. If we'd have played for another week, they wouldn't have scored.

Shaqiri cost just £13m from relegated Stoke City. In that eight-minute spell against our bitterest of rivals, he more than repaid that. The Kop simply played out the game by taunting the United supporters and board. 'Don't sack Mourinho' they sang ironically, before reminding the enemy that 'Liverpool, Liverpool we're top of the league.'

James Pearce's match report summed up the significance of the win: 'The scoreline massively flattered Manchester United. But for the heroics of David de Gea and the wobble the Reds endured after Alisson Becker's howler enabled Jesse Lingard to cancel out Sadio Mané's opener, this would have been an absolute annihilation.

The gulf in class was immense as Jürgen Klopp savoured securing the league scalp of United for the first time. These are two clubs heading in very different directions. The contrast could hardly be greater.'

United would turn to Ole Gunnar Solskjaer to dig them out of their hole. Decent results against poor opposition sides aside, the former United hero would make little progress. Liverpool, though, were on the road to much bigger and better things.

Liverpool's supporters show the world that 'hunger and fear don't wear club colours'

In December 2018, Klopp's Liverpool were busy setting new benchmarks in the club's glorious history. Records were broken with ruthless regularity and the team found their form in spectacular fashion. They played eight games in a month usually known for separating the wheat from the chaff in the title race, and they won all of them.

Liverpool had scored 23 goals and conceded just three. That meant they would enter the New Year facing a titanic battle with champions Manchester City as the only unbeaten team in the league, and six points clear at the top of the table. City manager Pep Guardiola, indulging in some pointless mind games and presumably attempting to cast his own expensively assembled team as underdogs, had hailed the Reds as 'the best team in Europe, maybe the world'.

There may have been a kernel of truth in his attempt at psychological warfare. Judging by the angst being unleashed on social media at the mere prospect of the men from Anfield ending their long wait for a 19th league title, Guardiola's wasn't the only mind in which the Reds were living rent-free.

Football on Merseyside serves many purposes for its people. It is a great unifier, an expression of civic pride and all too often an escape from the daily misery of life. The winter of 2018 was a grim time for many people in Britain and the city of Liverpool was no exception.

The roll-out of a controversial benefit system, known as Universal Credit, meant that thousands of families on Merseyside faced a terrible Christmas. Hunger and homelessness stalked the streets in what resembled a Dickensian dystopia being played out in the sixth-richest nation on earth.

The country felt deeply divided on issues of Europe and immigration with Brexit dominating the nightly news and newspaper front pages. Against this backdrop Merseyside felt like an oasis of unity and humanity.

Supporters of both the Reds and the Blues rallied to help alleviate the suffering of their fellow citizens. Under the banner of 'Hunger Doesn't Wear Club Colours' they collected food donations at every football match, organised a conference on mental health and held out the hand of friendship and solidarity to asylum seekers, who had risked life and limb to reach safety in Britain. Away fans also took food parcels to grounds across the country, dropping them off at food banks when they arrived.

On 28 November, Liverpool had made their way to France to face the nouveaux riche upstarts Paris St Germain. The trip had proven another thrilling away day for supporters, at least off the field, but had ended in disappointment on it. The Reds slumped to a 2-1 defeat and the performance was a pale imitation of their Premier League form.

However, Liverpool fans have always understood there is often as much treasure to be found on their travels, as there is in the destination. The trip to and from France for this fixture was filled with enough tales to fill an entire volume, let alone a chapter. But, perhaps the greatest of them involved a coachload of big-hearted Reds and a couple of daring stowaways.

Peter Jones, a 24-year-old from the Wavertree area of the city, was on that coach trip home. Peter writes for the official matchday programme and had travelled to France with friends for the game against PSG. He described how, exhausted and yearning for sleep, he and others began their weary journey back home after the disappointing defeat.

However, his attempts to get some shut-eye had been disturbed by a strange knocking sound coming from under the bus. It grew louder and then he could hear someone shouting 'hello'.

At first there had been laughter among the travelling Reds, but soon the realisation dawned that something serious might be happening. Peter made his way to the front of the bus to convince a sceptical driver that he needed to stop the coach.

Eventually the bus pulled over on the motorway. Peter explains what happened next: 'As soon as we stopped this fella got out from the hold. He looked like he'd gone through an ordeal as his coat was all ripped apart with the inside all hanging out.

'Everyone had their phones in hand, trying to capture the moment. We all cheered and celebrated. The lad didn't run or anything, just looked made up to have made it, stretched his arms out and was very calm.

'We walked him on to the coach and the cheering continued. People moved aside and let him sit down. Crisps, drinks, sweets and sandwiches were all passed to him. It was amazing how calm and happy he was, we all expected him to run as fast as he could when he got out, but he was just so happy to be out of the cavity near the engine.'

The drama wasn't over though, and soon another stowaway would emerge from the luggage hold. What followed was an emotional reunion, with the Liverpool supporters cheering and applauding their unexpected guests.

Peter continued: 'The hold was lifted, and another young lad was hiding with our luggage. We were all cheering, and the first lad pushed past everyone and ran to his friend or brother. They embraced and started crying and I think everyone stopped and just realised that they must have gone through so much to get there.

'I think we realised how huge it was for the two of them. People started getting pictures of the lads and we had the group picture that made the front of the [*Liverpool*] *Echo*. We invited them back on to our coach, where the food and drink were flowing. They were with us for around ten minutes and then a police car came and took them.'

Peter was overwhelmed by the public reaction, and the way the story was picked up on social media. However, some didn't see things quite the same way.

'Some other British people questioned whether we would be happy if they were terrorists and if they did something bad while they're in the country. I can't fathom that reaction,' said Peter. Those two lads wanted to risk everything to get here and they deserve the rewards they get. The reaction of everyone on the coach didn't come from a debate or a show of hands, we all wanted to help as much as we could.'

Peter's words speak from an ethos on Merseyside that, while not unique in the UK, has become synonymous with the region. It speaks from a belief in welcoming others and offering solidarity to people less fortunate. It is not limited to supporters of the club either, with the players also showing their compassion over the festive period.

Club captain Jordan Henderson, along with Virgil van Dijk, Adam Lallana and Alex Oxlade-Chamberlain helped organise events at Anfield for underprivileged and disabled kids. In addition, local lad Trent Alexander-Arnold had joined with Andy Robertson in supporting food banks and other charities aimed at alleviating the effects of austerity.

Several journalists were moved to contrast the ethos at Anfield with poverty mocking-chants sung on the terraces of rival supporters. Henry Winter, writing for *The Times*, hailed the efforts of its fans and players off the field as well as on it. He called for all supporters to celebrate should Liverpool eventually secure the league title, citing the many altruistic and charitable acts carried out by players and supporters alike, before declaring, 'So ignore the tribal screams; Liverpool should be seen as a model club in many ways.'

This may seem fanciful. After all, many see following their team as a tribal act rather than act of communal expression. Others turned their ire on the behaviour of Liverpool's rival supporters, pointing out the self-defeating nature of working-class supporters turning on their own in times of need, by singing about poverty on Merseyside. Simon Hughes, writing in *The Independent*, bemoaned the culture of turning such suffering into a source of terrace banter, especially when those singing these songs suffer themselves. He said, 'Football supporters are betraying their backgrounds, shared histories and struggles, as well as the dedication of some who follow under the same sporting banner as themselves whenever they mock the poverty of other places.'

It's a sentiment shared by lifelong Liverpool supporter and local Labour councillor Ian Byrne. Along with Evertonian Dave Kelly, Ian has been instrumental in setting up Fans Supporting Foodbanks, a voluntary organisation which collects food donations at every home game on both sides of Stanley Park.

Ian told me, 'The singing of the song "feed the Scousers" fills me with great sadness. To me it's a betrayal of working-class solidarity between fans. These fans fail to see the real enemy waging war on our class. Our enemy is not the fan from Salford, Gallowgate or Wolverhampton, our enemy is the neo-liberal ideology which has caused austerity and the pricing out of huge swathes of the working class out of the game they love.

'Football activism should always be focused on challenging this ideology and its consequences. This is the ethos we have built fans supporting Food banks on and the working-class solidarity we have built off the pitch with many fellow supporters of clubs is one of our proudest achievements.

'On Merseyside our two great clubs have come together on many issues including Hillsborough, Rhys Jones and working together to challenge ticket prices among other things. This solidarity has led to FSF and is an example of fans working collaboratively to aid our communities, hence the hashtag hunger doesn't wear club colours.'

All clubs are afflicted by a minority of fans who let their sides down. Liverpool is no different. However, few could argue that the people of Merseyside are among the most politically aware and organised in the country. They remain true to the socialist principles of one of football's greatest managers, Bill Shankly, and remain fervent advocates of solidarity and collective effort to solve their problems.

This spirit is naturally reflected in the attitude of the city's football teams and their supporters. I suspect it always will be. It seems these great supporters have shown that singing 'feed the Scousers' is utterly redundant. No matter how tough times get, Scousers will always strive to ensure that nobody goes hungry, no matter where their allegiances lie or where they come from.

Sixties hero and wing wizard Peter Thompson passes away at the age of 76

On New Year's Eve 2018, with Jürgen Klopp's Reds topping the league table, the club and supporters alike were rocked by news of the passing of one of the original Shankly boys. Peter Thompson, a veteran of the league- and FA Cup-winning team of the 1960s, had passed away at the age of 76.

Thompson, born in Carlisle in 1942, rose to prominence as a highly sought-after winger plying his trade at Preston North End. In 1962 his team were pitted against Liverpool in the FA Cup and the pacy youngster caught the eye of Bill Shankly, after he had knocked the Reds out of the cup with the only goal of a tie that had gone to two replays.

The Liverpool manager quickly snapped up the 20-year-old, paying £37,000 for his services on 14 August 1963. However, the deal very nearly fell through at the last minute. Many years later, Peter gave an interview to lfchistory.net, in which he told the hilarious tale of how he was given a hero's reception on his arrival at Anfield, but almost messed the whole thing up.

Such was the buzz surrounding his capture that supporters had turned out in their droves to catch a glimpse of the new arrival. Thompson had been so taken aback that he asked the boss, 'What are they all here for?' Shanks looked at him, puzzled, and simply replied, 'You.'

It was a whirlwind experience and the player was immediately whisked away on a tour of Melwood, before finally finding himself in the chairman's office, where a pen was placed in his hand. This was a momentous moment in his football career. He was about to sign for a team that would go on to conquer all of Europe and become a household name all over the globe. It was the opportunity of a lifetime.

However, perhaps flushed with the hype surrounding his arrival on Merseyside, he almost threw it all away by asking for a signing-on fee. The manager's face darkened and, you can imagine, so too did the atmosphere in the room, as player and directors held their breath.

Shankly grimaced and his face turned puce. In his trademark gravelly tones, he bellowed, 'You what? I am giving you the chance to play in the greatest city in the greatest team that is going to be in the world and you want illegal money. Get out!'

Imagine the scene. These were the days before agents, when managers and their clubs held all the power. Having played his hand so badly, Thompson was staring at a painful journey back to Preston with his tail between his legs. What a terrible thing that would have been for him and Liverpool Football Club.

Fortunately for both men and for Liverpool, Thompson thought quickly and grabbed the pen from the great Scot's hand, immediately signing the contract before Shankly could give him his marching orders.

He would go on to play 416 times for the club, scoring 54 goals and winning two league titles, in 1964 and 1966, and Liverpool's first FA Cup in 1965. The latter achievement brought such joy to the Red half of Merseyside that many supporters of that generation rank it as the greatest in the club's history.

He would also be a runner-up in the European Cup Winners' Cup Final in 1966 and was on the bench for the 1971 FA Cup Final defeat to Arsenal. Peter also tasted disappointment at international level, having been cut from the initial 28-man England squad for the 1966 World Cup.

His reputation for beating his man on the wing and then going back several times to beat him again, would delight and frustrate in equal measure, and some complained that Thompson didn't score enough goals for a player of his ability. His manager, though, knew exactly what he brought to the team, saying, 'He could run forever, but more importantly in football he could run with the ball – probably the hardest thing to do. He could run every minute of every game, every week, every year better than anybody else.'

Ray Carrick, a Red for more than 50 years, recalls watching Thompson from the Boys' Pen, in the old standing Kop in the 1960s.

'Liverpool were an absolute joy to watch back then. For us kids, whenever Peter Thompson got the ball, magic followed,' he says.

'He was fast and clever. He could dribble through a crowd of opposing players effortlessly and in school, on a Monday morning, we all imitated Peter Thompson in the playground.'

Injury eventually ended his time at Liverpool with the boss forthright in letting him know that his days at Anfield were over. Shankly famously had no time for players who were injured and pointed out, 'Men who worked on the docks were paying good money to watch him play,' and pointing out that his injuries meant he was a 'cripple'. It seemed the boss wanted the player off the wage bill as soon as possible.

Nevertheless, Thompson was granted a testimonial by the club, and despite his previously brutal assessment of Peter's abilities at the ned of his Anfield career, Shankly was more than happy to eulogise about his former winger in the match programme: 'His work rate was outstanding, his fitness unequalled, his balance like a ballet dancer. I have no hesitation in placing Peter up among the all-time greats – alongside such players as Tom Finney, Stanley Matthews and George Best. They say he didn't score enough goals, they said his final pass wasn't telling enough. Well, if he had scored goals as well as everything else he did, he would have been in the same category as Jesus Christ!'

Whatever Shankly had said behind the scenes, it was no doubt motivated by the greater good of the club. He would have been in no doubt that in his prime, there were few who could match the prowess on the wing of Peter Thompson. He practically invented the role of the wing wizard so coveted by teams today.

Liverpool has lost a player who indeed belongs to a pantheon of great Reds heroes, men who worked tirelessly to build the footballing empire we adore today and footballers who made the people happy. May he rest in peace.

Wolves at the door as Jürgen bloods his cubs

The start of 2019 ushered in the third round of the FA Cup. The Reds' opponents were Wolverhampton Wanderers and many feared that with Liverpool having bigger fish to fry in a season of promise, the boss would field a team of sheep. In the end he put out a team more than capable of winning the tie, but that wouldn't stop the vultures from circling.

Klopp's men had just suffered their first defeat of the season to Manchester City, a 2-1 reverse at the Etihad. While Guardiola's men deserved the three points, Liverpool had been unlucky. They had hit the woodwork and thanks to goal line technology found themselves millimetres from a point. It was just one loss against a great team, but it was enough to create despondency in some quarters and give rivals hope that Liverpool could be starting to wobble.

Certainly, given their celebrations at full time, you'd think City had already won the league. This was the backdrop to the visit to the Midlands and a clash with Wolves.

The so-called 'magic of the cup' has long since faded from view. Where once there was crackle and fizz around the

FA Cup, now there is talk of fixture congestion and squad rotation. A trophy once regarded as the pinnacle of English, even world football, is now a sorry third on the honours wish list for a club like Liverpool.

It may not be a truth shared by all Liverpool supporters, particularly those who can remember the thunderstorm of emotion and revelry that accompanied the club's first cup final triumph in 1965, nor those who can recall the bitter price paid for that 1989 victory. Then there are those like me, who will always feel that winning trophies, whatever they are, is a good habit to have. There are many who bemoan the relegation of a once prestigious competition to also-ran status.

However, there exists an ever-growing generation of more pragmatic supporters. An army if you will, whose eyes have not seen the glory of a league title win, and who see the FA Cup as a distraction.

Others, those who got their football education in a different time, see winning trophies as a habit. More than that though, we see the FA Cup as something integral to our history. These feelings found expression in online debate and even poetry.

Lee Walker, a local author and survivor of Hillsborough, penned the following words on social media:

The FA Cup, La

The one that resonates across the path of our history.
From my much-missed dad crying tears of joy in 1965

To tears that poured like waterfalls
24 years later
Never mind all that it doesn't matter shite
It does

It fucking does
And don't let those who run modern footy tell you
any different
It matters for the 96

For those who, by the grace of God, got out
Physically safe
Though not in mind or spirit
Or soul. Nah, not in soul
The FA Cup – It matters

However, as Jürgen's Reds got set to face Wolves on 7 January 2019, it was approaching 29 years since the club had lifted a league championship and 14 since they lifted a European trophy. These are the treasures the modern-day supporter craves.

Broadcasters, try as they might, can't hide the fact that they bear some of the responsibility for the slow and depressing demise of a cup competition that has been wrapped up in the history of our game for more than a century. Yet some of them, Jermain Jenas and Alan Shearer in particular, seemed bemused that Klopp may select a team that entirely reflected the competition's ranking in his list of priorities.

Jenas moaned, on live television, that Liverpool looked lacklustre. He was seemingly oblivious to the fact that Jürgen had made nine changes to his first-choice XI, including adding three players who weren't even born at the turn of the century, and that he had lost his only recognised centre-back after five minutes.

The game kicked off on a freezing cold Monday evening in Wolverhampton. Thousands made the trip from Merseyside, boosting the attendance in a stadium peppered with empty seats. Wolves did their best to generate an atmosphere with a huge firework display prior to kick-off and the tannoy system blaring out the song 'Hi-Ho Silver Lining', which was dutifully lapped up by the home crowd.

For their part, the Reds decided to take the night off, at least in the first half. The performance was grim and there was little to cheer for those who had travelled to support their team despite their pockets having been emptied by December's festivities. Wolves had gone a goal up thanks to Raúl Jimiénez after 38 minutes.

He had pounced on an overhit pass by the usually dependable James Milner, who in the opening exchanges was not alone in simply going through the motions. Jiménez gleefully lapped up his opportunity and raced towards Simon Mignolet, who was deputising for Alisson Becker. His finish was unerring and the Reds were facing a half-time roasting at the hands of their manager.

There are many who claim Klopp didn't want to win this, but it's hard to argue that he wasn't furious watching his side go a goal down. As they returned to the field for the second half, several minutes earlier than their opponents, it was clear that they had a collective 'flea in their ears'.

Whatever the manager said, it seemed to have an immediate effect and it took Liverpool just six minutes to level the tie. They had finally found their mojo and an incisive pass into the box by Xherdan Shakiri found Milner with his back to goal. The veteran spun round and unleashed a shot that was blocked. Fortunately, it fell to forgotten striker and derby-day hero Divock Origi, who controlled it expertly and unleashed a sublime strike past the despairing John Ruddy in goal.

Game on!

Or so it seemed. Sadly, the Reds' joy was short-lived and just five minutes later Ruben Nevez unleashed a 30-yard strike that beat Mignolet at the left-hand post. Despite a thunderous free kick from Shakiri in the 69th minute, which crashed off the upright, Liverpool never recovered.

Whatever the 2018/19 season was to bring, it wouldn't deliver an FA Cup for Liverpool.

Klopp reflected on Liverpool's bad luck in losing Lovren so early, on the changes he had to make and, of course, the performance of his youngsters. It was, however, hard to hide the frustration. The sense that the magnificent bubble of December had just been popped was all around.

Perhaps, though, there is still a little magic to be found here, in the misery of a third-round defeat. This was a decent Wolves side who had troubled some of the finest outfits in the

Premier League, beating both City and Chelsea. Liverpool, despite their deficiencies and below-strength team, could easily have taken the tie to a replay had Shakiri's goalbound effort been millimetres to the left.

We may not be telling stories of another raucous trip to Wembley come May, but we might one day remember when Ki-Jana Hoever became the youngest Liverpool player to wear the shirt in the FA Cup, at just 16. Could we be reminiscing about how, after being thrust on to replace the injured Dejan Lovren, he showed an air of confidence that belied his youth? After all, he wasn't even a year old when the Reds' oldest player, James Milner, made his league debut. Was this the launch of another hero of the Kop's career? Who knows?

Maybe, in years to come, we'll talk fondly of a young Scouser called Curtis Jones who showed no fear and even outshone his elders, or of how 18-year-old Rafa Camacho demonstrated maturity beyond his years against much more experienced opponents.

We might.

But in the aftermath of this 2-1 defeat, the Reds' second in consecutive games, all the talk was, on one side, about opportunities missed, bottling it and disrespecting the cup.

On the other, it was about prioritising the league title and how the cup no longer mattered. It was a debate summed up by contrasting views aired by various ex-players and managers on social media and in newspaper columns.

Alan Shearer found himself in reverie about the days when Liverpool competed for every trophy, while Jamie Carragher talked about the boost to the Reds' title chances, now that they would have a few free weekends to rest. Roy Evans and John Aldridge felt it was a chance of silverware blown and some fans simply shrugged their collective shoulders and looked forward to seeing their heroes fresh for a title campaign that was shaping up to be one of the most exciting for years.

So, as 2019 cranked into gear, Liverpool found themselves out of both the League Cup and FA Cup. They were also looking forward to a huge glamour tie against Bayern Munich in the Champions League. But crucially they were sitting pretty at the top of the table; four points clear of their rivals Manchester City.

Were things really that bad?

Fear and loathing in L4: Reds frustrated by the ice, the referee and the Foxes

The first month of the year came to an end with a flurry of snow and ice. On Wednesday, 30 January supporters shivered and shook as they made their way to Anfield. The visitors were Leicester City, an age-old bogey team. Almost 24 hours earlier, the Reds had been gifted a golden opportunity by their closest rivals, Manchester City, and an old friend, Rafa Benitez.

The former Liverpool boss and hero of Istanbul had pulled off something of a miracle by leading his team to a

2-1 victory over City at St James' Park. The Geordies had gone behind after just 24 seconds and it had looked like another routine win for Pep Guardiola's men. Benitez had been reading a different script though, and just as he had done in Turkey he oversaw the unlikeliest of second-half comebacks to take all three points.

In the context of a relegation dogfight, it meant the world to the Toon army. To Liverpool fans, riding the wave of an unexpected title challenge, it was a gift from the gods. Liverpool could have been going into the game against the Foxes ahead by a single point; instead they sat comfortably on top of the table four points clear, and with an opportunity to stretch their lead to seven.

Hope soared on Merseyside. At least among the Red half; Blues were despondent but beginning to resign themselves to the 'unthinkable'. Yet, despite the open goal being presented to Liverpool and the fact that they had beaten every side outside the top six so far this season, the overwhelming sense among Kopites was one of anxiety.

The endless memes on social media thanking Rafa Benitez, and even a poster in the window of Anfield bakery, Homebaked, declaring 'Ta Rafa La', felt like the thinnest of veneers. It did little to hide an underlying feeling of nervousness.

The call went out to get to the game early and the usual crowd turned up on the corner of Anfield Road and 96 Avenue to welcome the team bus. The feeling was if we treated the game like a cup final or a European night, we could roar the boys to an easy victory. Klopp's pre-match press conference spoke of the need for the home crowd to give his team an edge. Sadly, it just didn't happen, on or off the pitch.

After the game the press thought they'd detected a nervousness about Liverpool, and it quickly became an editorial line with former Manchester United defender Rio Ferdinand seizing on his opportunity to introduce doubt into Liverpool's title bid. In truth they were right, to a point. It's just that the edginess was in the stands and not on the pitch.

In the Cabbage Hall pub, situated within earshot of the Kop, crowds assembled ahead of the game as they do every week. Roma and Fiorentina were playing out an irrelevant, from our point of view, match. Not even the extraordinary scoreline, which saw last season's Champions League semi-final opponents destroyed 6-1, could distract us from the issues at hand. Could Liverpool finally look a gift horse in the mouth and still take all three points?

The Reds have waited 29 long years for a league title. They've had too few genuine challenges, but those that have come our way, have seen the team fall agonisingly short. So accustomed are fans to disappointment that they often feel like they can hear the beat of its hooves from a mile away. Instead of excitement and anticipation, phrases like 'banana skin' and 'slip up' filled the air amid the clatter of glasses.

It was all so unnecessary. This was after all January. Liverpool still had another 15 of these 'must-win' encounters to negotiate, but such is the fragile nature of a Liverpool supporter's psyche when it comes to the league title, none of us could truly enjoy the moment. That nervousness would leave the pub with us, it would take the short trek to Anfield alongside us and it would sink its icy claws into every one of us as the game unfolded.

As kick-off approached, the crowd waited, watching through the glimmer of floodlights as a deluge of snow fell from the heavens. The pitch was looking more hellish by the second and in the stands we shivered. And it wasn't just the frost that chilled our blood and twisted our guts into knots. Memories of so many false dawns filled the minds of supporters eager for some sign, an omen that the wait for glory would soon be over.

Within two minutes of the start it seemed like we had one. The ever-dependable Andy Robinson fed Sadio Mané in the box and the Senegalese striker gave Kasper Schmeichel no chance at the Anfield Road end. It was just what we needed, the earliest of goals that would maybe tempt Leicester to break with their defensive game plan and force them into having a go at Liverpool.

Teams had by now come to realise that 'having a go' at Anfield usually led to an avalanche of goals and certain defeat. Even Guardiola had turned in a defensive masterclass during an earlier visit in the season. He had banked on his players taking advantage of even the rarest of opportunities. When his team were gifted a late, late penalty he must have thought his strategy had worked a treat. When Mahrez missed, he turned a disappointing home draw into something that felt like a victory to every Liverpool fan in the ground.

Would Leicester boss Claude Puel's men be stung into action, or would he bide his time like City's master tactician had? Puel is a good manager and the Foxes mid-table stupor was hard to explain, at least on the evidence of this game. Instead of going gung-ho, Leicester dug in and set about frustrating Liverpool.

Firmino, Salah and Mané all missed opportunities, before referee Martin Atkinson added to his many crimes and misdemeanours as far as the Liverpool faithful were concerned. Again, Mané and Robinson linked up superbly, with the rampaging Scot feeding the striker with a sublime through-ball. Sadio was on it in a flash, but covering defender Harry Maguire hauled him down. Mané had been racing in on goal and a second looked inevitable. However, instead of the expected red card, Maguire saw yellow.

Fury erupted in the stands as Atkinson's decision was greeted by a cacophony of howls and shouts of 'Manc bastard'. Sometimes incidents like this can act as a spur. They can stir the Anfield cauldron into a maelstrom of noise and power, and the resultant whirlwind can sweep opposition teams off their feet.

But this only tends to work in an Anfield that is pumped up with pride and self-belief, one that feels the hot breath of destiny on its neck. Think of nights under the floodlights against sides like St Etienne, Chelsea, City and Dortmund. European classics when L4 sneered at the seemingly impossible and roared the men in red to improbable victories. Sadly, on a cold and frosty night in the Premier League, the weight of history can be completely debilitating.

On nights like that, when Kopite minds are haunted by images of calamity and a sense of deep foreboding, the cathedral that is Anfield has the opposite effect. Worry is all pervasive and doubt clasps its chilling fingers around Red hearts.

And so, it came to pass. On the stroke of half-time, with the crowd having moaned and groaned its way through every stray pass or scuffed shot, a man who should not have even been on the pitch levelled for Leicester. As Maguire strutted in front of the Kop, sheer rage rolled down the steps of the famous old stand. However, whatever rage filled our souls, only a fraction of it was aimed at the defender. This was mainly self-loathing.

The players received the customary applause as they trudged off the pitch, but they faced a second half of frustration and pain. The groundsmen would do their bit in the interval, adding to the story of the night by only clearing the Leicester goal of ice and leaving the Liverpool penalty area a treacherous place for Leicester's attackers. It would be an act that filled as many column inches as the game itself and Klopp himself would have to argue that he hadn't ordered this to happen.

Despite their efforts it wasn't the snow and ice that robbed Liverpool of a winner and a priceless three points, it was the referee. Once more, Atkinson drew ire from the crowd by denying Naby Keita a stonewall penalty in the 57th minute.

The Reds had opened up Leicester and with Keita clear through on goal, he appeared to be taken out with only the keeper to beat. Pundits and ex-referees alike would later agree that it was a penalty, but such was the fear and loathing in the crowd that the anger was turned inwardly. Some accused Keita of 'bottling it' with the goal at his mercy and others bemoaned Liverpool's wastefulness.

In truth this was a difficult game against a tricky opponent in terrible conditions. Liverpool's players were showing maturity and patience as they probed and prodded the Foxes' backline. Unfortunately, such calmness was in short supply among the supporters.

We'll never know of course, but I left the ground with an overwhelming sense that the crowd, so often the pivotal cog in the Reds' machine on nights like this, had not been at their best. Had we shown a fraction of the maturity Klopp and the team had done, they may have had the nerve to snatch a deserved winner. Instead, frustration and fear grew ever larger and we became our own worst enemy.

Rio Ferdinand may have been right to identify that nervousness had took hold of Liverpool's title bid too early, but he was wrong to single out the players and staff. While Klopp and the team were the epitome of patience, Anfield was filled with fear and loathing.

While such impatience and anxiety may be understandable in the context of 29 long years without a title, it had been revealed as the single biggest obstacle to Liverpool ending that long wait.

A storm is weathered but that golden sky proves elusive as Liverpool surrender top spot

We're entering March 2019. Merseyside is battered by wind and rain, as Storm Freya wreaks havoc on the region. The hopes and dreams of Reds supporters everywhere are being buffeted in the high winds of a narrowing title race.

There are now two clear front runners, Liverpool and Manchester City. After successive goalless draws, in successive away games to Manchester United and Everton, the Reds had surrendered top spot for the first time in three months.

The post-mortem was in full swing, even though the body was still alive and kicking. Liverpool had been seven points clear at the top of the table a matter of weeks ago. Now they were a point behind City. Rival supporters rejoiced at their 'demise' and journalists and pundits chewed over 'failed substitutions' and Klopp's alleged 'conservatism'.

At Goodison and Old Trafford the bunting was out. It was party time. Their teams had secured monumental goalless draws, at home, to Liverpool. Their celebrations were both comical and telling.

United's lack of ambition on home soil was a testament to Liverpool's progress under Klopp and their demise since the loss of Alex Ferguson. Meanwhile, the jubilation among Everton supporters and their belief that they had robbed

Liverpool of the title, in March, with nine games remaining, spoke from a genuine fear among their ranks that their rivals were on the brink of a return to glory.

Whether it was to be this season or not, there is no doubt that this Liverpool team is closer to the 'holy grail' than any assembled over the last 30 years. Why else would the old enemy rejoice so much in taking a solitary point from us on home soil?

However, where there was joy and ecstasy at the other end of Stanley Park and the East Lancashire Road, there was almost unfathomable despair within the ranks of Liverpool's massed army of supporters. Fans took to social media to declare, with 27 points to play for, and with the Reds just a solitary point off the top, that Klopp and his charges had 'bottled it'.

He was too cautious, they argued. Liverpool couldn't and wouldn't win the title. Debates broke out on social media, across the globe, and in pubs, as to whether our pint glasses should be half empty, or half full. In truth, it wasn't the manager or his players who were losing the plot, it was their fans. Support for this argument came from surprising sources. One of them was Chris Sutton, a Premier League winner with Blackburn Rovers and Celtic.

'To me the Liverpool fans seem to be bottling it, not the players and Klopp,' he told the BBC.

'Can't we just say that Liverpool and Manchester City are two great teams – it's a brilliant title race. This will go to the wire. When Manchester City lost earlier in the season to

Palace and Leicester and Newcastle, did we say Manchester City are bottling it?'

The answer was obviously no. Admittedly, City had recent pedigree for winning the Premier League and a squad that was the stuff of fantasy football wet dreams. Liverpool supporters were also dealing with three decades of title pain. They had been nearly men too many times, only to fall agonisingly short. The spectres of the near-misses under Rafa Benitez and Brendan Rodgers still haunted our dreams. Until a title win could exorcise those ghosts, periodic meltdowns were seemingly inevitable.

It was a point that Raheem Sterling had made, as the former Reds prodigy had indulged in some mind games before the 233rd Merseyside derby had even kicked off. From across the M62 he had mused on how, during his Liverpool playing days, the anxiety among the Anfield faithful had sowed doubt in the minds of Rodgers's charges and ultimately cost them the title.

Reflecting on the draw with Everton, lifelong Liverpool supporter and co-founder of the *Across the Park* podcast, Phil Roberts, summed up the mood during and after the game among supporters forced to endure the games from their armchairs or in pubs and bars across the world.

'The atmosphere in The Church [a pub near Anfield stadium, on Walton Breck Road] was one of excitement and confidence until the team selection came out. There were some groans that Klopp had gone a bit negative. Still, we thought we'd still have too much for them.

'It was a pub full of Reds and the van Dijk and Bobby songs were getting a good airing for the first half hour. Then the mood turned, and supporters were becoming increasingly frustrated. There was an overwhelming feeling of dread that Everton, of all teams, could have put a dent in our title challenge.'

While some may argue that this is evidence to support Sutton's and others' criticisms of the Liverpool support, writing for ESPN, Dave Usher, editor of fan site 'The Liverpool Way', questioned the whole 'bottling it' narrative applied to the team, the manager and the fans, arguing, 'Liverpool have kept five clean sheets on the spin, so the players aren't "bottling" anything. The forwards are spluttering but, in truth, they haven't looked quite right all season and therefore talk of the team wilting under recent pressure is nonsense.'

Addressing criticism of the fans, Usher continued, 'As for the fans, how can they "bottle" anything? Liverpool's travelling support at Old Trafford and Goodison was terrific, but they can't put the ball in the net for their misfiring team.'

For Usher, the rantings of supporters on social media or on radio phone-in shows, even their despair in pubs outside the ground had little or no bearing on what happens on the pitch. That's almost certainly true, so long as the manager and players pay no attention to it. We know Klopp never has, so what's the problem?

For supporters with an appetite to consume every column inch of analysis and every tweet ever written about their beloved club, it was always going to be much harder. Some had become convinced that the title was lost in March, despite being one point behind the leaders and with 27 still to play for. As Usher suggests, this was entirely understandable when weighed against the Reds' decades-long quest and recent history of near misses. That didn't mean they were 'bottling' anything though.

Nevertheless, it remained true that after that disappointing draw against Everton the mood among many on the Red side of the city took a nosedive. That wasn't the case for those who travel to support Liverpool though. They seemed as ardent in their faith as ever. However, among the rest, it seemed that belief remained fragile. For them, four years after Klopp's arrival, the doubter continued to lurk close beneath the surface.

Success in football is of course the result of a delicate interplay between talent, mentality and tactics. The players arguably provide the talent and the manager provides the tactics. Achieving the mental strength to power past your rivals in a race is perhaps the most complex aspect of this 'holy trinity'.

If a player is blessed with a single-minded focus and unshakable belief, no matter what the odds, then it almost doesn't matter what is happening around him. However, footballers are human beings and prone to doubt and nerves. Those who can steel themselves and rise above it all on every occasion are rare. Only a team filled with seasoned title winners can boast such qualities. Experience breeds confidence and belief, but you must first gain that experience.

Here the supporters play a part, as does the manager, in creating an atmosphere in which doubt is never allowed to take hold. In this department, Liverpool's travelling support was rapidly becoming the benchmark. Even after the draw against United at Old Trafford, where they were locked in for what seemed like an age after the final whistle, they could be heard singing loudly, 'Liverpool, Liverpool, top of the league.'

Their passion and refusal to be bowed drew praise from both Jürgen Klopp and club chief executive Peter Moore. The latter took to social media to thank them, while the manager eulogised about them in his programme notes before the game against Watford, which had ended 5-0 to the Reds. He wrote, 'I always go to thank the fans for their support after every game but at Old Trafford my gratitude was even stronger than usual, that was because the 3,000 Liverpool supporters in a crowd of almost 75,000 had somehow made themselves sound like there were ten times as many in the away end.

'On Sunday our supporters were still in the away section. I loved the reception. There was a defiance in them I really love. They were shoulders back, chest out and proud – the attitude and mentality we need.'

He went on, 'As well as pride at representing people who support Liverpool in this way, I also felt a powerful responsibility to bring them the success that they deserve.

'This is something that I feel every day and it will never go away but at that moment it felt as strong as ever.'

The atmosphere at Watford also proved that such passionate support can prove to be the vital ingredient in Klopp's alchemy. Of course, it is still only one ingredient and the manager and players must do their bit, but that is always much harder without that support.

With five home games remaining in the title run-in, would the Anfield faithful be able to provide it? Time would tell, but, as February was blown away by Storm Freya, many Liverpool supporters were still struggling to see that famous golden sky.

Bayern Munich swept aside in Germany, as the Reds power their way into the quarter-finals

If you believe the strange science of punditry, Liverpool were enduring something of a mini crisis as they prepared for the Champions League quarter-final second leg against Bayern Munich. Their passage was far from assured as they had, according to some, squandered the home tie by drawing 0-0. Apparently, such expertise comes at the expense of realising that Munich had failed to score an away goal.

However, there was more. As a result of drawing very winnable games away to Manchester United and Everton, Liverpool had 'bottled it'. There was a time when a draw away to those sides would have felt entirely acceptable. However, this was before Manchester City spent north of £1bn and coincidentally became virtually unassailable.

There had been some succour though. Among the wreckage of the games at Old Trafford and Goodison, were towering victories over Watford and Burnley. The Reds had thrashed the Hornets 5-0 and put four past Burnley.

Sadly, there was no margin for error anymore and many saw those four dropped points as fatal. So, with the destiny of the title no longer in their hands and facing a difficult tie away to one of Europe's premier teams, some felt like the season was unravelling.

Fortunately, the Champions League would prove to be the perfect tonic for their domestic ailments, just as it would do in June.

Munich clearly fancied themselves. They had celebrated their goalless draw at Anfield and must have thought they could finish the job off at the Allianz Arena. They had every reason to be confident. The Reds had been poor away from home in the Champions League.

Not so in Germany. This was a consummate performance of breathtaking skill and tactical brilliance. Miguel Delaney, writing in *The Guardian*, summed up the scale of Liverpool's achievement on foreign soil: 'Liverpool don't so much surge into the quarter-finals, as soar there. That's how easy this 3-1 win away to Bayern Munich eventually was. So much for this club representing something of a complex for Jürgen Klopp. By the end, Bayern were crumbling – having been initially torn apart by fine goals from Sadio Mané and Virgil van Dijk – in what looked real end-of-an-era stuff.'

After 26 minutes, Mané would get things started with a goal of sublime impudence. The sheer invention and audacity of it had the travelling Reds in raptures.

Virgil van Dijk deserves plaudits for the accuracy of his assist, which landed at Sadio's feet, but the striker's control was awe-inspiring. Goalkeeper Manuel Neuer was so far off his line, that the net was virtually begging to bulge. Mané deftly sidestepped him, but as he did so he was faced with a pile of onrushing Bayern defenders.

Lesser players would have flapped at it, not Mané. He simply turned and lifted the ball over all of them and into the net. Liverpool had an away goal and suddenly that goalless draw at Anfield wasn't looking like the beachhead Munich thought it was. Then the fates conspired, as they so often do when it comes to Liverpool, to make life difficult for the Reds. Firstly, they lost Henderson to injury. The captain was replaced by Fabinho. Then Joél Matip became embroiled in a disappointing own goal. It felt cruel on the German-born Cameroon international, who had been imperious after deputising for the injured Joe Gomez.

Liverpool looked furious. Not necessarily with themselves. The goal felt freakish. No, they were angrier with Bayern for having the cheek to score. Instead of gaining the upper hand and feeding off the energy of the home crowd, the Germans seemed to shrink from the fight.

Salah and Mané were giving Neuer and his rearguard a torrid time, when in the 69th minute Liverpool won a

Jurgen Klopp salutes the hordes of Liverpool supporters at Queens Drive

The Strand, along Liverpool's historic waterfront, is packed out as an estimated 750,000 people to welcome the players home

Trent Alexander-Arnold holds the European Cup aloft as the parade passes the neighbourhood where he grew up

The people's cup. A city and a club united in belief, as supporters and players share in the collective joy

Back in Liverpool whole streets showed their support for the team who would make their dreams a reality

The iconic Mathew Street erupts in celebration as Liverpool clinch their sixth European Cup

Klopp hoisted into the air after leading his team to victory in Madrid

Cast's John Power leads a haunting rendition of 'You'll Never Walk Alone' in Madrid fan park, Plaza Felipe II

A Liverpool supporter leads the singing in Plaza Felipe II, as fans turn Madrid red

Jordan Henderson becomes immortal, as the fifth Liverpool captain to lift the European Cup

Liverpool fans in the Wanda Metropolitano Stadium. They will remember this place all their lives

The Egyptian King Mo Salah shows off the cup to his adoring supporters

Anfield awaits. The Barcelona team bus arrives to a cauldron of crimson pyro. They never stood a chance

A Liverpool supporter watching the semi-final unfold through the window of a packed Anfield pub

'At Liverpool Football Club, there is a Holy Trinity of manager, players and supporters,' said Bill Shankly. Decades on, Jurgen Klopp has rekindled the bond

This image of Messi, the world's greatest footballer, looking small against the backdrop of a pulsating and mighty Anfield, perfectly sums up the magic of that night

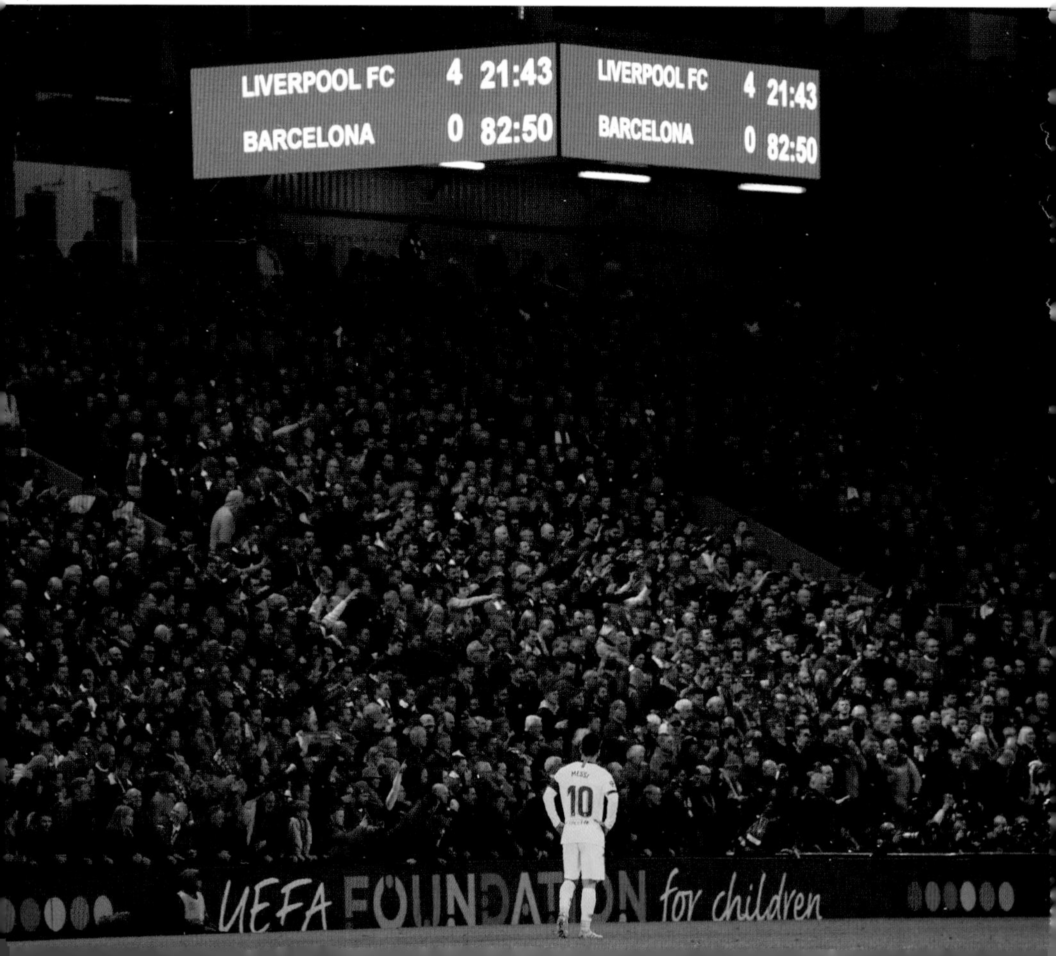

corner. Milner lobbed the ball into the air and the towering presence of van Dijk outmuscled all around him to head the ball into the net.

The Dutch master had contributed to both goals now and Bayern Munich had no answer to him.

Then Mané finished them off with his second, a headed goal six minutes from the end. Liverpool fans would sample the delights of the Bavarian city, celebrating in fan zones and draining steins as they toasted Liverpool's march into what would prove to be an epic quarter-final tie against Porto.

Klopp was ecstatic as he celebrated in front of the near 4,000 Liverpool supporters who had made it into the stadium. Each of his now famous three fist bumps were greeted by a huge roar. The Bayern fans simply left in an orderly fashion.

Klopp was becoming a master of the two-legged tie, having never lost one during his managerial reign at Anfield. Writing in the *Liverpool Echo*, James Pearce reflected on another incredible European night for the red men: 'This was a special performance from a special team. From the grit and desire of the first half when Sadio Mané's stunning opener was cancelled out by Joél Matip's own goal, to the swagger of the second half when Virgil van Dijk's header was followed by Mané's second of the night.'

Some Kopites were beginning to dream of Madrid. Others were booking their flights.

Carragher declares 'Salah's a dancer' as Reds rearguard contributes to epic victory over Spurs

It's Sunday, 31 March; a 4.30pm kick-off against Spurs and another must-win battle awaits Liverpool. Two weeks earlier, Liverpool had managed to dig out a crucial win with virtually the last kick against Fulham at Craven Cottage.

The title race was becoming so tight, so tense, that an away draw was no longer acceptable and potentially disastrous. After Sadio Mané had put Liverpool in front, a routine and comfortable victory seemed to be on the cards. However, the Reds would settle into the sort of pedestrian display that had supporters tearing their hair out.

Fulham had punished Liverpool for their lethargy in the 74th minute, and the goalscorer was as gutted as any Liverpool supporter. Just as Ryan Babel, a hero of the Rafa Benitez era, was about to capitalise on a Virgil van Dijk error, the camera focused in on his face. He looked almost apologetic as he stroked the ball into the net. That made it 1-1 and every supporter watching could see their title dreams evaporating before their eyes.

To make matters worse, Mané had hit the bar just a minute earlier. Football can be cruel and as Liverpool would find at the end of the season, it's often the fine margins that define the big moments in football. Previous incarnations may have withered at this point, but not this one.

Yet somehow the team found it within themselves to raise their level once again. Those who have played the game professionally will tell you that this is a hard skill to master. When you fall into a pattern of play, it is often difficult to suddenly switch gear. However, that's what this Liverpool team did.

Under Klopp they have plundered hidden reserves of strength and persistence so often, it is becoming a character trait. Fulham's goalkeeper, Sergio Rico, made a hash of a Salah shot. The ball fell to the feet of Mané and the stopper's bungled attempts to rescue the situation saw him bring the Senegalese striker down. It was a clear penalty.

James Milner and Salah briefly argued over who would take it and the Yorkshireman won. Mo was desperate to score but James wanted to atone for the misplaced pass that put Virgil in difficulty, leading to Babel's leveller.

Milner is no stranger to high-pressure moments, but if his finish was calm, his celebration was anything but. With nine minutes left, the Reds were 2-1 up. They'd ground out another win while playing poorly. It was becoming a habit and, at Anfield, in the spring sun, another London team were about be on the receiving end of it.

On the eve of their encounter with Spurs, in the United States, Liverpool's ownership team were chatting to NBC News about their hopes and dreams for the season. Tom Werner, the club's chairman, was talking about how tense the title race was becoming, how exhausting it was. Director Mike Gordon summed up the challenge facing the Reds. 'Manchester City just aren't going away,' he said.

In truth, City supporters were probably saying the same thing about Liverpool. The race for the Premier League title was turning into the equivalent of the world's most nerve-shredding penalty shoot-out.

The Reds had claimed top spot prior to the international break two weeks earlier. That came courtesy of a last-gasp penalty winner at Fulham. It probably felt harsh on the home side, but I wasn't in the mood to stare any gift horses in the mouth.

In any case it gave Reds fans yet another chance to sing about being top of the league, at least until after the international break. City would make their own trip to Craven Cottage on the Saturday before our encounter with Tottenham and duly knock us off the top of the pile with, it has to be said, a much more comfortable victory over Fulham than we had managed.

The pressure had shifted back to Anfield. Advantage in the title race was shifting back and forth between either ends of the M62 at a dizzying pace, and there was not a single sliver of room for error. Seven games now stood between Liverpool and that elusive Premier League title and as I prepared to make the pilgrimage to my seat on the Kop, I felt just like Tom Werner, exhausted.

Given Spurs' penchant for blowing up at precisely the wrong moment, I had foolishly viewed the game as a banker home win just weeks earlier. They had been right in the title race at one point but had slipped away just as they so often did. Prior to their trip to Liverpool, they had lost nine times and were facing an uphill slog to stay in the top four.

However, as the referee signalled the start of the game, the magnitude of the task was beginning to dawn on me. Spurs were a side full of quality with a great manager in Mauricio Pochettino. Players like Dele Alli, Harry Kane and Son had all hurt us in the past. Suddenly, the game wasn't feeling as easy as I had allowed myself to believe.

The Kop was in full fury, ablaze with banners and flags and 'You'll Never Walk Alone' thundered *a capella* into the Anfield air as George Sephton turned down the volume on Gerry Marsden's recorded rendition. It may have been the loudest I've heard it in an age. As the fluttering in my gut surged and the almost involuntary 'Come on you Reds' spewed from my throat, I realised that this was going to be another 'cup final', one more energy-sapping clash that could so easily destroy a title dream.

An almighty roar greeted the kick-off, the Reds were attacking the Anfield Road end and the hopes and dreams of 50,000 Liverpudlians in the stadium and the countless hordes at home and abroad hung in the balance. As supporters we live a dual existence. We simultaneously crave and fear the tightrope of victory and defeat. It energises and depletes us in equal measure, but we would never be without it.

Ninety-five minutes later I surveyed the carnage that lay all around me. Supporters, some of whom barely knew each other, were locked in passionate embraces. Fists pumped the air and throats were stripped in primal screams. This was joy. It was ecstasy, but that huge cacophonous bellow that followed the final whistle spoke of the sheer relief felt by every supporter in the ground. Liverpool had done it again, in a way only we can and at the expense of countless frayed nerves.

James Pearce, writing in the *Liverpool Echo*, proclaimed, 'The roar was deafening. Pure euphoria swept around Anfield. The celebrations were wild. It was a snapshot of what this title race means to Kopites. And it was created by a Liverpool team to cherish who simply refuse to give up.'

Those few words perfectly capture the moment and its importance. The Reds had almost snatched defeat from the jaws of victory. However, in a glorious throwback to the halcyon days of the 1970s and '80s, they simply refused to surrender.

They'd done it against Everton, when Divock Origi chased a lost cause into the Everton net in front of the Kop. They'd managed it also at Craven Cottage, when James Milner, cold as ice, slotted his penalty down the middle of the goal to deny Fulham a point. Now at Anfield, in front of a baying home crowd they had done it again, with another last-gasp winner. When all had seemed lost, Liverpool found something deep within them to grab the points and send their supporters into a frenzy of celebration. It was the stuff of legend.

The first half had offered no hint of the drama that was to follow. Spurs looked bright, as we expected them to, but Liverpool were fashioning chances and in the 16th minute Roberto Firmino converted one of them to put the Reds in front.

Much was made before the game of Klopp's decision to play Milner in preference to Fabinho. The Brazilian had been immense since the start of the year and many, me included, couldn't understand why he was being rotated in such a crucial game. It's been a running conversation, at least among the massed ranks of football's punditry class that Liverpool's midfield lacks creativity. The sight of Henderson and Milner in the middle of the park did little to assuage concerns.

Henderson had been immense on international duty, putting in a performance that had largely gone unnoticed and Milner has an engine that defies his age. However, Fabinho's ability to spot a pass and win vital tackles was going to be missed on a day when mistakes would be hugely expensive.

What many of us had failed to notice though, was the fact that much of Liverpool's creativity this season has come down the flanks. The Reds' full-back dynamos, Trent Alexander-Arnold and Andy Robertson, had been rekindling memories of a bygone age, back when the marauding defenders joined the attacks and turned draws into victory.

Both men had been contributing an astonishing number of assists and it was more than compensating for Klopp's more workmanlike midfield. By the end of the game, both would have added to their tally.

The first of these came courtesy of Andy Robertson. His whipped cross in the first half was steered home expertly via the head of Firmino. The breakthrough had come and from that moment on it felt like Liverpool would run riot. However, as the half ended, Spurs had regained a foothold in the game and nerves began to jangle in the Kop. Spurs supporters, sensing they were still very much in the game, even mustered a song on 44 minutes.

The second half continued in similar vein, and slowly Liverpool's confidence began to ebb. The crowd became nervous and frustrated as we seemed to surrender possession too easily and the midfield became sloppy. Time and again the Kop rallied with great chants of 'Liverpool, Liverpool'. They went through their full repertoire in an attempt to buoy their heroes, but an equaliser was coming.

We could sense it. You get those feelings during a game. I don't know what it is, but something changes. Whether it's a mood in the stands that transmits to the players or vice-versa I don't know, but it's the closest thing to precognition I have ever experienced.

In the 70th minute our worst fears were realised. Spurs won a free kick and Harry Kane took it quickly, too quickly as it transpired. TV screens would later show us that he kicked it while the ball was still moving and should have been told to retake it. He got lucky. So what, just 20 minutes later Liverpool would be even more fortunate.

From the set piece, the ball was swept out wide and then whipped into the middle where Lucas Moura, who smashed the ball into the back of the net. The Spurs fans erupted in wild celebration. The mood had changed again.

Had the ghosts of title challenges past returned to haunt us? Was this another 'slip'? Could this be another 4-4 against Arsenal in the 2009 title run? Or was it the eerie doppelgänger of the collapse against Chelsea in 2014? It would prove to be neither but not before a few more scares.

Spurs sensed their opportunity had come. With Liverpool rocking and the crowd stunned they mounted attack after attack. Klopp would say it was the best response to an equaliser by supporters he had ever experienced but from my perspective we were shell-shocked. The crowd attempted to roar the lads back into life, but I felt utterly deflated.

Tottenham chances came and went at an alarming rate and I turned to the fella next to me and said, 'We'll be lucky to get a draw here.' It's not like me to be pessimistic, but the Moura leveller had hit me where it hurts.

Alli and Kane both squandered opportunities to grab a winner, but by far the best chance to break Kopite hearts fell to Moussa Sissoko. In a moment that may well become Virgil van Dijk's finest hour in a red shirt, Spurs carved Liverpool open.

Sissoko and Son were both through on goal with only Liverpool's Dutch maestro standing in their way. The crowd held its breath as it seemed inevitable that Sissoko would slide the ball to his right and Son would smash home his second.

What happened next defies belief and perhaps marks van Dijk out as the greatest Reds centre-back since Alan Hansen. Perhaps.

The Dutchman would later explain that he knew Sissoko was right-footed and was aware of Son to his right. If Sissoko managed to pass the ball it would be game over, shepherd him to the left and force him to take the shot on his unfavoured foot, however, and you never know.

Van Dijk jockeyed the Spurs man, shielding him from his partner and the Frenchman blazed his shot over the bar. It was a huge let-off but one that owed itself to a defensive masterclass. How any player, embroiled in the pace and power of a Premier League game can find time to reason in this way is beyond me, but when you find one who can they're priceless.

With the game heading towards what would have been an agonising draw and City fans already celebrating, it was the turn of another Reds defender to turn provider. Liverpool won a corner on the left, facing the Kop. At this point we were all standing.

To their credit the players had kept going, looking for a winner in a game they could easily have lost, and the crowd responded, roaring them on as they launched wave after wave of attacks.

The initial in-swinger from Trent was cleared by Kane but only as far as Robertson, who swept the ball back outside to Alexander-Arnold. The youngster drove a cross to the far post where it was met by Salah. In truth the Egyptian's header was weak, and Lloris should have caught it easily. Instead he fumbled it into the path of Toby Alderweireld, who somehow shinned it towards his own net.

Time stood still and, for a moment, from my vantage point, it looked like the ball would be bundled away. However, my friends standing directly behind the goal would describe how it rolled slowly over the line avoiding the desperate clutches of the Spurs keeper.

There was a nanosecond of silence and then an almighty explosion of noise. We leapt into the air, we hugged each other, and we roared with all of our might. The Spurs defence fell to their knees, ours were imperious and the game was won.

In a moment of sheer delirium, Jamie Carragher, who was on commentary duty for Sky Sports, declared 'Salah, you little dancer!' It made no sense, but neither did this result. Who cared?

It was inexplicably, yet strangely predictable. The Reds had done it again. In that moment, I had no idea if Liverpool were going to win the title, nor if I was going to survive this nervous run-in. However, I did know that there was no place I'd rather be and no team I'd rather support.

Farewell to the Anfield Iron: A complicated hero who left behind a legacy of glory

On 12 April 2019, Tommy Smith, a former Reds captain, league title and European Cup winner, passed away. He left behind glorious memories after carving his name into Anfield folklore during a career that spanned 16 years, from 1962 to 1978.

This has been a tough chapter to write. Tommy was a player and a man whose career and life were riddled with contradictions. While I want to pay a fitting tribute to a man who was a tireless servant of the club and a childhood hero, I feel there is a duty to acknowledge his problematic attitudes off the pitch.

As a kid growing up in Liverpool, I idolised men like Tommy Smith. They were tough, craggy and supremely talented, and they wore the shirt with pride and distinction.

In my eyes the Liverpool stars of my childhood, including Tommy, could do no wrong. They were gods and beyond reproach.

Delving into Smith's life, I'm confronted with a much more complicated story. One that is more akin to Robert Louis Stevenson's *Strange Tale of Dr Jekyll and Mr Hyde* than a *Roy of the Rovers*.

However, before we confront Smith's troubling alter ego, it is only right that we begin with the brilliance of his football. Even here, we find there are two sides to the story.

Tommy Smith earned a reputation for being a Liverpool hard man, fierce in the tackle and uncompromising in the cause of the Reds. Such notions are fuelled by honorifics, such as the Anfield Iron, and testimonies from former team-mates, opponents and managers.

Bill Shankly famously said, 'Tommy Smith wasn't born he was quarried.' He also bemoaned the fact that his tempestuous charge 'could start a fight in an empty room'.

Norman Hunter, of Leeds United, who was also famed for being something of a hard case, remembers many encounters with Tommy: 'Come near me and I'll break yer back, was his catchphrase. But he's actually a very nice man, honest!'

Of course, Smith took pride in his notoriety, as Bob Paisley would observe: 'Tommy hated losing and was quite prepared to put himself through all manner of pain and suffering to avoid it. There was an element of notoriety about it which I think he quite enjoyed, but if any opponent cared to put that reputation to the test, Tommy didn't disappoint them.'

This fearless and sometimes brutal devotion to winning was part of the makeup of the archetypal Liverpool player of the 1960s. The philosophy at Melwood went along the lines of nobody should be allowed to bully a man in red, on the pitch or anywhere else for that matter.

No team could want victory more than a man who played for Liverpool either.

'For a player to play for me, he has to be prepared to run through a brick wall, and come out fighting on the other side,' said Shankly.

Smith certainly fits the bill, but it is unfair to talk about him purely in those terms. After all, this was a player courted by none other than Matt Busby, and Bill Shankly once threatened journalists who failed to vote for Smith as Player of the Year with being sent to the Kremlin. He also saw fit to make him the club's captain from 1970 to 1973.

Smith was more than a hard man. He was also a man who could play the ball and get forward when needed. You need only watch his performance in the 1974 FA Cup Final against Newcastle United to understand that this was a player with true footballing ability.

His role in Keegan's second goal is something to behold. Smith, running down the right wing, arrogantly plays not one, but two one-twos off first Brian Hall and then Steve Heighway, before racing to the by-line and playing a stunning cross for Keegan to tap in. This is sublime stuff.

Then there is perhaps his greatest moment in a Reds shirt; the goal he scored in the 1977 European Cup Final, in Rome, against Borussia Mönchengladbach. With the tie level in the second half, Tommy rose majestically in the box to head home powerfully from a Heighway corner.

Tommy regularly defied the stereotype he had created for himself. Therefore, growing up, I saw Tommy as a hero.

Here was a player, born within earshot of Anfield, who was feared by strikers throughout the land and who could also play great football.

Smith played 638 times for Liverpool and scored 48 goals, a decent haul for a defender. His trophy collection would be the envy of many a modern footballer, consisting of four league titles, two FA Cups, two UEFA Cups and a European Cup.

This is a record that has rightly earned him the title of Liverpool legend.

However, there's an adage that goes along the lines of 'never meet your heroes as they may have fists of iron and feet of clay'.

Perhaps you shouldn't delve too deeply into their private or public utterances either.

This is where we painfully, but inevitably, must confront the Mr Hyde side of Tommy's personality, specifically his attitudes on race.

Tommy Smith was undoubtedly cast from iron on a football pitch, he was also possessed of brilliance with the ball, but there were many times when he was standing on feet of clay off the field.

It is true to say that the world in which Tommy grew up was very different to the one we occupy today. The sort of casual racism uttered on television and lapped up on sofas in the '60s and '70s wouldn't be tolerated now, but it was commonplace back then. However, the effects of prejudice and bigotry were no less damaging then than they are now.

In his autobiography *61 Minutes in Munich*, Howard Gayle gives a compelling and depressing account of how the young black player's progress was made more difficult by Smith's racist abuse at Melwood.

The youngster had been an admirer of the man of iron, who he had idolised from the Kop, but had been disappointed and disillusioned by the reality.

Writing in his biography of John Barnes, *Out of His Skin*, Dave Hill reveals appalling comments Tommy made to him during a taped interview at the Adelphi Hotel in Liverpool.

Smith had said he wouldn't have wanted a black neighbour, or for his daughter to marry a black man. More worryingly he had felt that, in saying so, he wasn't being prejudiced, but just being truthful and normal.

In the interests of balance, Tommy did threaten to sue Hill after the book was published. However, he didn't proceed, and the author has since stood by his work and maintains that the entire interview was taped.

There are those who put forward the defence of generational racism. This is an argument that suggests it's unfair to judge the attitudes of people in the 1970s against modern-day standards. However, this ignores the very real harm caused by such behaviour.

In any case, while the context may offer an explanation, it cannot surely provide an excuse.

Tommy's utterances on race were doubtless shared by many in the game at the time, including at Liverpool Football Club. And, despite our desire to bestow almost supernatural qualities on our heroes, they remain depressingly human and subject to the same imperfections and frailties as the rest of us.

However, none of that protects the victims of racism from its damaging consequences. You need only look at how long it took for England to award a black player a cap to see that the very best players were being held back by attitudes to race.

Tommy Smith was awarded an MBE for services to football and after he hung up his boots, he carved out a career as a respected columnist with the *Liverpool Echo*. He was admired by his peers in the press in just the same way as he was by fellow professionals.

Tommy also battled bravely with arthritis and disability, a consequence of his all or nothing approach to football, perhaps. Through all that he remained devoted to his family.

So, in appraising the life and career of an Anfield icon and legend, it seems right to celebrate his many talents as a player, his ruthlessness in search of glory for our club and the many treasures his efforts bestowed upon us.

It is also important to remember he was a man, with a family, who loved him dearly and miss him terribly. They should be justifiably proud of his many achievements in the game, as should we.

We can do all of that, while acknowledging he was flawed as a person. Tommy Smith, it seems, was always a man of many sides, who has had a career and a life filled with contradictions. However, when he crossed the boundary between dressing room and field of play, there are few men in the history of the club who fought harder for Liverpool Football Club.

Rest in peace, Tommy.

Adversity and triumph on the south coast: supporters and players endure wild ride to the top of the table

It's 5 April 2019 and Liverpool are in the grip of one of the closest and most intense title races of all time. Jürgen Klopp was going toe-to-toe with Pep Guardiola's expensively assembled Manchester City and neither side was showing signs of crumbling. Liverpool had recovered from two damaging draws against Manchester United and Everton and a win on the south coast against Southampton would take them back into first place. The Reds were no longer in control of their own destiny and were praying for a Manchester City slip-up.

Following a goalless draw at Goodison, they had returned to winning ways in the league and knocked Bayern Munich out of the Champions League with an impressive 3-1 victory away from home. On the domestic front they had won three on the spin, scoring eight and conceding just three.

Nevertheless, with the pressure of the run-in mounting, a trip to St Mary's' was a daunting prospect and had 'banana skin' written all over it. And, it almost proved to be just that until Liverpool's now famous powers of recovery, and penchant for late goals sent them soaring back to the top of the table.

As the game got under way, it looked like the worst fears of the travelling Kop were about to be realised. The Saints were in front in under ten minutes, and they thoroughly deserved to be.

Paul Doyle, writing in *The Guardian*, summed up Liverpool's ragged start: 'They started like a team stunned to be confronted by opponents who treated them as they like to treat others. Which was a surprise, given that Jürgen Klopp is very familiar with Ralph Hassenhüttl, both having been on the same coaching course many years ago and having preached similar tactics ever since. But for 30 minutes the visitors were rendered ragged by hosts who pressed and thrust far better than them. Outfought as well as out-thought,

Liverpool were terribly uncomfortable or, to be fair, plain terrible.'

Disaster struck for the Reds when in the ninth minute Ryan Bertrand broke down the wing. His cross was flicked on by Pierre-Emile Højbjerg, and somewhat uncharacteristically Andy Robertson misjudged the flight of the ball and Shane Long smashed the ball into the net. The home fans were ecstatic and in the away end Liverpool's hardcore support looked worried. Could this be the moment the league finally slipped from their grasp?

Mané went close after that, but Liverpool laboured, and Southampton could sense blood. For almost 20 minutes frustration threatened to consume the Reds, then Trent Alexander-Arnold, playing his 50th game for the club, laid yet another delightful assist on a plate for Naby Keita in the 36th minute.

The young right-back, who was locked in a battle with Robertson over who would record the most assists of the season, lofted a great ball into the box and Keita headed home. It was the second goal of his Liverpool career and hugely significant. Waves of relief washed over Liverpool's travelling support. It was game on, at last. But they would be made to suffer for their win.

With the tension threatening to smother the life out of Liverpool's title challenge, Southampton took Klopp's men all the way to the 80th minute. The Reds should have had a pen after Keita was felled in the box, but the referee waved away the resultant appeals. Replays showed it was a clear foul. It all added to a growing sense that this just wasn't going to be Liverpool's day.

Then Klopp made a decisive move, bringing on James Milner and Jordan Henderson for Georginio Wijnaldum and Alexander-Arnold. The Reds had been lacklustre to say the least and were in need of a severe kick up the backside.

Milner and Henderson would do just that, grabbing the game by the scruff of the neck and shaking the life out of it. Then something truly magical happened.

Southampton won a corner and anxiety levels reached fever pitch. The ball sailed in and it was cleared. Mo Salah latched on to it and raced almost the length of the pitch with the ball seemingly glued to his boot. The Saints chased him all the way but his pace was electric.

Salah was in a battle of his own, after nine games without a goal and chasing the record for the fastest Reds player to 50 league goals. There was a sense that he almost wanted it too much, and where he had once possessed the golden touch in front of goal, he was now overthinking it and snatching at chances.

The sense of mounting anxiety as the Egyptian raced towards goal was palpable. Fifty-six-year-old Liverpool fan Terry Murphy, a tour guide at Anfield, was in the away end that day. He had already endured an arduous journey from Liverpool, which involved a broken-down coach and a £120 taxi ride to the stadium. A disappointing draw would have capped a miserable day, but his luck was about to change.

Terry explains, 'When Southampton scored, we were all a mess, but you know when you're sure of something but not quite sure, that was how I felt. Then we equalised. The second half was pure gut-wrenching tension. Then, with ten minutes to go, Salah is running and we're screaming "pass it"! He ignores us, then bang! Goal!

'I admit, in that moment, in my head, I was 16 again running down the front and going wild. Then "Angry Jordan" scores. All bets are back on.'

Jordan Henderson would seal what, on paper at least, looked like a comfortable 3-1 win. Firmino broke into the box on the right-hand side of the Southampton penalty area and squared the ball to his onrushing captain, who stuck it away with relish. The travelling support exploded.

Henderson, who had endured great criticism from a section of Liverpool's online fans, showed everyone watching exactly what the goal meant. With fists clenched, he roared into the skies above St Mary's, his face wearing the look of a man ready to go to war.

Terry would enjoy the ride home but would get little sleep. 'Who needs sleep when we have this Liverpool team to enjoy. I'm 56 going 16 again.'

Writing in the *Liverpool Echo*, James Pearce would praise the side's sheer bottle and will to win.

'The bottle of this team Klopp has assembled is staggering.

'As the stakes keep getting higher, the size of the cojones on display are immense. There's a powerful sense of unity, spirit and belief – coupled with an abundance of quality – which is powering them towards the finish line.'

Liverpool were top of the league again. They would take City all the way and, in the process, they would make the people happy. And, for the moment, that would do.

Liverpool breeze past Porto during a momentous and emotional April

April would turn out to be a momentous month for Liverpool. After their heroics on the south coast, they faced two games against Porto and sandwiched in between them was yet another must-win game, against Chelsea. That tie would fall on the eve of the 30th anniversary of the Hillsborough disaster. The poignancy and emotion of it all clung to every fixture.

After the victory over Bayern, any poll of Liverpool supporters would have demonstrated conclusively that Porto was the draw they all wanted in the quarter-final, and that's exactly what they got. The mood of relief was not shared in Portugal though. Liverpool were once again one of the most feared teams in Europe, and for good reason.

Liverpool had thrashed Porto 5-0 in the first leg of the tie just a season earlier, on the road to Kiev. The Porto coach, Sérgio Conceição, tried his best to play down any inferiority complex his side may have, by claiming that they had put any 'negative thoughts' behind them. Perhaps they should have hung on to them; it may have reminded them of the dangers Liverpool posed.

In the end the first leg was over inside 26 minutes, thanks to Naby Keita and Roberto Firmino. It wasn't as if Porto were poor. They started brightly enough. It was just that Liverpool were so assured. The only note of disappointment was that the Reds didn't put their dominance to good use. Another rout of European opposition might have filled us with confidence as we geared up to face Chelsea.

Perhaps Klopp's men were simply holding something in reserve, and maybe that was wise. So in control were Liverpool that Jürgen was able to rest Firmino and Mané for the closing stages of the game.

It could and, in the opinion of everyone on the Kop, should have been 3-0 when Henderson's delicious cross was volleyed expertly under Casillas. Thanks to the referee and the annoying VAR system, the goal was ruled out for the most marginal offside decision. We would have to wait for a week and the second leg, for our rout.

That would take place on 17 April, in the Estadio do Dragao. This was the birthplace of the now totemic anthem, 'Allez, Allez, Allez', which has accompanied the Reds on so many European journeys and carried them through an astonishing league campaign. It would also prove to be yet another launchpad to greatness.

Liverpool simply cruised past the Portuguese outfit, treating their travelling support to yet another incredible victory over the Portuguese champions. The *Liverpool Echo*'s James Pearce describes the emphatic nature of the

Reds victory: 'Pity poor FC Porto who felt the force of Jürgen Klopp's ruthless, rampant Liverpool once again. The Portuguese champions were ripped to shreds on home turf by the Reds for the second successive season as they were routed 4-1 on the night and 6-1 on aggregate. Having survived an early bombardment at the Estadio do Dragao, Liverpool showcased the array of firepower which has made them feared across the continent.'

The goals came courtesy of Sadio Mané, Mohamed Salah and Roberto Firmino, who came on for Divock Origi at the start of the second half, before Virgil van Dijk smashed home the fourth six minutes from time. A 68th-minute header from Éder Militão was nothing more than an annoyance and scant consolation for the home fans.

Liverpool now faced FC Barcelona in the semi-final of the competition. Despite the size of the task and the reputation of the opponent, fans were supremely confident. A general refrain went along the lines of 'they'll be just as scared of facing us', or 'bring it on'.

Andy Hunter, of *The Guardian*, summed up the night: 'It was a fight before it became a procession and, in keeping with the story of the season so far, nothing could derail Liverpool from their objective in Porto. Resilient and reactive when necessary, incisive and clinical when opportunity arose; the attributes that make Jürgen Klopp's team feared throughout Europe were all on display as they marched into the Champions League semi-finals for a second year running. Messi awaits.'

As tough a test as the Catalan giants and their talisman would undoubtedly be, especially on home soil, all of us knew that if we could at least give ourselves a chance after the first leg, then anything was possible at Anfield in the second.

The back page of the *Mirror* captured the spirit of optimism abroad among Liverpool supporters and their players. 'LIVERPOOL IN MOOD TO LEAVE MESSI IN A MESS' it declared. Of course, we would, but not before he would deliver a masterclass of finishing in the Camp Nou.

However, none of us had any idea of what we were about to experience at Anfield; neither did Barcelona and Messi, and nor did the world of football.

Messi and Suárez humbled by the power of Anfield: Furious Reds secure their place in Madrid final

There are great Anfield moments that I have experienced as a Liverpool supporter, which will echo in eternity. I will take their memories to my grave. There are St Etienne in 1977, Olympiakos in December 2004, Chelsea in May 2005, and Dortmund in 2016. All of them were spellbinding, wondrous and awesome. However, none of them were as inexplicably magical as the one I witnessed on 7 May 2019 against Barcelona in the second leg of the Champions League semi-final.

As I stood at the back of Block 109 in the Kop, my head clasped in my hands to keep it from exploding, and surveying the scene of utter carnage all around me, I could not explain what I had just seen, nor could I believe it. On the pitch, players lay collapsed on the turf, and the Catalan stars stared to the heavens as if cursing the gods of football who had forsaken them in the most humiliating fashion possible. The Reds had done the impossible and beaten Barcelona 4-0 to reach their ninth European Cup final.

The Liverpool bench, substitutes and coaching staff alike, raced on to the field of play, their fists punching the air and huge grins on their faces. All around me people stared in disbelief, eyes wide, mouths open. Others twirled their scarves in the air and soon they were singing 'Allez Allez Allez'. We conquered all of Europe, they declared.

It seemed to cycle around the ground, starting up independently in different parts of the stadium. My mind tried to catch hold of it, and just as it would, I'd lose track as another group of fans were singing it out of step and in their own time. I was in a daze and all around me supporters were standing on their seats, desperate to catch sight of their heroes and join in with the singing.

Then my eyes focused, and I realised I was staring at the guy in the row in front of me. He too was agape. My mouth opened, but the words were weak and croaky. I realised I had stripped my vocal cords through 95 minutes of shouting, whistling and screaming with joy. Or was it that my hearing had gone? The ringing in my ears was loud and I could still hear the boos and the whistles that had accompanied the last ten minutes of the game, as Barcelona had chased the killer away goal.

'How the fuck did that happen?' I asked.

He stared back at me, tears streaming down his face and juxtaposing the huge smile on his face.

'Only here,' he said. 'Only fucking here does that happen. Nowhere else.'

And, amid the chaos and the improbability of that unbelievable fightback against the world's greatest players, his was as good an explanation as any. Not in the wildest dreams of any Reds player or supporter could we have imagined a scoreline so comprehensive.

Liverpool 4 Barcelona 0. It had been the stuff of fantasy just 95 minutes earlier. Now it was the stuff of legend.

Only one man had believed such a superhuman feat was possible. That man was Jürgen Klopp. During the player's pre-match meal in the aptly named Hope Street area of the city, Klopp had risen to his feet to deliver a speech. It would turn out to be the greatest of his life and it needed to be.

In the aftermath of this titanic victory, players would talk of how they had never seen him like this before. Of how it lifted them and filled them with belief. Belief; that word again. Jürgen's elixir. He had called for it right at the very start. Could it really have been that simple? Maybe.

He had become more than a manager now. He was an alchemist; creating gold from rough cuts. A sorcerer, casting spells and conjuring the impossible with astonishing regularity and the one simple ingredient that ran through every one of his spells, was belief.

Liverpool had endured a terrible night in the Camp Nou, Barcelona's iconic stadium. Though they had turned in a first-leg performance of flare and endeavour, they had not been able to turn their dominance into goals. The Catalan team had simply picked Liverpool off.

A goal from Luis Suárez and two from Lionel Messi created a scoreline that seemed cruel on Liverpool and barely represented the reality of the game. Barcelona made one terrible mistake though. They didn't score a fourth. That was all Klopp needed.

As he stood staring out at the faces of his players, he summoned the words that would drive them on to victory.

To the media he had played down his side's chances. There was no bluff or bluster. Instead he talked of losing in the most beautiful way possible, with pride intact. However, when eyeball to eyeball with his team, Klopp showed a steely determination.

Every one of them would repeat the phrase verbatim after the game, showing just how much it had meant and how it had resonated.

'If it were anyone else, I would say it is impossible,' said Klopp, referring to the task of overturning a three-goal deficit while preventing the greatest player on the planet from scoring. 'But, because it is you, I think there's a chance.'

He believed in them. They believed in themselves. They were Liverpool. This was Anfield. Impossible was nothing.

The streets around the ground were rammed hours before kick-off. Supporters gathered once again to cheer their idols into the stadium and remind the opposition what they were up against. Vast swathes of people and pyro walking through plumes of red smoke and singing their hearts out made for an awe-inspiring sight. Some of that Klopp magic had found its way to Anfield Road.

At kick-off the air was thick with anticipation. Stomachs churned and hearts soared as the referee blew the whistle, and every one of us, players and supporters alike were like one hive mind. The roar was incredible. It would be surpassed at full time, but in that moment, I don't think I'd ever heard one so loud.

Then Jordan Henderson lit the blue touchpaper and the ground almost lifted out of its foundations. Somehow, he found the ball at his feet and he burst into the penalty area. His shot was parried and 50,000 people gasped simultaneously. It was as if the rush of air sucked the ball on to the foot of Divock Origi, who slid his effort past ter Stegen and into the net.

Anfield was a wall of sound and a mass of flailing limbs and swirling scarves. People jumped into the arms of strangers, hugged and cried, though none could believe it. Liverpool still needed three goals to progress, but in that instant, that felt like a mere detail.

The rest of that half remains a blur. Barcelona would trouble the Reds' defence, as we all expected, but Liverpool's backline was equal to them. Alisson was inspired. At the final whistle many would laud the outfield stars who made the win possible. Their performances were stellar, but it seems harsh that they should outshine the brilliance of Liverpool's goalkeeper.

As they grew increasingly frustrated, Barcelona's stars would resort to the darker arts. There were several Oscar-winning performances from players who could turn the simplest of challenges into something akin to assault with battery. That, coupled with a series of sly kicks and digs, would only serve to incense the crowd.

With every perceived injustice the noise levels were cranked up, until soon none of us could hear ourselves think. When a Luis Suárez kick put Andrew Robertson out of the game, the Kop bellowed 'FUCK OFF SUÁREZ!'

The player who was once the darling of the Anfield faithful would stop at nothing to win. Neither would we. This was war and in the heat of battle, he was already dead to us.

We knew we were getting to them and they were losing their heads. In the second half they would eventually crumble altogether, and it was a joy to behold.

Liverpool's second came just nine minutes after the restart. Trent Alexander-Arnold raced down the right wing, attacking the Kop. He seemed to lose the ball, then won it back. His determination drew a huge cry of approval from the supporters. Then he whipped a brilliant cross into the box.

Barcelona's defenders could do nothing, and Wijnaldum, racing into the box, struck a powerful shot that flew under the keeper. Cue bedlam. None of us would see Gini race into the goalmouth to yank the ball from the keeper's hands. We were too ecstatic, too locked in embraces and too deliriously happy to notice it.

Messi had gone. Suárez was broken. They were still leading in the tie overall, but in their heads, they were well and truly beaten. Two minutes later, the tie was level and the away section may as well have made its miserable journey to the airport half an hour early. Instead they stood transfixed, like rubberneckers gazing upon a car crash, they couldn't drag themselves away despite the horror.

We barely had time to reset and get ready for the next onslaught when Shaqiri found himself with the ball out on the left. His looping cross found the head of Wijnaldum who scored Liverpool's third and his second and levelled the tie overall.

Anfield went nuclear. If raw emotion and passion could find physical form, it would have appeared as a huge mushroom cloud hanging over the stadium and visible for miles. It felt like we had won and to all intents and purposes, we had. All that remained was for Origi to rubber-stamp the victory in the 79th minute.

The winner was an act of impudent genius that made a mockery of Barcelona's defence and an instant legend of Trent Alexander-Arnold. I don't even think I saw it. In my mind, I was somewhere else, contemplating the corner and wondering how my heart would cope with extra time. Then the ball was in the net.

It was inexplicable, incredible and few of us could work out how it had happened. The visiting team wore similar perplexed expressions on the pitch, as the men in red danced in front of a jubilant Kop. It was 4-3 and Liverpool, if they could hang on for another ten minutes plus stoppage time, would be on the road to Madrid.

That would prove an agonising feat, but somehow all of us survived it. In my pocket, my phone was vibrating like crazy. I didn't want to look at it, I was so transfixed on the game. I worried that if I took my eyes off it for a second, we would lose our grip on it. Somehow, on nights like that, you do feel like you are contributing in some way, that your actions matter.

Later, sat at home, I surveyed text messages that told their own story of disbelief, incredulity and sheer joy.

'Oh. My. God!' said one.

'Trent you fucking beauty!' said another.

'I'm in tears here,' said a third.

They were legion and a beautiful record of a magical night. As I walked home, I was convinced I had never seen anything like it in my life and not sure I ever would again. Images of the players in communion with the Kop and both them and us singing OUR song will stay with me forever. My thoughts turned to absent Reds, people and places. I'm not a religious man, but in my mind, I spoke to them all that night and I imagined them all grinning back at me, their eyes glistened with tears, just as mine were. It was a beautiful fantasy, and one fitting of such a magical night.

Writing in *The Guardian*, Daniel Taylor captured the mood of everybody connected with Liverpool Football

Club: 'Of all the incredible nights at Anfield, where does this one count? It has to be at the very top, presumably, given who they were playing, the importance of the occasion and the overwhelming feeling, despite everything this stadium has witnessed over the years, that Liverpool have never quite managed anything this spectacular before, with the floodlights on and the European Cup as the target. That is some honour for Jürgen Klopp and his players when you think of all the occasions here that have helped to shape Liverpool's reputation. They have won this trophy five times and now, for a second successive year, they will be going to another final with the chance to make it six. It was nothing short of extraordinary –one of the all-time Champions League comebacks and a reminder, amid all the euphoria, about the greatness of this sport, with its capacity to surprise and conjure up barely conceivable storylines.'

Katie Price, a disabled supporter who sits in the Kop, had felt the full force of this incredible night. It had moved her deeply. Katie travels the world with her father, supporting the Reds, but she says the victory over Barcelona will live with her forever.

'I forgot I was in my wheelchair,' she told me. 'I felt just like every other supporter, dancing like a lunatic. In that moment, at full-time, I wouldn't have wanted to be anywhere else in the world.'

It was a game that we will remember all our days and those who gave us these wonderful moments will be immortals.

We were going to Madrid.

Mixed emotions as Reds fall agonisingly short after record-breaking season

We arrive at the end of an incredible Premier League season. Liverpool have been involved in an epic tussle with Manchester City. Both sides had gone toe-to-toe in their quest to lift the league title. Top spot had swapped places more than 20 times, and the race had gone down to the final game.

Both teams had played the same number of games, and City sat one point clear at the top of the pile. Liverpool had won 29 games and lost just one as they prepared to face Wolves on the final day.

The Reds would end the day having amassed 97 points, a record for the club and the third-highest total in the history of the English top division. Their goal difference was +67 and they had conceded just 22 goals. Two of their strikers would earn the Golden Boot and their keeper the Golden Glove. Liverpool were also unbeaten at Anfield.

Football is cruel but the league table rarely lies. Manchester City were marginally ahead of the Reds. Despite having the wealth of a nation behind them, they were just a single point better than we were at the start of play and that's the way it would stay after the game was over.

There was no shame in that and there was much for Liverpool fans to be proud of, but that didn't completely ease the disappointment of going so close only to end up empty-handed. We would have to win the Champions League to get rid of that gnawing ache. Fortunately, thanks to one of the greatest European ties in their history, Jürgen's men had given themselves a great chance of doing just that.

So, as we gathered in the Cabbage Hall pub for one last time during the 2018/19 season, we were hoping for another miracle. For Liverpool to clinch their first league title since 1990, they would need to overcome Wolverhampton Wanderers and hope that Brighton and Hove Albion could upset the odds and not lose at home to City.

It was incredibly unlikely, of course, but this had already been a season full of improbable outcomes. The beer flowed and the chatter switched back and forth between possibilities. Whatever happened, we still had an amazing game in Madrid to look forward to.

The mood around the ground was carnival-like. There was so much to be grateful for and to look forward to. As 3pm approached we said our goodbyes and headed into the ground promising to meet afterwards, come what may. As I climbed the steps to my seat the sound hit me. It was a noise that had almost been the soundtrack to my life as a Liverpool supporter. That hum that represented the chatter of tens of thousands of hopeful Reds, punctuated by song and the swish of flags and banners. It filled my soul to bursting and I took my seat and dispensed the customary handshakes and nods of recognition with those around me. This was my other home, where I truly belonged and a place I will continue to return to until I leave this world.

Liverpool were in front in under 20 minutes, thanks to another goal from Sadio Mané. The Senegalese hitman was having his best season in a red shirt. The tension inside the ground evaporated in that moment. All of us could face missing out on the title, so long as we won this game. Doing so would enable us to hold our heads up and high, knowing we had done all we could.

Then something changed. Across the pitch, in the Main Stand, a small section of Liverpool supporters began to celebrate, jumping up and down and punching the air. Then the Kop began to roar. Someone in front of me shouted that Brighton were winning. It was bizarre, not because they weren't at that moment in time, but because they were a few moments later.

However, for the briefest of periods hope sprang eternal. *Guardian* journalist Daniel Taylor captured the moment in his post-match report: 'For two minutes, at least. The next roar crackled round the stadium like electricity and this time it was real. Up in the directors' box John Barnes was pumping his fists. Kenny Dalglish was checking his phone, grabbing the arm of the person in the next seat. His phone told him: Brighton 1 Manchester City 0.'

Nobody knows how that initial rumour circulated. Perhaps it originated with a Kopite premonition. A mysterious sixth sense. Probably not. These things have happened before. Sadly, our joy was short-lived as City equalised quickly and then went ahead.

Amazingly, and without a hint of irony, a group of supporters who had never seen their team win major honours, attempted to make themselves relevant by singing relentlessly about how Liverpool had messed up another title race. The Kop simply bellowed back, 'WHO THE FUCKING HELL ARE YOU!'

As a rebuke it may have lacked subtlety, but it seemed entirely appropriate. Wolves had gate-crashed mid-table, Liverpool had gone into the final day still with a chance of winning their 19th league championship and looking forward to a ninth European Cup final. None of us had any time for Wolves' *Soccer AM*-style banter.

By half-time we knew that the destination of the title had been settled. All that remained was for every Red to get behind the lads and let them know just how much we appreciated them and give the greatest send-off we could, as they prepared to jet off to Spain.

Taylor, in *The Guardian*, noted how determined the supporters were to give the team their full backing: 'Of course, Liverpool being Liverpool, they were determined not to let everything fizzle out with a sudden, damp silence. Anfield was far too proud to sulk or stew.'

They would be rewarded by a second Sadio Mané goal in the 81st minute. This was the first time in almost 40 years that Liverpool had not lost a home game in successive seasons. Anfield was a formidable fortress and that would stand them in good stead as they go again next time.

The game was won, but the league was lost. Yet this was a remarkable Liverpool team; one to cherish and a side that compares to some of the great Reds sides of the glory days. We can thank Jürgen Klopp for that. The club was gripped with self-doubt when he arrived. On the final day of the 2018/19 season it was powered by vast reserves of belief.

A lap of honour has rarely been so deserved at Anfield, especially for a side that had fallen short in the domestic campaign. That didn't matter and we all knew we had been lucky enough to watch something special develop and grow and everybody stayed behind to show their appreciation.

'The manner in which Anfield collectively responded to the gut-wrenching heartache of their Premier League title dream being dashed told you everything about where Liverpool Football Club are right now.

The *Liverpool Echo*'s James Pearce summed up the mood at Anfield perfectly: 'Talk about a show of deafening defiance. Rather than lament what might have been, they raised the roof when the final whistle sounded. "We shall not be moved" boomed around the stadium before "Allez, Allez, Allez" was followed by a stirring rendition of the club's iconic anthem. Kopites paid homage to the extraordinary work of Jürgen Klopp and those heroes in red who have strained every sinew over the past nine months. They chanted with glee about their impending trip to Madrid where Tottenham stand between the Reds and a sixth European crown. This was no scene of devastation.'

No, it was not and in three weeks' time, Liverpool would ascend to the summit of European football. As the Kop sang, 'Porto, Barcelona, who the fuck you trying to kid? We're the mighty Liverpool, we're going to Madrid.'

Allez. Allez. Allez.

A new generation of Reds baptised in glory as Spurs are defeated in Madrid final

Finally, we arrive at Saturday, 1 June 2019. The domestic season had ended three weeks earlier and the build-up to the biggest game in world football had reached its peak. Across Liverpool, indeed across the globe, anxious, excited Reds supporters prepared to watch their heroes take on Tottenham Hotspur in the Champions League Final.

This would be the club's ninth European Cup final. They had won five already, beating the likes of Borussia Mönchengladbach, Bruges, Real Madrid, Roma and AC Milan. For us the competition is special because it allows us to face off against teams from far-flung destinations and experience different cultures on foreign shores.

Somehow though, a final against an English rival didn't feel quite right. A lot of Reds would have preferred to face the beaten semi-finalists, Ajax of Amsterdam.

Nevertheless, this was a chance to claim a sixth European Cup. Every one of us felt that lifting that trophy would be a fitting end to an incredible season. The disappointment of missing out on the league title, despite losing just one game and securing a club-record 97 points, still lingered. Winning the biggest game in European football could exorcise that.

Liverpool have had a special relationship with this competition ever since Bill Shankly decided he wasn't content with dominating English football. After all, why settle for being a king of England when you could rule over an entire continent?

Success in Europe is now synonymous with the club and, under Jürgen Klopp, the Reds had once more become the most feared and respected club in the tournament. Anfield was legendary and visiting supporters spent as much time photographing and filming the Kop as they did their own teams.

Kopites love a European night under the floodlights and the prospect of an away day, or a final is so enticing they will move heaven and earth to be there. Steven Gerrard was quoted as saying, 'If they played a game on the moon, our fans would find a way to get there.' He was right. It's not just the supporters either.

Jamie Carragher told me that as a player he always enjoyed testing himself against the European teams and sampling those incredible nights.

'There's something about the atmosphere on those nights,' he said. 'Travelling away. I remember one of the games under Houllier, I think it was Roma away. I remember after the game going out on to the pitch and the floodlights were still on and the place looked amazing, and I just thought, "Wow, I've arrived." This is the pinnacle. Now I'm not playing, I love travelling away with my lad, as a fan. These games are just so special with everyone together, enjoying themselves.'

I wondered what it was like for the early pioneers. Paisley's men were the first to bring home 'old big ears'. Surely those days must have been magical, breaking new ground for the club and setting new standards. Jimmy Case agrees.

Recalling how Liverpool dominated Europe in the 1970s, he said, 'In the beginning, when I was involved, I'm talking 1976 onwards and starting off by winning the UEFA Cup, there was a fantastic feeling, a real buzz. Then following it up with back-to-back European Cups in '77 and '78 was just incredible you know.

'European games at Anfield had an intensity and an eagerness to them. It would kick-in straight after the final whistle of the Saturday league game. And it wasn't just the supporters but the players and everyone at the club.'

But why are those games so special?

Case continued, 'From a supporter's point of view, I think in those days the teams we came up against, there wasn't a lot we knew about them and you didn't know a great deal as there wasn't a lot of the likes of TV coverage back then. But everyone knew they were good sides because after all they had to qualify by winning their respective leagues. I think the supporters relished the fact of watching the unknown team and to see how we deal with them. I think that adds to the excitement of the night.

'For me, they're still magical. You can feel the intensity of the support from the fans and that gives them a fantastic lift going into the dressing room. Players love playing in Europe because there's always a great tactical battle. The games tax your brain.'

Listening to Carragher and Case, I'm left with the sense that there is a great synergy between players and supporters, and perhaps that goes some way to explaining how this is a club that regularly delivers the seemingly impossible on a European stage. This is why fans will go to such incredible lengths just to be near to the action.

Football writer Steven Scragg is a case in point. A lifelong Red, he travelled to Madrid without a ticket, and he described the exodus of supporters from all over the globe as an 'absolute invasion'.

'There must have been ten Liverpool fans to one Spurs supporter,' he told me. 'The fan zone was mental. John Barnes doing Rapper's Delight is one of the greatest things I've ever seen.'

Scragg endured a 22-hour drive to get to Madrid and stayed in a picturesque town called Pastrana, an hour outside Madrid.

'When we arrived, there were loads of long-term regulars without tickets. One watched it in a betting shop near the Bernabeu. I heard of one coachload of fans where only two of them had tickets,' he said.

Steven was able to revel in the atmosphere in the squares and bars of Spain's capital, and tells me that some felt the atmosphere outside the ground was better than the one in it.

'I was told that the atmosphere in the ground was quite sedate, by our usual standards. But, in the city centre it was biblical. Locals got swept up by it. I bumped into half a dozen souls that I had travelled to Istanbul with. It was part reunion, part street party. The game wasn't a classic, but the result was. There is nothing in football that can match Liverpool winning the European Cup.'

Many fans went to the Spanish capital, even though they had not been able to get hold of a ticket. For them, it was about being part of the atmosphere and as close to the action as possible. Phil Roberts was one of them. He talked about the lengths he had gone to to get there, and his feelings about the final.

His journey to and from Madrid involved four planes, four coaches and hours of travelling. He wouldn't change a thing.

'Despite not getting a ticket, I couldn't have wished to be in a better place for the game,' he told me. 'The city of Madrid was a sea of red and Plaza Felipe was a vibrant ball of positive energy. I felt no nerves. We were the favourites and this time it felt different.

'After the game the scenes were epic. You'd see a stranger in red and instantly hug them, start jumping around and singing together. We were congratulated by Spurs fans and it felt like we bonded, like two heavyweight boxers, who had spent 12 rounds smashing each other around a ring, only to have discovered a new-found respect for their opponent.

'All in all, I am glad I went. I wouldn't have missed it for the world.'

For Tony Zeverona, a veteran supporter who has seen all of Liverpool's European Cup victories, the decision to travel was made after the quarter-final against Porto. He was sitting in a plane with his son Joe and friend Peter Collis.

'We made a decision to book flights for Madrid because we felt we would beat Barcelona in the semi-final. I had booked the hotel as far back as June 2018 just in case,' he explained.

Tony's journey was typical of so many Reds, and it involved multiple stops, an overnight stay in Brussels on the Thursday, and then on to Madrid on the Friday morning. Once there, it was party time.

'The bar we were in made a huge mistake,' he recalls. 'They had a loyalty card and it said if you buy five pints, you get one free. The beer of choice was Stella and we proceeded to drink the place dry.

'The local busker had an amplifier, which he plugged his phone into. That meant we had our own jukebox and one of the lads, Connor Hill, became the DJ. He went right through the BOSS Night [a series of party nights in Liverpool] playlist and the place was bouncing.'

Another Red, Graeme James Strain, describes his trip and his childlike excitement and anticipation in the build-up.

For Graeme, the journey began in the early hours of the morning of the game.

'The alarm went off at 3am,' he said. 'It felt like Christmas morning when I was a kid. There was a sense of anticipation that I haven't had since Istanbul. A feeling that something huge was going to ignite this red juggernaut.

'I arrived in Madrid and immediately started the search for my mates.

'I'd already consumed a load of ale on the way there but heat was madness and so it was off to Puerto del Sol square. That's where the party really started. The atmosphere was incredible. Jamie Webster and the BOSS Night lads took care of that.'

Back home in Liverpool, and across the world, supporters were treated to an endless supply of videos depicting Liverpool fans painting Madrid red. The squares and fan zones were rammed, and the air was filled with smoke and song.

In Liverpool, crowds gathered at the waterfront Echo Arena. Ten thousand people filled the convention centre to watch the game on a giant screen and roads were closed as the city centre streets filled to bursting.

At the Sandon public house, historic birthplace of Liverpool Football Club, 5,000 people packed out the car park to watch the game, and at Aintree Racecourse there were similar scenes.

It seemed like the whole city was in the grip of cup final fever. In truth this pattern was repeated across the world. This was a global game and the Reds were playing not just for a piece of silver, they were carrying the hopes and dreams of millions on their shoulders.

Perhaps it was the weight of expectation, maybe it was the heat or possibly the loss of rhythm on the pitch was due to an enforced three-week gap between the end of the domestic season and the final showdown with Spurs, but the game itself failed to live up to expectation. It had threatened to, when after 22 seconds, Liverpool were awarded a penalty.

The Reds broke quickly from the kick-off, attacking the end where the Tottenham supporters sat. Sadio Mané teased the defence and attempted to lob a pass into the box from the right. For reasons only he can explain, Moussa Sissoko stretched out an arm and the ball struck it via his chest.

It was a clear pen and even an obligatory VAR check confirmed it. That didn't stop rival supporters from claiming Liverpool had been lucky, but Mo Salah didn't care and smashed the ball straight down the middle of the goal. Hugo Lloris almost got a hand to it, but the sheer power took the shot straight past him.

In the Liverpool end the supporters exploded with joy and relief. Arms flailed in the air and people embraced as it began to sink in. With barely two minutes on the clock, Liverpool were in front. What should have followed was a demolition job. After destroying Barcelona at Anfield, Liverpool fans could have been forgiven for dreaming of a rout. Instead the game would settle into a dull pedestrian affair.

Tottenham had all the possession but failed to take full advantage. Liverpool dealt with everything Spurs threw at them. Alisson, who was rarely troubled, was impeccable when called upon. Just like Bruges in 1978 and Madrid in '81, the game was dull but the Reds would emerge victorious. And, as far as every Liverpool fan was concerned, that was all that mattered.

Divock Origi, on for the tiring and uncharacteristically lacklustre Roberto Firmino, would add a fine gloss to the result in the 87th minute. From a corner on the right, in front of the Liverpool supporters, the ball bounced around the box and found its way to the feet of Joél Matip.

Matip slid the ball to Origi on the left. The Belgian had a lot to do and the angle looked difficult. However, Divock had been here before and he passed it into the right-hand corner of the Spurs goal with aplomb, and past the outstretched arm of Lloris.

As the ball rippled the net, a huge roar filled the air as Liverpool supporters ascended to football heaven. Surely this would be enough, surely Origi had just secured Liverpool's sixth European Cup. He had. Five nail-biting minutes of injury time could never be enough for this misfiring Spurs outfit to find a way back. In the stands, behind the Spurs goal at full time, the emotion of it all got to Tony Zeverona: 'It was a great start, but then it felt like the longest game of our lives.

'We were looking back and forth at the clock. Then, when Divock scored, it was the loudest roar I have ever heard. At the final whistle it was total bedlam. There were loads of tears. People were really emotional. It took me back to Rome in 1977.' The feelings of supporters in the stands were mirrored on the pitch as players hugged and cried. Virgil van Dijk fell to his knees, tears streaming down his cheeks. Jordan Henderson ran to his father Brian and the pair embraced. Trent Alexander-Arnold celebrated with the cup and his family, who were pitch-side.

For Jürgen Klopp, who was treated to 'the bumps' by his players in front of their exultant Liverpool supporters, this represented vindication for both him and his captain. Klopp went out of his way in the post-match media scrum to emphasise how Henderson had proven his doubters wrong. He was a European champion, and no one could ever take that away from him.

Klopp had also freed himself of his own demons. Having lost his previous six finals, a seventh defeat was unthinkable. His joy was obvious. 'Let's talk about six baby,' he sang, grinning ear to ear, after a journalist had asked him to share his post-match thoughts.

The scenes on the pitch were incredible, as players and staff sang along with the supporters in the stands. Jose Mourinho, working for beIN SPORTS, would describe the sights and sounds as 'more beautiful than any words we have.'

Arsene Wenger agreed, describing it as unique, saying, 'Liverpool is the city of music, the working class and football. And that is why they are always able to make miracles.'

An emotional Jordon Henderson told the *Liverpool Echo*, 'My dream as a kid was to win trophies. My best friend sent us a picture this morning of me kissing a trophy when I was about ten so that gave me even more motivation. It's obviously emotional. We have come a long way as a team, and we have had so many knock-backs. To finally get over the line, it's so special.

'We have come back from so many disappointments and finally won a big trophy. Hopefully we can use this to win more in the future.

'It gives us confidence to know we can win the Champions League and together we can move forward and hopefully win more trophies as well.'

This was a hugely significant victory for so many reasons. Liverpool's sixth European Cup success would ensure that they were now officially back among the big boys. It felt to all of us as though a corner had been turned and that this could be the prelude to something much bigger.

Of course, in terms of the financial rewards on offer, the win would establish Liverpool among the world's financial as well as its sporting elite. That meant talk of an Anfield Road expansion and another plunge into the transfer market. However, there are intangible benefits associated with such an epic night. For many supporters, the impact of this win and the whole run to the final went beyond a mere sporting victory. Instead it meant so much more and had a positive effect on their lives, lifting them and giving them hope in the broader sense.

Joe Goulding, my son, explains 'Last summer I was struggling with stuff, but those Tuesday and Wednesday nights, going out with my mates and watching the Reds in Europe, the atmosphere generated gave me something to look forward to. Then, after Kiev, it was back down to earth with a bump.

'So, I can't put into words what it feels like to see Liverpool win it. The pay-off is so massive. I feel like I've been on a journey with Jürgen and the lads. They've got me through so many tough times. To see them win it live in the stadium, well I can't put it into words.'

His friend Sean Macgregor, who also travelled to Madrid, felt similar emotions and points out that fans of all generations found the experience profoundly moving. 'It was just boss. I cried at the end. So many older men were crying too. It was unreal. I hope we kick on now and the next few years will be really special. But I don't think anything will top Madrid for our generation.'

Matt Ladson, editor of *This is Anfield*, writing for the popular *FourFourTwo* magazine, felt the win restored pride to the club and its supporters and aimed a shot at Alex Ferguson, who had once bragged about knocking Liverpool off their perch.

He said, 'After glory in Madrid, players had tears in their eyes and looked on in amazement as an estimated 750,000 supporters lined the streets of the city to welcome back their heroes. Derided by some outside of the club, the marketing slogan of "This Means More" was actually there on display, and proven prophetic. This, for Liverpool, does mean more.

'It means being able to move on from the Gerrard slip, Karius in Kiev, Ramos on Salah and mockery for achieving 97 points but not winning the league. It means Liverpool are well and truly on their way to being back on their fucking perch.'

However, we must leave the last word to a jubilant Jürgen Klopp, who had kept a promise he made after the defeat to Madrid in Kiev a year earlier. Following his team's heroics the night before, the Reds manager was caught on video holding the European Cup and singing a new song. It went like this:

'We're sending greetings from Madrid
Tonight we made it number six
We brought it back to Liverpool
'Cos, we promised we would do.'

Liverpool basks in glorious sunshine as it gets set for triumphant homecoming

For hours we waited in the Liverpool sunshine. The Strand, a highway that traverses the city's resplendent waterfront, was awash with a jubilant mass of humanity. Red smoke billowed from the top of the Liver Building. We watched, mesmerised as it swirled around one of those iconic birds that had stared out over the city for over a century. Then the skies exploded with the sound of fireworks.

I'm reminded again of how tourists clambering on to the Mersey ferry are regaled with tales of how one of the birds looks out to sea, to see when the sailors are coming home, the other inland to see if the pubs are open. On 2 June 2019, both birds were getting ready to welcome home an old friend – the European Cup. It was the city's sixth, thanks to Jürgen Klopp and his Liverpool team.

And how we welcomed them. Earlier, supporters, transfixed with their phones, desperately searching for updates of the progress of the open-topped bus that was weaving its way agonisingly through the city streets, groaned as a van bedecked with loudspeakers announced the team were three hours away. Still it had been 14 years since we'd last tasted such joy, we could wait a few more hours.

The parade had been a glorious outpouring of emotion. Fans clambered on to rooftops, bus stops and traffic lights. They had even used cherry pickers with platforms raised high into the sunny skies to catch a glimpse of their heroes. On pavements below, young kids, parents and grandparents strained for any sight of the team that had fulfilled their dreams. On the top decks of that bus, players, officials and owners stared in amazed bewilderment at the throng.

The scenes witnessed, remarkable though they were, would pale by comparison with those witnessed on the Strand. At Childwall Fiveways a great tumult had shocked players and reporters alike. Writing in the *Liverpool Echo*, Joe Thomas, who was riding on the press bus behind the team, had this to say: 'How do you describe a day like that? I'm not sure it's even possible.'

So magnificent was the welcome that seasoned journalists had been left open-mouthed. Joe continues, 'It was beautiful chaos, gorgeous carnage, a wonderful mess of shirts and flags and banners and fireworks.'

The mayor of Liverpool's office would later say that 750,000 had turned out. That's a colossal figure, given that over 100,000 had travelled to Madrid with at least half that number still out there. However, those who were there to witness the parade and those who watched it on their TVs would put the figure much higher than that.

This was something few people had ever experienced before. Newspapers and broadcasters would fill screens and front pages with glorious images of the Reds' triumphant return. Mingling among the players on the top deck of their bus was LFC TVs Peter McDowell. As he moved among the players and staff, he would capture an emotional Jürgen Klopp staring in disbelief at the assembled crowds. His face beamed with his now trademark infectious smile and his eyes were filled with emotion.

'How important are scenes like these when it comes to signing a player or even keeping a player? Why would you want to play for any other team?' McDowell asked.

Jürgen nodded and laughed. 'You need to make a good film of this. I haven't used my phone yet. I only watched,' he replied. 'You make a film and we will use it for the next signing.'

Of course, those of us waiting on the waterfront would need no persuading of the virtues of following our club. That said, we could only imagine the joyous scenes that were greeting the players. We knew nothing of the difficulties encountered as the team attempted to wind their way to them. Phones fizzed in pockets, and told of gridlock at the Jolly Miller, a pub and restaurant on Queens Drive and pandemonium on Tuebrook.

Eventually we heard that the bus was on Islington and that the crowds were still growing. Our heroes were 45 minutes away. So, we just waited, basking in the sunshine and sang our songs.

Liverpool was Red. It was exultant. Less than 24 hours ago they had witnessed their heroes earn the honorific splashed across the cover of the local paper, the *Liverpool Echo*. Immortals, it screamed. They were now.

Then, after waiting for more than four hours, those of us on the Strand would finally catch a glimpse of the team and that famous trophy. Amid another volley of fireworks and clouds of crimson smoke the buses emerged. First came the press pack and then the one carrying the team. They were emblazoned with the words 'Champions of Europe' and 'European Royalty' and they were here, finally, to greet their adoring subjects.

As the bus turned on to The Strand, the Liver Building looming like a great monument to a city's ambition, towered above them. Pyrotechnics erupted from its roof, confetti filled the air and the vast swathes of people screamed with joy. 'You'll Never Walk Alone' blasted from speakers on a truck travelling in front of the bus, and players and supporters joined in.

Huge cheers filled the air as Jordan Henderson lifted the cup aloft, then again slowly, milking the crowd's affections. Smiles filled faces and tears rolled from eyes. Mine were full. I'd seen his before. As a child, I'd come to expect it. I grew up thinking such parades were an inevitable finale to every season. Then there were the barren years, punctuated by the magic of Istanbul. That had been 14 years earlier, and we'd dined on scraps since then.

Now, all around me, children too young to know what Istanbul was, much less Rome or Paris, were witnessing some of the glory my own eyes had witnessed. They had heard our tales and maybe thought they were fanciful. Now they knew. Now they had seen for themselves the awesome majesty of their city, their team and the power of Liverpool Football Club in all its glory. They would remember it for their whole lives and the emotion of all that was simply overwhelming.

However, it wasn't just Liverpool that would witness jubilant celebration. In Madrid, many had stayed behind to party. Ticketless fans, who had travelled just to be part of the moment, would help Spanish street cleaners to clear up the mess, and others partied in Bilbao and Benidorm.

Reds all over the world posted videos of delirious celebration. In Denmark thousands packed into a stadium to watch the game and in New York the streets outside Carragher's Bar were shut down as citizens of the 'Big Apple' could barely contain their joy. Similar scenes were repeated in San Francisco and Boston. In Indonesia, pyro filled the night sky and tens of thousands celebrated in the streets, as did the Reds in Lebanon, Australia, Canada and Ireland.

As I watched the scenes in Liverpool and beyond, in television reruns, I was struck by the magnificent diversity of the crowds. Liverpool in 2019 is a truly global club with a fanbase to match. It is a joy to behold.

My hope for them all is that this is just the beginning, that they will come to know the almost mundane success enjoyed by my generation. But if all they must feast on are these memories, they will be able to dine out forever.

However, it would be wrong to leave it there. There is one more moving tale to tell. It involves a survivor of the

Hillsborough disaster, 30 years ago, and an incredible gesture by James Milner.

After the crowds has dispersed, and with the open-top bus speeding towards Melwood, Milner instructed the driver to make one more stop, outside the home of Andrew Devine. Andrew, now 53 and living with his parents in South Liverpool, was crushed in the Leppings Lane end and is now wheelchair-bound.

The *Liverpool Echo* reported: 'When the bus pulled up, Andrew was outside, and Milner leant over the side of the bus to show him the gleaming trophy.'

It was a truly magical moment that epitomises perhaps more than anything else, the special relationship between this squad and its supporters. It says a lot about the calibre of James Milner.

Liverpool Football Club is back. Feared and respected across an entire continent and drawing fascinated glances across the globe. It has once more established a bond with its army of fanatical supporters and has a charismatic leader at the helm. Together, we have conquered all of Europe and we're never going to stop.

We conquered all of Europe
We're never going to stop
From Paris down to Turkey
We've won the fucking lot
Bob Paisley and Bill Shankly
The fields of Anfield Road
We are loyal supporters
And we come from Liverpool
Allez Allez Allez

Afterword

There are those who would have you believe that the turn of the century brought a period of misery for Liverpool Football Club. They point to the absence of one trophy and suggest that this negates the winning of ten others. To them, Liverpool are a club in perpetual decline and living on past glories.

Maybe there was a grain of truth in that. Maybe. After all, Klopp has talked of the need for his charges to create their own history and of the suffocating weight of the club's illustrious past. I agreed with him that the key to future glory lay in unburdening ourselves from the past.

However, to suggest that the last 19 years have been a barren wasteland for the club, as many do, is revisionism of the worst kind.

The Premier League trophy may still prove elusive, but during that period the Reds have played in four Champions League finals, two UEFA Cup/Europa League finals, three Super Cup finals, three FA Cup finals and five League Cup finals. They have amassed ten trophies from that lot, and many of those singing about Liverpool as also-rans would kill for that level of 'failure'.

In truth, there will always be something in the DNA of this club that drives it towards finals and silverware. There is an arrogance about us, but one based on a belief in who we are and where we belong. As Bill Shankly once said, 'You must tell yourself every day that you're the best in the world. Then go out and prove that you are.'
Arrogant? Maybe. However, it is exactly what is required to be successful in the game and it has served this club well for more than 127 years. Jürgen Klopp has rekindled that attitude. Under his leadership, Liverpool and its army of supporters are no longer doubters. We now believe in ourselves, just as the legendary Scotsman had believed in us, and an eccentric genius from Bavaria does today.

In 2019, that belief brought its first taste of glory under Jürgen. We have been here before. In 2001 the club failed to capitalise on their incredible treble-winning season under Gerard Houllier. Again, in 2005 and in 2009 the hierarchy failed to make the most of a Champions League win and a Premier League challenge under the guidance of Rafa Benitez. Then came the title tilt of 2014 under Brendan Rodgers. That was squandered with the sale of Luis Suárez and the failure to replace him.

On each of these occasions Liverpool punched above their weight. They showed what was possible, if only the club could create the right environment and invest wisely. Sadly, we lacked the leadership and ownership structure off the field to deliver success on it. All of those advances would prove to be false dawns.

It was these failures that had sewn doubt into the minds of the club's devoted followers and handed ammunition to its detractors. Those days are over.

In 2019, Jürgen Klopp's Liverpool is a much different animal. Far from overachieving, they look and feel like a team that belongs at the very top. On the field of play, they are blessed with world-class talent. Our players fill the ranks of many a pundit's world XI and we have a defender, in Virgil van Dijk, who is spoken of as potential Ballon d'Or winner.

Up front, Liverpool's attacking line-up is the envy of European football and we have a manager coveted by teams and supporters across the globe. This is now a club built to succeed in a way it hasn't been since the 1980s.

There is an air of stability, of quiet effectiveness and progress in all areas of the club and the results are there for all to see. Liverpool's sixth European Cup has been delivered. In the coming months there will be more showpiece finals and chances to add to our tally of silverware.

When Alex Ferguson arrived at Manchester United all those years ago, he came with a mission to 'knock Liverpool off their fucking perch'. He succeeded, for a while.

However, Jürgen Klopp has drawn us level once again. Both clubs, with 45 major trophies, are the most successful in English football. Imagine that. It took Ferguson and his 'impossible dream' decades to overtake Liverpool, and in just four years Klopp has restored us to the pinnacle once again.

Once again, we are European royalty, and there is every reason to believe that we stand at the threshold of another glorious era in the club's history. May our Red Odyssey be eternal.

You'll Never Walk Alone.

FINAL